The Job Promoters

The Job Promoters

A journey to a new profession

R. Meredith Belbin, MA, PhD, Hon FITD

Foreword by Sir John Cassels, *formerly Director of the Manpower Services Commission and Director General of the National Economic Development Office*

Heinemann Professional Publishing

Heinemann Professional Publishing Ltd
Halley Court, Jordan Hill, Oxford OX2 8EJ

OXFORD   LONDON   MELBOURNE   AUCKLAND
SINGAPORE   IBADAN   NAIROBI   GABORONE   KINGSTON

First published 1990

British Library Cataloguing in Publication Data
Belbin, R. M. (Raymond Meredith), *1926–*
    The job promoters: a journey to a new profession.
    1. Great Britain. Unemployed adults. Training
    I. Title
    331.2592

ISBN 0 434 90065 6

Filmset by Latimer Trend & Company Ltd, Plymouth

Printed in Great Britain by
Billing & Sons Ltd, Worcester

Contents

Foreword

The man on the Clapham omnibus probably doesn't realize and would be astonished – and ultimately enraged – to hear that there are plenty of professional economists around who think that it is essential for between one and two million workers to be unemployed in Britain. They have the best of causes in mind – the economic health of the country. Bring the figure down below, say, 1.5 million, they think, and inflation will get out of hand and everything will go to pot.

The man on the Clapham omnibus doesn't like inflation either, and he is right. But he would also be right to hang on to the belief that, for all their argumentation, economists are talking nonsense when they say this, and all the more appalling nonsense because a sense of outrage at the effects on people and communities of enforced idleness is so entirely lacking. (How many economists are at risk of long-term unemployment?)

And of course economists, like other people, do get it wrong and they have particularly, many of them, got it wrong in recent times through simplistic notions of how unemployment and wage inflation interact. Beveridge thought that about 3 per cent was as much unemployment as was unavoidable for the economy to function properly. We managed with a lower level than that for many years after the war. I fully expect to see unemployment head below one million well before AD 2000, hotly pursued by a crowd of economists explaining how that had proved possible after all without prices soaring out of control.

The great merit of this book is that Meredith Belbin largely – and perhaps resignedly, but certainly wisely – ignores this learned economic chatter and goes straight for the problems that puzzle and give anguish to ordinary people. What can be done to help people with no work to get it? What can be done to help business to fill jobs, expand and create more jobs?

I find persuasive Meredith's thesis that a new kind of profession is emerging, that of the 'job promoter'. We are not talking here about macro-economic decisions by governments which inevitably affect the prospects of tens of thousands of businesses and millions of workers. Nor are we talking about the strategic manoeuvring and takeover ambitions of big business or the march and countermarch of the trade unions. The task of the job promoter is to deal with much more finespun webs: with the potential and the crankiness of small businesses, the determination and the loneliness of the self-employed and the skills, experience and unfulfilled abilities, as well as the foibles, self-doubt and weakness, of individual people wanting work – and the way all these relate to each other.

The labour market is a crude mechanism – too often short on imagination and flexibility, and crucially and continually short on information. It is that crudeness which creates the need for the job promoter and it is the skill of the job promoter to take difficult job situations and alleviate or cure them simply by enabling the latent potential present in all such situations to be spotted, developed and put to work.

A bold claim? Read on.

John Cassels

Introduction

This book is about the human side of job creation with special reference to those with a mission to bring about jobs in the localities where they are most needed.

The approach taken in this book is directed to a neglected part of an important but complex problem. Some things on the wider front we are bound to take for granted. Few would dispute that the creation of jobs demands certain pre-conditions in society: people must feel free to trade and conduct business and develop new ideas and products; a stable economy along with stable money provide an ideal framework for expanding work opportunities; and, not least, the growth of employment to match the needs of job seekers depends on a steady supply of those with the incentive and special talents needed to start up new job-creating enterprises.

Yet we will argue that reliance on any given set of favourable conditions alone is not enough to resolve all the problems of a shortfall in employment. Where jobs are regarded only as a by-product of business, there is an ever-pressing risk of a gross unevenness in the development of economies, that pools of unemployed people will gather in areas in which the business community has little interest.

When that happens the plight of the jobless is apt to be perpetuated. Misery abounds for those who have little prospect of earning a fair livelihood. That unhappiness is compounded by a knowledge of the wealth that exists elsewhere beyond their reach. It is an ugly blot on a civilized society if the majority enjoy their prosperity in disregard of the privations of a minority debarred from participating in ordinary life because they have no work. Allowed to foster and grow, their grievances provide the fuel for tyrants. The repercussions can set in motion mighty conflicts that know no natural boundaries.

On such criteria the promotion of jobs is a subject worthy of existence in its own right. It demands to be spearheaded by appropriate professionals who by study and experience can devote themselves to this important field.

Such people are already to be found. But so few in numbers are the members of this occupation that they carry no acknowledged title and we have had to invent one – the job promoters – to embrace the activities in which they engage.

How is it then that a book has come to be written about what many would regard as a phantom profession? My answer lies in both a practical consideration and a vision. The former is a recognition that the labour market, left to itself, works too crudely and inefficiently to cope with the insistent demands of the modern world. To compensate for its imperfections, the job promoter's task is to harness its potential and to harness too unused human talents so that as many people as is possible or desirable can gain an income through employment. The latter consideration – the vision – is that this band of professional pioneers may one day play an essential part in contributing to the future peace, security and happiness of the world. That outcome depends on how well their skills are developed and recognized as being complementary to those of politicians, employers and entrepreneurs – who between them bear prime responsibility for the general state of employment.

Some may argue that in rich countries the problems are more marginal and certainly less pressing than in the less developed world. Economists and politicians have combined to build up an effective social security system with a guarantee of income for those who lose their livelihood.

The solution however is part of the problem. It is true that social security removes the more obvious hardships. But in the long run another price has to be paid, just as it was in Ancient Rome with bread and circuses for the jobless masses. Then as now the option of an alternative to work, which unemployment benefit allows, has the effect of inflating the numbers of the unemployed along with its associated ills. And so a counter-pressure builds up. Because the cost of supporting the unemployed falls largely on the shoulders of the working population, there are growing numbers who favour reducing this tax burden by getting people back into work, quite apart from the conviction that it is socially desirable to do so.

In principle conditions are now ripe for the emergence of a profession that can bring to bear expertise on the many difficult problems raised: how those long out of work can be brought back into employment, how economic activity can be fostered in rundown areas, how jobs can be modified to match the skills and attributes of individuals and how individuals can be trained and developed to match job demands.

In practice in most countries no coherent public body addresses itself to all the interrelated and demanding human issues that are involved. While functions are centralized, responsibility is fragmented. An unstable system has stabilized.

The elaborate systems of the social security, being departmental in nature, have a vested interest in their own continuity. 'The dole', as unemployment benefit used to be termed, is routinely ladled out to the unemployed, not with the soup-spoons of old, but with forms, cheques and computer programs. There are officials to assess the eligibility of the workless for the many benefits to which they are entitled and which are often too complex for them to understand; there are information gatherers and there are snoopers on the trail of false claimants. Others in public service focus on collecting and supplying 'labour market information' often to bewildered clients who with only limited personal assistance make from it what they can. There are instructors, trainers and training administrators who process job-seekers through the various programmes available, but who are separated from the issues that govern their subsequent placement. There are many who provide a service in the various fields of health or social welfare to cope with the mental, physical and social ailments of those who sink, unwillingly at first, but later often with resignation, into a condition of long-term and sometimes chronic unemployment. And from this group that fails, in spite of all these efforts on their behalf, to establish a work role in society, a new underclass comes into being. The problems of this latter group eventually prove far more exacting than those who experience merely the misfortune of losing a job.

Of the great army of public servants drawn up to cope with the ramifying problems of the unemployed, what percentage is charged with dealing with the core problem – of getting people back into work – rather than with its peripheral features?

The answer I believe is smaller than it should be in nearly all countries. In the public service job promoters are to be found, working here and there in small numbers, often widening, unofficially, their terms of reference in spontaneous initiatives entered into because they believe in the importance of what they are doing. Yet they belong to no professional organization that formally recognizes and encourages them and helps to develop their skills in this key undertaking. In private industry, and amongst voluntary bodies, job promoters are less restricted by circumstances and more conspicuous in their public activities. There are many examples of individuals and small organizations that display dedication and skill in helping those in need to improve the job prospects and position of those out of work and in rendering help to job-creating new enterprises. Yet is it not surprising how many individual job promoters from this background turn out to be unpaid workers or engaged merely in some temporary assignment?

What is the fundamental reason that renders society keener on spending huge sums of money in administering unemployment than on creating new jobs in particular places? What new outlook and brand of expertise is needed to enable the jobmaking process to flourish and for unemployment to wither? And if the few job promoters who do exist can produce beneficial results – as I believe the contents of this book will demonstrate –

is it not time that a new framework was found whereby this largely unrecognized breed can operate to advantage?

This book might have encompassed data collection and analysis, using the approach that accords with a respected scientific treatise, or it could have been treated like a chronicle of the period, detailing the dates and circumstances of the public events that figure in the book. Instead, I have opted for a greater measure of freedom by choosing an informal narrative style and relating a story of a personal apprenticeship through a newly developing subject. I confess to a sense of need to apologise in advance for the autobiographical tone of this book. Yet the account of my journey through many trials and tribulations has at least prompted me towards conclusions that otherwise would never have been reached.

It is only through working with a range of people from talented entrepreneurs, the unemployed and those who service them that I have come to see unemployment as a potentially self-perpetuating condition, yet also one that is reversible. The guarantee of a job plus the availability of professional resources in vocational training, placement services and enterprise formation have the power, I believe, when properly balanced to restore near full employment in places in which all hope has been lost. So too it is only as a result of assignments in developing countries that I have come to realize the value of establishing the conditions in which human skills and aptitudes can contribute to business growth and job creation and how widely these have been neglected in favour of emphasis on straight financial aid.

Before I start the story it is fitting to present my credentials.

Most of my working life has been spent as an industrial consultant in the private sector of the economy. But I have always kept in working touch with the public sector due initially to my academic involvements. The connection started almost fortuitously as a consequence of my doctoral dissertation in the University of Cambridge on 'The employment of older workers in industry'. A few years later I was invited to undertake an assignment on behalf of the Organization for Economic Co-operation and Development (OECD) to set up demonstration projects in the training of older workers in its member countries. The Deputy Director of the Manpower and Social Affairs Division of OECD at the time, Solomon Barkin, whom I had long admired as a pioneering figure, is one to whom I owe much as a mentor. Barkin made sure that the projects were well chosen and imaginatively conducted, especially in the United States, where, as an American, he had special knowledge. My other projects were located in Austria, in the United Kingdom and in Sweden, one of the world's leading pioneers in manpower policy. As a young man working with greyheads my varying experiences made a considerable impression upon me – even more so years later when the lessons had sunk in.

After writing two short books for OECD in the series 'Employment of older workers', I was invited to become a member of various OECD working parties on manpower policy. I gained much personal benefit by working alongside the small number of experts involved in this area. Under a gifted director it was not true, as I had always been led to believe, that all experts disagree. On local and wider issues OECD working parties reached a high level of agreement on what types of measures were or were not effective. One important factor here was the value that could be extracted from demonstration studies — the only means of proving whether new employment strategies did or did not work in practice.

Later the Industrial Training Research Unit (ITRU) in Cambridge became the body under whose auspices we were able to set up the first experimental demonstration studies in the United Kingdom into cost effective ways of creating new jobs. This work of the ITRU was financed by the Manpower Services Commission (MSC). Following a change in its leadership, the Commission eventually took a more limited view of the problems it should tackle and finally ended up spending most of its budget on training poorly educated and unemployed persons for semi-skilled work. Research and development into cost-effective ways of creating new jobs was cut from the programme. At this point we made our departure from the ITRU in order to set up the Employment Development Unit (EDU). With the benefit of the research and development work already undertaken we were able to establish new types of operational project in local authority areas. In particular we concentrated on setting up and running a programme called CEBEE (the Combined Employment and Business Expansion Enterprise).

These various experiences have led us to think strategically about the prospects for the jobless and where society's aims should lie. As the world prepares to enter a new century the welfarers, the worksharers and the job promoters will become the principal voices to be heard pressing their rival claims. The outcome of this debate will be enormously important for the world's growing population.

Meanwhile the primary aim of this book is to stimulate interest in operational approaches to unemployment among a broad section of readers: executives of firms who believe they have some degree of responsibility for the job prospects and security of their employees; public servants concerned with employment issues, whether in central or local government; and finally those who are actively involved in politics of whatever calling and aware of the need to respond positively to constituents who ask: 'What can be done to create more jobs in our community?'

R. Meredith Belbin

1
The missing tradesman

There is nowhere more traditionally prosperous than the Green Belt, that exclusive outer zone of commuter land which serves the more distant travellers in the Metropolis. And there is no place more inscrutable; for on what does that prosperity depend? There are no visible signs of its origins, like smoking factories or rushing lorries. Instead, well-dressed people proceed about their unknown business in quiet and untroubled surroundings. Eternal order reigns.

Sevenoaks, the town in Kent in which I was raised, has its counterparts in many parts of the world that lie adjacent to a major centre of population. This leafy and affluent corner of England might hardly seem on the face of it to belong to the subject of this book with its focus on one of the more troubled sections of our population, the jobless. Yet, in examining a problem there are advantages in starting from a distance. Much of what we learn comes about through contrast and comparison and the consequent sense of wonder that prompts us to account for differences. And so it was that in such a secure place I took the first tentative step on what was to prove an eventful journey.

The clue to the past and present prosperity of Sevenoaks lies in its physical features and location. Any cursory examination might start with the Vine, reputedly the oldest international cricket ground in England. From there, we should proceed through the broadest of highways, St Botolphs, a stately curving avenue lined with huge chestnut trees under which small boys have always scurried to collect conkers at harvest time, and down to the very lifeblood of the town – Tubs Hill Station with its offering of a fast train to and from the City.

The urban sprawl of London is separated from the Kent countryside by the North Downs. Through this dividing range runs the connecting link, a long tunnel with its exit set, unseen, amid high banks hard by a local landmark, the broad tree-girdled chalk-pit of Pole Hill. Every evening with unfailing regularity the fastest express of the day would announce its homecoming as it broke into this rural world with a billowing of steam and the

1

accompaniment of an ear-splitting whistle. A few minutes later, at Tubs Hill, doors were flung open and, before the train had come to a halt, out leapt the smart, grey-suited gentlemen, each clutching a rolled umbrella and folded newspaper. Deftly finding their feet on the approaching platform they streamed towards the ticket collector and patting their season tickets as they passed, disappeared into the streets outside.

Each day at set times the denizens of Sevenoaks departed for and returned from the City. Unlike their wives who periodically indulged in major shopping sprees, these travellers carried nothing tangible back from their routine journey. But what they did bring home from their offices was the invisible harvest upon which the town's fortunes depended. The commuters spent money on their homes and families, they patronized the local shops and places of entertainment and they fed the coffers of the local authority. The long tunnel at Pole Hill supported a first, second and third order of beneficiaries. Derivative income and prosperity passed from one set of hands to another. The process that operated then continues to this day, for it shares the same basis.

The workers in the City mainly earned their living dealing with a commodity unlike any other – money. The demand for it was permanent and assured. Money was banked, invested, dispensed through insurance, borrowed and paid back. It was always on the move, yet its very movement guaranteed the job stability of those who handled it. It was rare to hear of someone in the City who had become destitute through a capricious downturn of trade. For if money ceased to flow in one direction it found another channel offering alternative business and employment. The workers in the City were adept enough in responding to the vicissitudes of business. In extreme circumstances they accepted cuts in salary and commission. But they had little difficulty in maintaining their established way of life even when business fell away.

The commuters were aware of their good fortune and the need to protect it. That solid phalanx of grey, which streamed to the station and back again at set hours, maintained its cohesion at election time when a fleet of cars, coloured in an identical fashion, delivered the commuters to the polling booths to register their approval of the system that had created their prosperity. So uniform was their behaviour that it became impossible to miss the exception. On one occasion an individual attired in a brown suit became the sole occupant of a waiting car, the posters on which announced it had a different political destination. This deviant aroused much curiosity but no hostility. He was said to work in the printing or publishing trade. Beyond that, nothing more was known. He was a centre of much speculation. To remark on the anomaly was a means of registering consensus. In a successful society all members are expected to belong to the accepted pattern.

For those who did not travel to the City the world held out fewer beckoning prospects of such an assured livelihood. One day, I remember, a carpenter came to our house. There are some workmen ever ready to share the benefits of their wisdom and knowledge of the world with those who are prepared to listen. He was one. His variety of experiences made the routines of the City workers pale into insignificance. Yet it was also marked with pain and grief. 'You don't know what it is like to be unemployed.' This climactic statement was made in the same tone as one relating a ghost story. I had to admit, horror-struck, that I did not. Indeed I could not have done. I was only ten at the time. But it was enough to strike a vocational chord.

Here was something strange. Problems of life appeared to fall into two categories, those that could be fixed and those that could not. Tiles that fell off a roof, machines that broke down, doors that became unhinged constituted problems requiring the services of a tiler, a mechanic or a carpenter. It was straightforward enough to call in the appropriate tradesman. Losing a job, however, fell into a category for which there was no appropriate tradesman or 'fixer'. Instead, the unfortunate person became processed through a system devised by the State.

That procedure, I was to learn later, meant presenting oneself at a Labour Exchange. There, behind a counter, a clerk would take details, sort through cards on which job vacancies were recorded, find one considered appropriate for his or her client and in due course note the outcome of the application. Unemployment benefit would be paid while the process continued. If the job-seeker were to turn down job offers from three suitable vacancies or fail to present himself, unemployment benefit would be withheld.

The clerk behind the counter was a person of influence and some power. He was expected to judge which job was suitable for someone out of work, he might offer guidance, he would assess whether a claimant was a malingerer and he was responsible for making the social security payment. It was not surprising that all this caused delays. The slow-moving dole queues which built up outside Labour Exchanges announced the aimlessness and the hopelessness of those who had lost their job and now depended on public benefit. These unwanted workers provided a highly visible message to the rest of the community. The dole queue became the symbol of the Depression.

The harder and more conscientiously the clerk behind the counter performed his task, the longer other people had to wait in the queue. However, the length of the queue was related not only to how thoroughly the clerk did his work but also to the *ratio* between the number of jobs available and the number of job-seekers. The clerk could hardly be blamed if the queue was long. Other ways have since been found for reducing the length of the dole queue, like paying claimants by a cheque delivered through the post, and allowing them to help themselves to information about job vacancies at an Employment Office. But in those days public reaction was less concerned about administrative speed than with the fundamental reasons for the under supply of jobs.

Adequate employment opportunities for all

When the Second World War ended there was a widespread surge of public opinion in favour of creating a society in which there would be adequate employment opportunities for all. The evidence that governments could conduct the vast and complex business of running a war reinforced belief that much of that organizational skill could be transferred to tackling the problems of peace. Providing jobs was top of the list of priorities in most countries which had become embroiled in the conflict.

But how was this ambition to be achieved? The intellectual base was provided by John Maynard Keynes. This distinguished economist had made his mark in the academic world by his treatise on money. Much of his writing is considered obscure. But his messages were clearly expressed whenever he felt like assuming — as he did intermittently — the role of preacher. Keynes postulated that government could exercise control over the economy in various ways to enable it to expand and to increase jobs at the same time.

Two concepts central to the Keynesian theme were *the management of demand* and *the generation of job multipliers*. Keynes argued that government could influence economic activity by the level of its own spending. The boosting of demand for goods and services should compensate for the effects of any downturn in the economy. New jobs would be created in those industries most directly affected. But additional demand would reach out to have a favourable but lesser effect on jobs in other industries. Like a stone dropped into a pond there were ripple effects though with each outer ripple being smaller.

The job-multiplier process needed to be delicately managed. Too much government spending could undermine the value of money, reduce savings and investment and result in economic stagnation. This condition did eventually come about and became known as 'stagflation'.

Just after the end of the war, when Keynesian doctrine was in its heyday, I became a university student. It did not take long to encounter the tracks of this historic figure.

Those who arrive in Cambridge by rail and take a bus ride from the station to the historic city centre pass Harvey Road, where Keynes once lived. The tendency for people to pride themselves on their local heroes and personalities is universal, and Cambridge is no exception. Keynes was revered as an intellectual and as a visionary who struggled in vain against the provisions of the Versailles Treaty which had placed such an impossible economic burden on Germany as, in his view, to endanger the peace. But he was also hailed as a man who had done much for the City and his College. The Cambridge Arts Theatre was founded through his energies and initiatives, partly it is said out of consideration for his wife, a famed ballet dancer. And as the Bursar of King's College he had demonstrated that theoretical intellectuals could also deliver the goods. During his steward-ship the finances of the College weathered the Depression and with economic recovery the College was elevated into the ranks of the richest in Cambridge.

The post-war world was so Keynesian that large-scale unemployment was talked about as if a spectre of the past and definitely avoidable. It could arise again but only through political mismanagement. What unemploy-ment did exist was termed *frictional*. In the main, people were in transit between jobs as old ones closed down and new ones started up. This frictional activity was calculated to generate about three per cent unemployment. The various provisions of the Welfare State would accommodate any human problems that might arise quite comfortably. Meanwhile the post-war industrial boom was pushing up the standard of living. More production was the formula for greater prosperity, given only a government that believed in fair shares for all.

Older workers in industry

With production now becoming the focus of attention, I was attracted towards making my way into industry. The opportunity eventually came about through my studies. After reading Classics and later Psychology I took up my first post-graduate appointment in the Nuffield Research Unit into Problems of Ageing under the direction of Dr Alan Welford, later Professor of Psychology in the University of Adelaide, Australia. The project on which I was engaged concerned the employment of older workers in industry. Alan Welford had accumulated experimental evidence from the laboratory which indicated that the nature of human skills tended to change with age. The corollary of this, if true, was that industrial operations that made different demands on workers would vary in terms of the ages of the people engaged upon them. Was it true that there tended to be a natural division between the work of older people, the middle-aged and the young – or was it all a matter of circumstance and experience?

In fact, the projections from laboratory studies turned out to be well-substantiated in the industrial field. Welford and his co-workers found that subjects in different age groups approached the operations set up in the laboratory in different ways, young people being faster in their responses, spending less time in planning and being more inaccurate than older people. In industry I found that similar distinctions could be drawn. Younger workers tended to be engaged in fast-moving production operations, especially those subject to piece-work, while older workers tended to gravitate towards inspection operations and planning functions.

The exceptions, however, were also notable. Small numbers of older workers were sometimes found on operations normally associated with young workers, provided they had learned these skills when young and maintained them. On the other hand, older entrants were seldom found where new skills, involving eye and hand co-ordination, had to be learned rapidly. It was not uncommon to find that those in charge of sewing-machine operations in clothing, footwear and allied industries reluctant to take on trainees in their late twenties. Too old at twenty-five was the maxim on some types of job. There was even evidence in industrial literature that on certain coilwinding operations trainees aged nineteen were inferior to those aged sixteen and that supervisors were reluctant to take them on! It was a reminder of the claim that those hoping for virtuosity with the violin need to start well before their tenth birthday!

The post-war period, being an era when many new industries were starting up and new skills were being learned, put a premium on youth. The words of one Managing Director in a hosiery firm I had visited were still fresh in my ears: 'We never turn down any sixteen-year-old who applies for a job at the factory gate'.

The converse of this promising vista for young people was that the prospects for older workers who had lost their jobs were correspondingly worse. Being seen as slower in learning new skills, they were discriminated against on a very broad front by employers.

Here then was an identifiable group of people who had difficulty in securing new jobs. From the employer's point of view there were some rational grounds for discriminating against them. On the other hand the methods which employers used to train older workers were based on those that had evolved to suit the needs and characteristics of school-leavers. This raised the problem of whether special methods could be devised to raise their employability.

My personal life, and subsequently my professional life, was now changed by matrimony. Eunice was a fellow student at university, and at the time of our marriage we were both engaged in writing up our doctoral theses. Mine was entitled the *Employment of older workers* and Eunice's was *The effectiveness of propaganda on recall, recognition and behaviour*. One of the findings of Eunice's experimental study was that people in different age groups responded to propaganda in characteristically different ways. Older subjects were observed to have distinctive learning styles. Under suitable conditions they learned rather well, incorporating changes in behaviour even if they could not recall what they had seen or heard. It was a topic we continued to discuss during such intervals as life allows between coping with a small baby and doing the household chores. We were already beginning to devise ways of training older workers for special skills based on a programmed Discovery approach.

We began to look for an opportunity to try out the new methods. However before we could proceed other priorities called. Now with the responsibilities of a family man I decided to apply for a 'proper job'. It had all come about as a result of attending a course at the Institute of Engineering Production at Birmingham with the aim of broadening my knowledge of industry. My name was passed on to Cranfield College for a possible appointment there.

The attraction of Cranfield was that Professor Jim Connolly was the Head of Department of Production, later to become the School of Management. Jim was Australian and totally free from British reserve. At the interview, Connolly invited me to bring in my wife and young daughter who soon proceeded to make nose-dive leaps over the back of the couch. Somehow Connolly managed to combine his share of rescue operations on the toddler without any interruption to his animated flow of conversation.

Connolly's enthusiasm for his subject had led him to set up demonstration rooms to illustrate to visiting industrialists what great gains could be made in productivity by setting up Work Study. Visitors were impressed and the College rapidly became a much favoured place for industrial courses. Cranfield imparted valuable technical lessons on how to raise productivity, to which a general message could be attached: increased output generates lower cost goods and increased profit. The latter may be distributed or reinvested so as to bring about further gains in wealth creation. The process seemed attractive, provided the market was continually expanding.

There was of course one reservation upon which the potential job promotor could alight. What about the displaced workers? If two workers can achieve the same output as three, someone is going to lose a job. Even here Connolly was confident that the problem could be handled to the satisfaction of all. One solution was an assurance of 'no redundancy'. Any displaced worker could be guaranteed another job within the organization. If that guarantee could not be given or if the displaced could only be offered lesser jobs, workers could be 'bought out'. In other words they would receive financial compensation for the job loss. The accent was on voluntary redundancy. If the money was attractive enough volunteers for redundancy would exceed the redundancies required. In practice that is exactly what happened.

A fluid job market is essential for any rapidly developing economy and the post-war booming world, fuelled on Keynesian economics, was still creating abundant job vacancies. Yet some of these jobs turned out to be unavailable to those in search of work, including those clutching their compensation packages. Older job seekers in particular seemed liable to remain — to use their own words — 'on the scrap-heap'. All this we fancied could change if there was some prospect of proving to industry that older workers could be as trainable as their younger counterparts given the right conditions.

Eunice gained the first opportunity to put these ideas into practice by setting up a long-running programme to train letter-sorters at the London Post Office. With time the programme became progressively more effective in meeting its goals and very many trainees passed through the new system.

The next challenge came from the Wool Employers Council in Bradford. The price of a piece of cloth is dependent on its quality. If the buyer can detect a weaving or spinning fault, he will look for a discount. That possibility prompted a great deal of time and effort being spent in the mills on rectification by operatives known as menders and burlers. Their scarcity resulted in vacancies being advertised outside almost every worsted mill in the area. The skill required sharp eyesight, a sensitive touch and an understanding of the configuration of the weaves which was often very difficult to see. Needless to say the mills were scrambling for almost every young school-leaver and experienced worker they could find.

Connolly took a generous view about giving time off to his staff for consulting work, believing that theoretical work and practical experience were best combined. And so Eunice and I were able to work closely in collaboration with Frank Hill, Director of Recruitment, Education and Training for the Wool Employers Council in setting up a school for burlers and menders in Bradford. Frank was bluff but charming and with all those qualities associated with Yorkshire grit. He would regularly rise early at his home in Oldham, drive over the Pennines and start work in the office before any of his staff arrived. Eunice and I were insistent that we should have a cohort of older trainees in the programme. In the face of the scepticism and opposition of many mill owners and managers, Frank obtained exactly the number of older trainees we required.

The industrial work we set in motion was conducted in an experimental setting. So we were able to compare the results of three different methods of industrial training: TWI (a method developed for use in wartime), 'sitting-by-Nellie', and the method we had designed ourselves.

Frank's capacity for application and speed of reaction was sometimes greater than we could cope with. When Eunice went into hospital for a minor operation, Frank was on the phone in a flash only to be told by the hospital that the patient had died in the night. The mistake was due to a mix up in names. But it did allow Eunice the rare privilege of collecting flowers intended for her funeral.

The new training methods widened the age catchment on the part of those entering the industry and ran unchanged for many years. The general lesson as far as employment policy was concerned was to underline the critical importance of individual skills for particular types of work. This view had dawned on me even as a boy. After all, the commuters at Sevenoaks who worked in financial institutions and mercantile operations in the City were not interchangeable with the building workers and shopkeepers who maintained the fabric and commercial life of the town. Jobs might be available in principle but jobseekers often had the wrong experience or aptitude, were in the wrong age group, belonged in some cases to the wrong sex and lived in the wrong place.

We had perhaps made a limited contribution in helping to get a group of workers disadvantaged in the labour market into jobs. But this result was no more than a by-product of our interest in research and development. No specific responsibilities had been involved. We were not jobmakers. Nor had we come across anyone in our travels who fitted this description.

Here was a subject that seemed to lie outside the everyday reach of economists, with their concentration on the broad fiscal and monetarist tools for the management of the economy. Could something be done about the unemployment that attaches itself to special groups? Was this the price that had to be paid for economic progress? Or was this a problem that could be 'fixed' just like any other matter requiring the appropriate tradesman?

2

A first sighting

After the post-war boom had faded the Organization of Economic Co-operation and Development, sometimes known as 'the club of rich nations', launched its Active Manpower Policy as one of its first initiatives. This policy placed an emphasis on promoting employment by direct investment in people. The recommended measure broadly fell into two types. In one the benefits were channelled towards *individuals*: these took the form of training facilities and financial allowances so that new skills could be learned for which there was an effective demand in the labour market; or relocation grants were made available enabling a worker to take his or her existing skill to a locality where it was needed. In the other approach, the benefits were channelled in the direction of the *employer*. Placement or training grants acted as inducement for employers to take on specified types of labour at a disadvantage in the labour market. For example, the German Federal Republic had made extensive use of these measures to absorb displaced coal miners into other industries.

The Active Manpower Policy was most notable for its emphasis on training, especially through the use of publicly financed training programmes to enhance the skills of the unemployed. The two problem groups were the young and the old, more notably the latter. When older workers lose their jobs they have difficulty in finding another. The reluctance of employers to recruit people in middle age, with or without training, was very evident in spite of the fact that much had been done in industry to make work 'lighter'. For them retraining could play a key part in securing another job.

This was the subject that had brought me to Paris. The letter inviting me was signed by Solomon Barkin (Deputy Director of OECD's Manpower and Social Affairs Division). That name may not mean much to most people. It meant a lot to me. During the exhaustive work of reviewing previous literature related to my doctoral thesis the writings of Sol Barkin had stood out from all the others. His major publication was *The Older*

Worker in Industry: A Report to the Joint Legislative Committee on Unemploy-ment, prepared under the Auspices of the Continuation Committee of the New York State Commission on Old Age Security. It had appeared as long ago as 1933. The author had an unusual background. Originally a trade official, he had become the Research Officer of the Textile and Garment Workers Union. After various public appointments he took up his position in Paris and later became a Professor of Economics in Pennsylvania State University. His writings indicated a man who combined scholarship with a grasp of the practical issues of life; who could bring out the intricacies of problems and also develop well-conceived solutions.

I had formed no clear idea of what sort of person I would meet. At the moment of introduction I was surprised to find someone in loose fitting clothes and a brown trilby hat and all the ostensible attributes of a character who might have stepped out of a pre-war movie about Chicago. Sol was straight talking and tough. He had throughout his career, as he explained to me with pride, regularly fired any inefficient people he found on his staff. He was equally critical of those with whom and for whom he worked. Unlike most international civil servants he had a habit of making others move whatever their level.

If ever I believed that seminars and conferences were little more than talking shops, Sol taught me otherwise. Those run by him always came up with clear-cut positive conclusions. His technique was to identify the most promising participants at an early stage and discuss with those individuals what ideally the outcome should be. He would then orchestrate the timing of each key contributor within a well co-ordinated framework. Minutes would be written up by a carefully chosen rapporteur. This formula resulted in good sense emerging from the most chaotic meetings. The published outcome would need the approval of everyone. If a fixer gets the results desired no one disputes the method.

After Sol and I had closely examined some of the employment problems beginning to emerge in developed countries, it was arranged that I would set up demonstration projects in the training of older workers in four or five member countries, and also be responsible for evaluation and for the writing of the reports.

Finding the right project was not easy. But after a number of overseas visits I was able to start up programmes in Sweden for the training of workers in engineering skills, in Austria for the training of stonemasons in a rural area where heavy snow regularly produced seasonal unemployment and in the United Kingdom where London Underground guards were learning to become train drivers. As far as the United States was concerned, Sol insisted that I would gain most in personal experience by working with one of the most go-ahead organizations in the United States: this was Community Progress Incorporated of New Haven, Connecticut. As I might have expected Sol's recommendation was well founded.

Community Progress Incorporated

The United States is a very large country. Its size means that only a limited amount of central administration is feasible. Indeed the constitution gives such a degree of autonomy to the State that the USA has in effect two governments, the State and the Federal. To the European and to the American the word 'State' has different meanings, one indicating central power and the other provincial power. Australia, almost a continent in itself, follows the American model. The practical effect of this power division is that a single country can encompass a broad range of systems and institutions for handling important issues in the public domain. This variety constitutes a strength. The weakness is that, unlike the situation in smaller European countries, success of one system or institution disseminates slowly. That is the price that has to be placed on having local institutions and local independence.

In American towns and cities mayors are very important people, whereas in the United Kingdom they are largely figureheads. In New Haven the Mayor had played a major role in setting up Community Progress Incorporated (CPI) and in liaising with the first Director of the CPI, Mike Sviridoff. CPI was set up to provide an integrated service to those in need of employment and social help, so that there was in effect a single local umbrella institution to which people could turn. That meant dissolving the power and influence of the many separate and uncoordinated bodies that provided welfare to the needy and which often resulted in half a dozen individuals visiting a single family without being aware of each other's existence. In an American town with a strong mayor that situation could be more easily remedied than in most European countries.

New Haven was a city with a problem. The centre was physically decaying, old industries had collapsed and there were not enough jobs to go round. The population suffering the greatest consequent hardship comprised ethnic minority groups, mainly negro and Puerto Rican. Crime and alcoholism were rife. Beyond the decaying city centre there was a good deal of prosperity. The wealth of this broader area meant that funds were available to improve the city. An extensive urban renewal programme was in full swing. Yet the view was taken that this initiative would not be a complete success without its counterpart: a human renewal programme embracing those who were caught up in the physical changes to the city. In long-depressed environments there is a natural scepticism about whether jobs can be created in adequate numbers and whether employers who are naturally reluctant to engage hard-to-place workers can be induced to take them on for the limited vacancies available.

Anyone who visits the United States on a work mission is likely to be surprised how long the day lasts. First of all there is the time change. Being met on arrival at New York my internal clock told me I should go to bed.

Instead I was taken out to dinner. This lasted until late in the evening even by American time. A point was reached when I almost slid under the table with fatigue. But it was not all a matter of time change. In the United States extended dinner and breakfast conferences can be taken for granted. It was all a great contrast to the gentle pace of life into which I had been introduced when first starting a job back home. During my stay in New York I was told about a British immigrant who had proved quite successful as a retail salesman – his manner and accent appealing to the customers – but who would not hesitate to interrupt a sale to take his afternoon tea at four o'clock! Perhaps the story was meant to introduce me to the new standards that were expected.

Americans work hard when they are committed and they were very committed at Community Progress Incorporated. This particular commitment sprang from a strong belief in the mission itself. CPI was one of a number of Community Action Programmes operating throughout the US with support from the US Department of Labor but designed locally and enjoying additional funding from local sources.

A distinguishing feature of CPI was its approach to enrolment. It is well known that those who have long been out of work become dispirited and apathetic. They cease applying for jobs, make poor use of local facilities and fail to take advantage of any opportunities that come their way. Further, as might be expected in a population of unskilled, under-educated workers, those with poor reading abilities or language problems fail to respond to advertisements.

All this was true in New Haven as it is elsewhere. The solution adopted in CPI was to bring people into its West Street Skill Center through the agency of neighbourhood workers. These neighbourhood workers had two approaches. The first sprang from contacts with social workers. This allowed problem families in the district to be identified. Often a critical factor for these families was the position of the husband and father. No longer the breadwinner he had, typically, lost his status in the family and his aberrant behaviour was compounding the difficulties faced by other members of his family. The favoured strategy was to call on the family head and to invite him to visit the Skill Center where he would be offered a 'job'.

The second approach was even more direct. Neighbourhood workers sought out and introduced themselves to the jobless whenever they could be found. Often they were lolling against brick walls in streets near their homes. Once personal contact had been established it was easy enough to bring them into the Skill Center, the merits of which could be assessed on the spot. Initially this street encounter population showed apathy towards almost everything. Later new flickers of interest in life developed as they began to appreciate what the Skill Center had to offer and for whom it catered. It catered for them.

The West Street Skill Center had a comprehensive plan for handling those it fostered: assessment, training, counselling and placement. Every newcomer had his skills, or more usually his deficiencies assessed at an early stage. There were some who had difficulty in reading simple measurements — necessary in many operator and craft jobs. But the *reasons* could differ. Individuals were innumerate or subnumerate, or they had acquired faulty techniques, like taking readings from the wrong end of a ruler; or they were bright enough but did not possess suitable spectacles. Here was the cycle of deprivation. Someone long out of work could not afford proper glasses and being unable to cope with application forms could not land a job. As a consequence poverty deepened.

Once an individual's capacity was assessed, the next step was to develop skills appropriate both to the person and to the job market. Reconciling the two was not that easy. For one thing the job market was slack and it was difficult to predict where the new jobs would come from.

The solution was to provide background training in likely fields. Common combinations were machine-shop skills, electrical work and data processing. Some contract work was brought into the Center. This meant that 'real' jobs were being performed. But there was also a strong training element. Inevitably individuals showed more flair for one job than another. When that happened more training and experience would be offered in the field for which aptitude was being shown.

Those who enrolled in CPI not only had skill deficiencies but many had personal problems too. The close relationship which training allows provided a means of approaching sensitive issues. So trainers had the opportunity to become counsellors. Counselling was especially important for one of CPI's programmes that catered for the young unemployed, many of whom had a delinquent past (and often present). Cases were quoted of some who were subject to violence and abuse at home or came from households where one or more senior members regularly engaged in crime. Wherever possible these young people were found accommodation in a hostel. Tackling a personal problem in a constructive way often brought progress and renewed interest in learning.

Counselling was thus an inherent part of a trainer's job. But with difficult cases specialist counselling was needed. Here Community Progress Incorporated was fortunate in having the services available of a distinguished counselling psychologist Dr 'Bernie' Berner. Bernie had a great capacity for talking to people and for collecting and interpreting other data about them. More unusually for those in the counselling field, he had an intimate knowledge of the job market. Further he had a great facility for seeing job characteristics in terms of the aptitudes and skills that his clients possessed.

Bernie was a modest man and many of his successes in finding jobs for seemingly unemployable individuals were mentioned by his colleagues in

CPI. However, the story which well illustrates his approach was told to me when we had dinner together.

Top East Coast salesperson

Joe had lost the use of his arms and legs when his car had driven into the buttress of a bridge on the turnpike or motorway. The accident was in fact a suicide bid. Joe had been a butcher and his business had begun to fail when supermarkets took over more and more of the meat trade. At the same time his marriage broke up. It was then that he decided to end his life. But he had failed there too. Joe was now in the situation where his prospects looked bleak and hopeless.

Joe was nursed back to health slowly. It was not long before he felt he 'wanted to do something'. However, despite his referral, Joe's physical incapacity barred him from any of their training or skill programmes. And so as a last resort he was passed over to Bernie.

This was one of Bernie's most difficult referrals. After all what job can society offer a quadriplegic and suicide case? Bernie set about giving Joe a battery of aptitude tests. Joe emerged as intelligent and energetic. He had strong social qualities and loved meeting and interacting with people. Bernie was also impressed with Joe's evident social skills at interview. The problem was how to capitalize on these strengths and to compensate for the man's physical disadvantages all at the same time? The solution devised by Bernie, with Joe's active co-operation, was to pursue a career in life insurance. Normally this would have called for a good deal of physical mobility in visiting potential clients. But Bernie established that much of the work could be done on the telephone. The trouble was that Joe could now no longer dial nor pick up and hold the telephone earpiece.

The solution was to have a special telephone made which Joe could use himself. Once that was done, Bernie made the first contact with a life insurance company, recommended Joe for a position with them and helped to set up the job. He also helped Joe to sort out his private affairs. Joe had met a nurse in hospital who had played a personal part in helping him to recover his self-esteem. Susan continued to see Joe after his discharge from hospital and was brought into the rehabilitation programme. Romance followed and Joe and Susan married.

Joe was a natural salesman. He would telephone potential clients, including those who had written into the insurance company asking for details. After a good deal of chatting up, agreement would be reached in principle that the client would take out a particular policy. Joe would declare: 'OK, I'll drive round and we could sign it up on the spot'. Joe, of course, had a driver who would take him there and escort him into the house. Clients were surprised to meet a paralysed company representative, but in general they took it in good part. Joe became so successful in his job that he won his company's award as the top East Coast salesperson of the year.

Bernie was the first true jobmaker I had met. He was a jobmaker in the sense that he made the job for this particular, highly disadvantaged person. Had Bernie confined himself to assessment, counselling and training, Joe would never have found employment or at least it would have been a near miracle if he had done so.

Job developers

Though it may not have been part of the original intention, CPI was in the jobmaking business. After all, that was the ultimate purpose of the 'human renewal programme'. Whatever techniques were used, what counted in the end was whether an unemployed person with poor prospects could eventually be found a job. Bernie was the shining star among jobmakers but he was not the only one. There were other important contributors in a related field. They were known as 'job developers'.

Job developers had a role to play in CPI that was complementary to that played by neighbourhood workers. In other words, while the West Street Skill Center needed neighbourhood workers to ensure that it brought in the target population, it also needed job developers to ensure that those leaving the Center could secure employment. Specialist personnel were required to cope with both the unemployed incomers and the outgoing trained workers of the Center. In fact the 'output' problems were at least as challenging as the 'input' ones. Trained workers need to be 'placed' or failing that, new opportunities have to be opened up, and that is where the job developers came in.

Placement involves matching the skills of those leaving with the demands of jobs available outside. This is a major undertaking in itself and one which proved very important for getting trainees into a job. But sometimes more was required than merely responding to published job vacancies.

Job developers visited all firms in the area with one query: 'Have you any job vacancies for which some of our trainees might be considered?' The usual answer was 'No'. This would then be followed by a second question: 'Is it possible that you might create some new jobs in the future? If so, what would they be like? We need to know because we try to develop our training programmes to take account of local needs'.

The West Street Skill Center created a good image for itself by asking this question. Firms took note of the fact that here was a potential source of supply of people with relevant skills. Sometimes the CPI's approach would even prompt a more immediate and positive response. 'We could do with an extra machinist for a few hours a week, but it would not be a full-time job. He would need to do his own machine setting, but most operators cannot manage that, We also have some work in our loading section, but that again would not justify a full-time appointment. Then there is a certain amount of invoicing work to be done. We are often delayed there. Still that calls for a different type of person.'

The job developers took the line that there were often hidden jobs about. The need was to bring out this hidden need and make the employer more conscious of it. This was the stage of *revelation*. The next crucial stage was one of *combination*. A bit of a job here and a bit of a job there could add up to one new job. This composite requirement was often difficult to project. A firm might advertise for a carpenter, a machinist or a storekeeper because everyone would know what that job meant. But how could one describe a job that carried no obvious title? The firm would not try. So it was understandable that an employer was generally glad to accept the services of an intermediary who could help to identify the requirements and find the right person to slot into one of these hard-to-describe positions.

Job developers need credibility and that can only be earned. The West Street Skill Center took great pains to ensure that it would send to new developed jobs only those individuals who stood a reasonable chance of making a success of the appointment. The chances of meeting a firm's expectations in this field were good because of the care that was taken. The eligibility of each trainee was considered in terms of a broad spectrum of available data on personal factors, special aptitudes and skills acquired in the Center. In practice CPI succeeded in gaining a high reputation in the New Haven area as an institution that did its research on jobs and supplied suitable people.

My own role as an OECD visiting consultant to Community Progress Incorporated was to set up training programmes suited to the special characteristics of older workers, including those who had been out of work for a long time. These people were prone to be cast aside as slow or even untrainable. What is more they were reluctant to submit themselves to demanding training programmes especially if these were technical in nature or involved fast-moving machinery.

The Discovery Method

We devised a number of ways of overcoming these fears. One of the most successful methods was to engage the men in ancillary work in the environment of the machines. Later when the fearsome nature of these mechanical monsters had worn off, we managed to persuade them to become trainee operatives themselves[1]. My main task, however, was to adapt training methods so that they would find learning easy and rewarding. Older trainees do not enjoy being treated like schoolchildren. They like to find out for themselves but they need guidance. The method we found suitable is called the Discovery Method. Our approach was described in my report[2] on the project as follows:

A training experiment

The Discovery Method cultivates understanding other than by verbal instruction or physical demonstration. Tasks and problems, graded in difficulty, are presented according to the trainee's existing knowledge and progress. It is in the solving of the problem that the trainee develops understanding, which can later be classified and reinforced by group discussion or by enunciation of the principle, if appropriate to the situation and if requested by the trainee.

The art of applying the Discovery Method lies in devising tasks which are not beyond the unaided accomplishment of the trainee at each stage in the learning process, even if he starts by knowing virtually nothing about a subject. The trainee may be helped to discover the response by reducing the complexity of the task as it appears in the real situation; for example, by introducing cues such as the use of colour to indicate which controls have to be operated on a complex machine and so leaving the trainee free to concentrate on other problems confronting him; or by offering hints devised to restrict the amount of information through which the trainee has to sort in order to reach his decision.

Sometimes 'discovering' is rendered possible by use of specially prepared materials. These retain essential features but eliminate non-essential features especially those irrelevant to or liable to interfere with progress in learning; or the critical features of materials may be enlarged to make it easier to perceive them and so more easily to observe the functional relationship of different parts of working tools and materials. In other words, the physical changes are designed to increase the prospects that the trainee will be able to discover something for himself.

The work undertaken at CPI was a scientific experiment as much as it was a demonstration programme. Younger and older trainees engaged in machine operating, electrical work and data processing were divided into groups trained separately by either the Discovery Method or a traditional method

[1] OECD (1965). Training Methods. In *Employment of Older Workers*, No. 2. Paris: OECD.
[2] OECD (1969). The Discovery Method: An International Experiment in Retraining. In *Series Employment of Older Workers*, No. 6. Paris: OECD.

and their results were compared on independently assessed performance criteria. Altogether, while I was there, 242 trainees participated in the experiments in twenty-one separate training groups. All this took some time to develop. A somewhat complicated pattern of results emerged but where notable differences in achievement did show themselves these were in favour of those trained by the Discovery Method. At any rate the United States Department of Labor, the main funding body behind the CPI, seemed pleased with the outcome. As a consequence we were commissioned to make a film about the methods used.

The fact that American fees were about to be paid on my next visit produced undreamt of visa complications. As I was to work under contract, the employing body, the US Department of Labor, had first to prove that no American was available to do the same job. The dynamic intermediary at the Department almost despaired of meeting the stringent conditions, one of which was that the final application form should be signed by a judge.

'Don't worry,' he said. 'I'll do my best and ring you again in twenty-four hours.' He was as good as his word. 'You can't believe what I've been through,' he gasped. Still, he declared he was holding the signed form in his hand.

Americans hate bureaucracy even if they create it. One well-known British training consultant after the last war secured contracts in the USA but ran up against formidable visa problems. There was no suitable heading to cover the reason for his business trip. The idea that a Briton could act as a consultant to American industry was unthinkable. 'Don't worry,' said an official. 'We'll put you down as a variety artist.' He did – and thereafter a leading British consultant became a variety artist on regular missions to American manufacturing industry.

The training results achieved at CPI may have been pleasing but I was conscious that training was only a means to an end. On the final page of my OECD Report I wrote (page 84):

> Finally, whatever evaluations may be placed on the research programme, some mention should be made of the outcome of the experiment for the trainees themselves, irrespective of training method used. Within a month of the conclusion of Phase I, over 75 per cent of the trainees completing the programme had been placed in suitable employment, most of them in jobs with better pay and prospects than they had ever had before. Three months later, 70 per cent of the trainees placed were still in their jobs. The trainees included a high proportion of people with physical handicaps or psychiatric histories and most had poor education and employment records. Informal estimates of those working in the State Department Employment Service had predicted an ultimate placement of not more than 20 per cent.

My experience with Community Progress Incorporated showed me that not only apparently unpromising people could be developed through training and counselling to take on demanding skilled jobs, but also jobs could be developed in a local environment even when there were ostensibly few around. Jobmakers were as important as trainers: in fact both occupations had an indispensable part to play in the overall package for getting the long-term unemployed and hard-to-place back into employment. In retrospect I felt very grateful to Sol Barkin for his foresight in choosing CPI as the place in which I should work.

Some conclusions

It is easy to believe in the inevitability of progress. The lessons learned at CPI seemed likely to spread, certainly through the USA and also through the rest of the developed world and perhaps on to developing countries, too. OECD provided the mechanism by which this might come to pass. Mike Sviridoff relinquished the Directorship of CPI to take up a similar appointment in New York where the challenge proved more daunting. Back in Paris, OECD was busy publicizing what had gone on, conducting international seminars and briefing its Council of Ministers on further ways in which its Active Manpower Policy could be made effective. In due course the general principles of the Policy received the assent of member countries of OECD and were put into operation under domestic programmes associated in the minds of the electorate with the governmental party of the day.

The transfer of a body of experience and methods from one set of people to another is never easy. It is made more difficult still if those responsible for the political administration of the programme decide to place their own stamp upon it, to simplify and to make such other changes as they consider desirable. The events that I was later to witness suggested that the principles of the Active Manpower Policy were misapplied by at least some of the governments that formally adopted them. The systems that produced good results on a small scale were to prove disappointing when they became standard national programmes operating under the aegis of a central bureaucracy. But before my hopes for the future were to founder, other valued experiences came my way.

3

Variants of the species

To have discovered a pocket of real jobmakers in the USA, operating within the broader tribe of job promoters, was as stimulating as it was unexpected. America has an image overseas of being a hire-and-fire country. New businesses boom or bust and the American worker shares in the see-saw economics of a volatile market. He may be fired at any moment but equally he is at liberty to pack his bags at any time and go off in search of a better paying job. In most countries the same truth applies but in the USA this reality is part of the legend that inspires the land of free enterprise. Each individual is a pioneer. And a pioneer is expected to make his way on his own in the world, unassisted by the State or the neighbourhood — especially where that neighbourhood may only be an arbitrary collection of immigrants with no common historically rooted sense of community. For all that, vigorous local communities in the USA have sprung up and have learned to tackle some of the major problems that affect their well-being.

While I had not expected to find such a diverse range of job promoters, in the USA, I had different expectations about Sweden, a country in which I was supervising another OECD project. Sweden has succeeded in establishing for itself in Europe and, to a lesser extent, throughout the rest of the world a reputation for leadership on employment issues and thinking. The facts support its position. Sweden has a sophisticated economy much of it based on engineering and with two leading car manufacturers, Volvo and Saab, in a population of only seven million; and Sweden is strong enough economically to produce its own weapons for its defence industry. Unemployment since the war has oscillated around two or three per cent and has never risen above four per cent even during the depression that followed the oil crisis. Sweden has had a major impact on international organizations through such distinguished figures as Dag Hammarsköld and Gunner Myrdal in the United Nations and Ghosta Rehn in OECD. Countries which have proved successful in ordering their domestic affairs, even if small in population, are capable of exercising influence on a world scale.

21

Sweden ought in theory, it has been argued, to have a high level of unemployment. Big firms dominate the economy (striving to become multinationals to escape the bounds of a limited home market) and the small firm sector is relatively weak. Incentives are low.

To understand something about the Swedish achievement and how the country reached its current position it is useful to take account of a leading figure less well known outside Sweden than some of his more celebrated compatriots.

Tage Erlander, as Prime Minister of Sweden, enjoyed twenty-three years of unbroken office, longer than that of any other European Prime Minister in this century in a democratic country. In an obituary in *The Times* Erlander was described as a man who 'guided the country to a succession of economic and social achievements that made Sweden the pride of social democracy in the western world. Here was a nation that was prosperous, well-ordered and blessed with extensive welfare services, even if it was also cursed with high taxation'.

Erlander had entered parliament as a Social Democrat in 1932. His party made important gains at the time of the Depression and Erlander, working on the Employment Commission, was to deal with unemployment at first hand. Before reaching the premiership he was in turn Minister of State at the Ministry of Social Welfare, Minister without Portfolio and Minister of Education.

On unemployment Erlander made his very radical mark by planning to avoid it. Firms were obliged to notify intended lay-offs six months before they took effect. Provisions were then made for emergency plans to be put into operation involving close co-ordination and consultation between central government, local government, industry and the trade unions. For example in one case with which I became familiar a company processing and trading in furs in a small remote forest town, where it was the chief employer, was faced with closure. The emergency committee, suitably funded, stepped in, found an established company in the furniture-making field that was interested in expansion, set up facilities in the town and provided training in the new skills. As a result the workers moved without an intervening break from the fur industry into training and straight into employment in the furniture-making industry.

The challenge in Sweden

At the time of my first visit to Sweden one per cent of the active working population was engaged in publicly-supported retraining programmes. Older workers were readily admitted into these programmes. A pre-existing interest in both training in general and our work in particular made it easy for us to start, and the facilities in Swedish training centres seemed very favourable for the conduct of a demonstration programme and an experimental study. The work to be undertaken was sponsored by the Board of Education and carried out in close liaison with the Institute of Applied Psychology in Stockholm under the direction of Dr Bengt Gustavsson. As seems common in Sweden, Bengt seemed to know personally everyone who mattered.

Our work was centred on adults being retrained in two engineering training centres, one in Tumba and the other in Norrköping. Groups of young adults and older adults were formed and were sub-divided on the basis of initial aptitude tests into the more able and less able trainees. The various sub-groups were trained by three methods: the Discovery Method, designed with the assistance of a team of Swedish colleagues assigned by Bengt to work with me, a programmed instruction method recently introduced by the Board of Education and the more traditional direct Instructor training. The results were compared in a careful evaluation by my colleagues.

From this a picture of some complexity emerged. The most important findings however were that the Discovery Method proved most effective where 'transfer of training' was measured (ie, the ability to tackle new test pieces), while traditional Instructor training was better where the test pieces were identical with or similar to the pieces used in training. The programmed instruction method was the least effective of the three, especially for the less able trainees.

These findings may have been of technical interest. But the salient fact of the matter was that whatever the method of training, those who had lost or, more commonly, were about to lose their job were absorbed anyway into new jobs already waiting for them. The explanation lay in the intricate network of manpower planning on which training rested, and which embraced private industry, local government and the central Ministries. Such an approach would have been unthinkable in the USA which depends far more on the verve of local community leaders and the distinguished professionals who reside in the area.

USA/Sweden: contrasts and insights

My visits to the USA and Sweden opened up new insights into the profession of job promotion. What became apparent however was that the Swedish job promoter was dissimilar to his American counterpart. The two were evidently different varieties of the same broad genus.

Why this should be was not absolutely clear. Eventually after numerous visits to both countries I began to form the view that part of the explanation lay in the fact that the USA and Sweden were contrasting societies with a contrasting set of expectations. Typically Americans are outgoing and impulsive while Swedes are reserved and thoughtful.

Americans are expected to look on the bright side. Boasting can be seen as a cheerful and positive feature, and not only in Texas. Almost the first information I was given about some of the distinguished Americans I met related to the salaries they earned, usually a closed subject in the UK. Swedes on the other hand decry their achievements. When visiting the most impressive up-to-date factories I was often told of all the mistakes that had been made. There was a virtual insistence that the factory was not as good as it should be, even if it was difficult to find anything at fault.

At dinner parties in the USA it was not uncommon for all the diners to be talking simultaneously so that it was difficult to think, let alone join in. In Sweden it was lack of talk that was embarrassing. On the occasions when I was invited to lecture in Stockholm, a stony silence followed at question time. This I attributed to language problems but was assured that this was not so. Apparently questions could have been taken as a form of impoliteness and indicate a lack of appreciation. Then there is the contrast in trust and the acceptance of conventions. America expects crime while Sweden regards it as an exceptional event. In New York a stroll out of one's hotel with a briefcase in hand can cause an encounter with the doorman checking whether you are trying to escape without having paid the bill. In Stockholm when leaving my hotel I happened to remark that I was travelling to Gothenburg but would be back later in the week. 'You can leave the bill till then, if you prefer,' said the wide-eyed receptionist. This was before the days when credit cards dominated one's life. Cashing a cheque provided another memorable experience. The weekend was coming up and I was running short of money. My OECD cheque was made out to a bank no branch of which existed in the city's suburb. The urgency to get back to central Stockholm was cut short by my Swedish colleague's suggestion that I cashed the cheque at another local bank across the road. 'But I don't have my passport with me,' I protested. Shoulders were shrugged. It was an in-and-out affair. A few minutes later I emerged with the cash in hand.

Sweden was the first country to introduce the green and red customs exits at airports, trusting passengers to choose whether or not they had anything to declare, and the first country to dispense with ticket collectors on the Underground.

While the USA and Sweden offer perhaps a sharp contrast to one another in style, policy and virtually in temperament, they share at least a similar record in other respects: both countries have long enjoyed a very high standard of living and both could claim to have led the way to economic growth from the depression that followed the world oil crisis with its massive rise in energy costs.

From the point of view of the job promoter, there seems to be more than one way to meet a given goal. The approach chosen is strongly influenced by the cultural characteristics of each society. In the USA unemployment tends to be seen as a failure to compete. It is common to find this handicap attributed to having an underprivileged background or to being a new immigrant unacquainted with Americanism. The remedy follows from the diagnosis. Much store is placed on further education, training and personal counselling. Americans are sustained by a belief that the jobs are out there to be found if only the individual is willing and motivated and has the desire to succeed. Anyone can make it. Yet help may be required. The helpers come in many shades and varieties and their range includes a small number of professional job promoters, some with an expert knowledge of the job market.

In Sweden, on the other hand, unemployment is seen less as a personal shortcoming and more as a socio-economic defect that is open to rectification. The combination of thinking that owes much to the long period of Social Democratic administration and the strong professional tradition in engineering in the country has combined to produce a *systems* approach to unemployment aided by project management.

The economy of Sweden is managed as a total system. The intention is to subject it to fine tuning. For example, Government freezes capital that belongs to companies so that it cannot be used for investment or distribution during a boom period when the economy is overheated. This capital is then 'unfrozen' when the economy is slack and needs fresh stimulus. Hence Swedish firms recover quickly from temporary recession: the means of doing so is in their own hands. By contrast in other countries it usually takes some time for the alternative approach to take effect where the aim is to quicken the pace of economic activity, based on higher government spending.

Another feature of Sweden's approach to promoting employment is its emphasis on *a high participation rate*. The work-load is spread out. Women are economically active – especially in comparison with, say, Holland and Ireland – and early retirement of either sex is not encouraged. Unemployment is seen as 'not participating economically', and on that account is theoretically and philosophically unacceptable. Those who lose their jobs are given every help to regain employment. If an unemployed worker refuses to accept a job or training place, his or her benefit can be stopped. This sanction is only politically acceptable because Sweden can guarantee the unemployed either jobs or training places. These mechanisms make it difficult for the unemployed to sit back and live 'on the dole'. The main emphasis lies in preventing unemployment rather than treating it through welfare.

One of the main aids to prevention is the early warning system introduced by Tage Erlander, to take early action in possible lay-offs. Representatives of central government, local government, industry and trade unions work together in a typically Swedish fashion to bring about an *ad hoc* solution to a threatened employment crisis in a particular locality. With funds available, they have the means to bring in or start up new enterprises and to retain workers before they lose the means of earning a livelihood.

Contrasts in job promoters

The job promoters in Sweden do not belong to any recognizable profession. Rather they are temporary members of a well established job promotion system. The members of these project groups develop clear mutual expectations based on shared objectives and a belief in the importance of their endeavours for the community.

Systems, however, have a way of perpetuating themselves. They have a life over and above that of the people who make them work. One of the factors on which Swedish labour economists place much emphasis is the flexibility of labour in meeting the demands of the labour market. Training is one means of making this happen. Another favoured method is to encourage the mobility of labour. In everyday language this involves inducing people to leave their homes and in effect destabilizes communities. This approach, in my view, seemed to work as badly in Sweden as it does elsewhere.

Unemployment in Sweden, as in England, is subjected to a North-South gradient. That unemployment should be relatively high in the North of Sweden is understandable since the North is not near anywhere in particular and suffers a long, very cold winter. Nevertheless for the people who live there it is home. To economists living in Stockholm it may seem self-evident that people living up North would wish to move South to a high standard of living and a better environment where jobs can be assured.

In the Training Centre at Tumba, south of Stockholm, I had the privilege of meeting some Lapps. The alternative they faced, as it was explained to me, lay in accepting a low standard of living up North with little prospect of advancement, or moving down South and, by being trained for engineering jobs, secure a promising future for themselves and their families. In the USA it would be left to the families themselves to make that decision unaided in terms of material assistance and unprompted by the government. In the Swedish Welfare State pressures built up to bring into the formal employment system those who had previously been semi-nomadic and who now realized they could technically claim to be unemployed. The Swedish government approached the subject with some magnanimity. Lapps were given free rail passes to come down to Stockholm to survey the scene and to visit the Training Centre at Tumba. Those who accepted training were given full financial support and regular free rail travel was provided for their visiting families. Generous relocation grants were available. Nonetheless the Lapps I talked to, while appreciative of the help received, were clearly very unhappy. They would have preferred to have had the same training and job opportunities back in their own territory. Their families, we were told, were equally unhappy too. The snow wastes and birch forests may not appeal to some people but they have a great pull on those who have lived in them for generations.

The major differences between the American and Swedish approaches to job promotion are now evident. Sweden works on a strategy that is conceived for the country as a whole and contains a great number of special provisions. But the strategy also operates in a flexible way with locally designed programmes that qualify for central government funding. The key job promoters who design and to a lesser extent operate the programme have a systems outlook. Professionally they incorporate people from different backgrounds but the principal operators are labour economists. The United States on the other hand, with the exception of the Franklin D. Roosevelt and John Kennedy eras, has not attempted to produce a coherent national strategy for jobs. Instead it relies on a buoyant economy to lift employment. Since the USA is amply supplied with enterprising people, this approach works reasonably well in many parts of the country, especially those well served locally by higher educational establishments. Pockets of unemployment create considerable problems in other areas and have given rise to a variety of community institutions and approaches. If, however, they share any characteristic in common it is that they tend to be person-orientated with a much higher personal counselling content than would be found in their European counterparts. All this is in keeping with the human resource characteristics of the USA. The large output from higher educational institutions of graduates in the behavioural sciences provides a ready supply of professionally qualified helpers who can direct their efforts towards individuals and small groups. The typical job promoter in the United States is someone who enhances skills, boosts confidence, improves presentation through grooming, imparts the techniques of applying for jobs and performing well at interview and comes to terms with the characteristics of the labour market in whatever form it is to be found locally.

The aim of the American job promoter — to get a client a job -- is broadly the same as that of the Swedish job equivalent. But they approach the subject from different ends of the spectrum. In the USA the accent is on individualism and in Sweden on holism. Job promoters in other countries approximate to a greater or lesser degree to one or other of these basic models.

Whatever national variations in job promoters exist they have at least enough in common to mark them out as members of the same species. In this respect they are to be differentiated from the more numerous public amanuenses who provide social security to the unemployed, assess their eligibility, dispense welfare services to them and enrol them in specialist programmes. To these may be added the administrators who help to keep the jobless occupied, provide information, or process them through educational methods and procedures that improve the job prospects of their clients. This group may be engaged in worthy activities. But the aim of helping people to gain viable jobs is never a primary purpose and seldom even an incidental purpose of their work.

Some time during the period when I discovered the two basic patterns of job promoter I had occasion to change my own job and move into a new environment, where as it happened, I was to encounter another member of the species.

The next stage in an apprenticeship

My contract had come to an end at Cranfield College and now I had to choose between continuing an academic life or moving into industry. Fate was to assist the choice. One of those who passed through management courses held at Cranfield was Michael Merriam, the youngest son of Sir Lawrence Merriam, Chairman of BX Plastics, then an independent company situated near the mouth of the Stour in attractive marsh country on the borders of Essex and Suffolk. Michael and I spent some time discussing problems of inspection, quality control and material efficiency. He felt I might be able to assist the firm and that was what prompted me to move for a long period away from academic and public work and into the private sector.

At the time, BX Plastics and its subsidiaries employed about 1800 people. Its main plant near Manningtree was remotely situated on a site deliberately chosen when the company had moved in 1883 from a densely populated district in Walthamstow on the eastern side of London. Xylonite or celluloid has only a slightly different chemical composition from gunpowder and the hazards of manufacture had alarmed townspeople as much as the production of nuclear energy does today. When the company moved it brought much of its work force with it – managers, foremen and workers. Now resettled in the villages of the Constable country – so named because the area figured prominently in the rustic paintings of John Constable – the immigrant population had settled down and intermarried with the locals. But still the old names continued, Merriam, Couborough, Jackson, Tabard, from one industrial generation to the next. The whole area as well as the leading families depended economically and socially on the continued prosperity of BX Plastics.

The Merriams were said to rule the company by divine right, that is to say they had held their position for three generations without ever holding a majority of the shares. Everybody expected their reign to continue indefinitely. All the Merriams went to Eton and did 'huntin', shootin' and fishin'' and were regarded as the local gentry. Sir Lawrence took a keen interest in his workers, was Chairman of the Joint Production Committee and successfully defused any potentially difficult issues threatening industrial relations. The factory operated on a three-shift system, seven days a week. Sir Lawrence never missed an opportunity following a late night theatre or formal dinner to inspect the night shift while clad in his evening dress regalia. He would ask searching questions on production matters and inquire after the families of all those to whom he talked. Incongruous though the inspection might have seemed at the time, the workers loved it.

All this information was conveyed to me by stout, middle-aged, white-coated tea-ladies. In the morning and in the afternoon their well-stocked trolleys trundled down the executive office block. The range of refreshments they served, much of which was home-made, far surpassed in quality the fare from canteen and vending machine which were to supersede them. The tea-ladies not only provided a service which avoided the necessity for the hungry or thirsty to move from their offices but were also controllers of 'the grapevine'. If someone was away ill, the reason could be instantly ascertained. Impending changes in appointments and transfers were often heralded by these ladies of the trolley before the news became generally available from official sources.

Managers, workers and tea-ladies belonged to the same rural communities and their families had been associated with one another for generations. Perhaps it is not unnatural therefore that jobcutting had not become the language of management. If productivity is to be improved, while demand for the company's products remains constant, there is only one solution that avoids job losses. That solution is to increase the range of a company's products. BX Plastics invested heavily in research and development at Lawford Place, an establishment perched on a small hill overlooking the factory and the Stour valley.

One of Sir Lawrence's notable actions was to provide the first scientific job for Margaret Thatcher, later to become British Prime Minister. We both started work in the company about the same time but did not meet. Any contribution Margaret Thatcher may have made to research at Lawford Place is lost in the shrouds of time. But she is remembered for having tried to start a staff association with herself at the head. Her persuasive powers had evidently not fully developed then for the other scientists would have none of it. Thereafter she left to embark on her political career.

When Sir Lawrence retired a new uncertainty arose on the part of the major shareholders about the management and future direction of the company. The era of the takeover bidders was commencing.

The company was to change hands several times during the period of a few years. The managers belonging to the old families were edged out, along with large numbers of production workers and all the tea-ladies.

Transatlantic management took over for a period. The company's research and development endeavours were greatly scaled down. Short-term financial improvements were registered but later the interlopers withdrew. Other managers were brought in to handle deteriorating industrial relations and an adverse trading situation.

Jobs and the family

The reluctance of family-run firms to sanction job losses, unless unavoidable is something I first observed while I was at BX Plastics. But I have noted the same phenomenon since both in various parts of the UK and in the rest of the world. In these cases human considerations play a part in the adoption of policy and determined efforts are made to explore redeployment through expansion into new ventures. The attitude of these family-based executives contrast with the new breed of professional managers, most of whom have no roots in the firm or the local community. Cutting jobs and therefore costs is usually seized upon as the first way out of a crisis and a quick way of registering improved performance. The subject is discussed not with distaste but with a burning zeal and almost a sense of pride. Macho management proves a man's worth and is often taken as the mark of a rising career. The social consequence of mass dismissals tend to be set aside as being a matter for government.

Family firms with dynasties tend to extend their interest in succession even to the families of workers. The largest privately owned company in the United Kingdom, until it was turned into a public company very recently, was Pilkington, the glass makers of St Helens. Pilkington has invested heavily in research and development over the years and one of the fruits of this endeavour has been float glass for which the company has developed a world-wide market. Even so, while many new jobs have arisen, job losses have occurred. But the effect of these on the local community, which lies in an area of economic depression, has been cushioned with Pilkington money to create the St Helens Trust which can justifiably claim to be the largest privately backed job-creation enterprise in Britain.

Perhaps the best-known country where large firms are run by dynastic families is Japan which has a very distinctive large-firm industrial culture. A high premium is placed on loyalty, which is a two-way business, with the employee gaining job security, a rare luxury at the present time. The Mitsubishi family-run company, for example, has only been able to provide job security by investing heavily in research and development, the prerequisite to new job-creating products and models. The result of this direction of effort has been the creation of vast numbers of new jobs to replace those removed by automation and robotic machines, not only in large firms but also in the small supplier firms which serve them. Japan is a highly populous industrial country of the type that many believe is highly susceptible to unemployment in the modern world. Yet its unemployment runs at little more than 2 per cent and reaches 3 per cent only on rare occasions.

Another country in which family firms are very strong is Switzerland. Its traditional watch-making industry has been hard hit by technical developments that have rendered obsolete the precision machinery and assembly skills that gave the industry its name. Switzerland is also characterized by its communes, small very stable local communities, which due to the decentralized nature of government in Switzerland, enjoy a large measure of autonomy over their local affairs. The small watch-making firms that operate in these areas have combined through their industrial federation to finance new types of product development, the effect of which is to protect jobs. The well-known Swatch is a product of that investment. Switzerland's unemployment is just about the lowest in the industrial world, operating usually at a little over 1 per cent. A number of other factors which affect this will be discussed later. Certainly one point which arose from our inquiries in Switzerland is the reluctance of those managing small firms to lay off workers who live in the same valley and are part of the same commune.

There is then a third type of job promoter who is to all external appearances, purely and simply an industrialist, but with a difference. We know that people act from mixed motives. But where an industrialist is part of the same community as those he employs there is an intrinsic tendency for his business decisions to be determined not wholly by the desire to make the maximum profit for himself but by some sense of need to develop plans that create job opportunities for others. It is virtually an understatement to refer to such a person as a job promoter since real jobs are being created directly. Here the title of jobmaker is more apt and may encompass those industrialists and entrepreneurs whose activities generate new employment, even if in some cases that outcome is only a by-product of their main endeavour.

Some conclusions

To summarize: we have detected three recognizable groups of job promoter who act with the intention of generating new employment.

The first group are the *systems scientists,* who by profession are typically labour economists operating within the machinery of government. They are nearly always advisers. And advisers are seldom in a position to undertake responsibility for the consequences of the advice they offer.

The second group comprises *people-helpers,* providing moral and technical support to those who are striving to secure new employment.

These helpers tend to be based on or may even run and manage local institutions set up with the express purpose of finding work or fostering and creating work for the unemployed. This group usually contains the most dedicated professionals. Their impact, however, is limited by lack of training, a scarcity of resources and more importantly by the fact that because they are not recognized they have to operate outside, and often in conflict with, the official systems run by the State.

The third group consists of *business men and industrialists* who accept jobmaking as having a place among their personal objectives. Their effect on employment, however, gains only scant recognition because in their public utterances they have to accept that the priorities of their business have an overriding influence on their decisions.

Job promoters in their various groupings can be fostered or they can be ignored. They can be offered an environment in which they can flourish, or they may find themselves facing conditions that discourage the exercise of their skills. At any rate this emergent profession had not yet arrived on the historical agenda. Other matters began to dominate public thinking on the various issues of employment.

4

An era of training

A belief that near full employment would continue with a rising standard of living for all was widely held in industrialized countries for a long time after the last war. The pre-war fears about mass unemployment were gradually dispelled as prosperity spread. Only the prospect that automation might eventually destroy jobs caused general concern. Even this fear began to recede once it became apparent that automation affected a restricted range of jobs, applied more to manufacturing and less to the service industries, wherein the largest growth of jobs was foreseen, and in any case was accompanied by a broadening in the range of job opportunities becoming available. The Active Manpower Policy of the OECD had stressed the importance of retraining, among a number of other measures, as the means of enabling those without jobs to move into the new forms of employment springing up. Training was seen as a force for growth in the economy, a beacon for lighting up the future. It was against this background that training became the primary focus of government manpower policy in most OECD countries.

The UK had developed its own specific approach to training and we soon became involved in the national effort. A good deal of work in the training field was being commissioned. While I had been conducting my OECD demonstration programmes, my wife, Eunice, had written two booklets, one dealing with her experiments on training adults in the Post Office and another a study of training in the clothing industry.[1,2] Both booklets had aroused widespread interest. So it came about that as a result of our joint activities and with the aid of substantial grants from the Ford Foundation and the DSIR we set up the Unit for Research into Problems of Industrial Retraining situated in Cambridge. As the national interest in training developed, the Unit grew in influence. Eunice was invited to

[1] Belbin, Eunice, Sergean, Robert. *Training in the Clothing Industry: A study of recruitment, training and education.* London: Twentieth Century Press.

[2] Belbin, Eunice. Training the Adult Worker. In *Problems of Progress in Industry.* London: Department of Scientific and Industrial Research.

become a member of the Central Training Council, the government body which supervised the operations of the newly passed Industrial Training Act.

Industrial training: the Act

Here some mention needs to be made of the intentions underlying the formulation of the Act. Essentially it was conceived as a way of overcoming the persistent skill shortages that beset industry, weakened the economy, held back the standard of living and restricted the growth of jobs. The problem arose in the first place because firms found they could acquire the skills they needed more cheaply by poaching from other firms rather than by financing training themselves. During a period of economic boom it was becoming difficult to retain a skilled worker, who might have been trained over a number of years, when a competitor was prepared to pay a higher wage. The dilemma was to lose the worker or to engage in a leapfrogging wages battle which had implications for the wages of all other employees. There was no obvious satisfactory solution to this problem. What happened in practice was that companies reduced their involvement in training.

The Industrial Training Act set out to break this cycle by introducing a number of measures. The first measure was to establish Training Boards which eventually became twenty-four in number. These Boards were set up to look at the immediate and long-term requirements for skills in the particular industries that fell within their province. The Training Boards devised appropriate training programmes, developed an industrial training service and appointed training advisers to liaise with companies.

The second important measure under the Act was the institution of the levy-grant system. The Boards were empowered to raise a levy in respect of each worker employed in industry. Companies were inspected by training advisers to assess whether they were making adequate provision to meet their own training needs. Those judged to be doing so were eligible to receive the return of the greater part, or even the whole, of that levy in the form of a grant. 'Poaching' companies, however, paid the levy but received no grant. Thereby the incentive for firms to train was re-established. At the same time Boards themselves provided much needed expertise, especially useful for firms lacking their own training resources.

The suddenness of the Industrial Training Act produced its own problems. At one moment the country was severely deficient in training. A year later a comprehensive system was operating embracing the whole country and most firms of any size. Could one find the skills and expertise to make such a great leap forward in so short a period?

The upsurge in the demand for training resulted in the appointment of training officers on a massive scale, many of whom had recently been complete greenhorns. Those with only limited pre-existing experience or knowledge of training found themselves cast as training advisers to the Training Boards with powers to make major decisions about the level of training in large companies. Inevitably, some firms reacted with indignation at this new imposition. The financial burden imposed by the levy was unwelcome and the introduction of an external inspectorate resented. Industry possessed a degree of influence over its Boards but the formula was that only one third of the board governors were industrial appointees. The other two-thirds comprised trade union appointees and independent members usually from the field of vocational education.

While the Industrial Training Act constituted a major step forward in increasing the supply of skilled manpower and safeguarding jobs in the future, the new measures introduced were clearly undergoing teething problems. From her position on the Central Training Council, Eunice became aware of the many things that needed to be done if the Act was to prove a practical success. We decided to broaden our specialized interest in the training of adults to cover training in general. So our Unit was renamed the Industrial Training Research Unit (ITRU). The problem of making a success of the Industrial Training Act, as we saw it, hinged on two issues: one was whether an adequate number of training officers could be trained to the standard which the Act demanded, and the second was whether the Boards had the expertise to make a significant contribution to the industries that they were designed to serve. On both counts ITRU was actively engaged.

One cannot have good training without having good training officers. How should they be selected? What should be the curriculum of the courses on which their skills are developed? How could their effectiveness as training officers be assessed and measured? We addressed ourselves to all these issues. In practice, however one learned a great deal from handling everyday problems under less than ideal conditions. On one occasion I found myself tying to prepare material for a group whose members included an experienced executive, a recent charge hand, a sewing machinist in a clothing factory and a Cambridge University graduate who had just completed his doctorate. With such a group there was no way in which one could please all the people all the time.

In retrospect, it may seem surprising that the type of industrial training system that Britain developed in this era progressed as rapidly as it did. As in war time a number of people responded quickly to the demands made upon them and set about their tasks with considerable dedication. The Training Boards were initially short of expertise in ways of analysing skill needs, in knowing how to design training programmes and how to choose a method within the range of training methods available to meet their needs; they lacked the theoretical knowledge and the practical experience to adapt standard programmes to meet the problems posed by special groups, for example, different learning styles, or those who had only scant knowledge of English; they were unsure how to assess the trainability of candidates presenting themselves for course programmes of varying complexity and sophistication; few Training Boards had the facilities for carrying out research and development studies that allowed them to treat issues fundamental to a specific industry.

This broad field provided an opportunity for ITRU which began to grow steadily in response to demand. Our work was made easier by the calibre of person we were able to recruit. Our location in Cambridge played a part in enabling us to attract very able research and development workers who could tackle challenging problems. We published a great deal, conducted seminars on specific topics, installed on-site development programmes, and, to cope with the additional demand for information, began to run regular Open Days for the benefit of training officers, training advisers, civil servants and visiting parties from overseas.

The Industrial Training Act had been set up with three principal objectives in mind: 'an increase in the quantity of training, an increase in its quality and a fair distribution of training'. It has been an enormous undertaking. When Barbara Castle, the first Minister to hold the new title of Secretary of State for Employment and Productivity, came to Cambridge to open the golden jubilee conference of BACIE (the British Association for Commercial and Industrial Education) she announced '. . . the development of industrial training over the past years is a success story!'

It was not an unjustified claim. Yet in spite of what had been achieved, the Industrial Training Act was not allowed to run in the way in which its designers had originally intended. Pressures to change the Act in its original form began to mount as the numbers employed in manufacturing employment fell, slowly at first and then more rapidly. The post-war boom was coming to an end. In addition the long anticipated shift from industrial employment to employment in the service section of the economy had started to take place. This trend did not in itself create any major problem. Yet the two factors taken together, resulting in a smaller intake of recruits into industry, detracted from the priority attached and the status given to training in the industrial community.

The training levy was now seen as a tax, comparable with and as unpopular as other taxes, rather than as an instrument for spreading the cost of training to the collective benefit of industry itself.

The coming of the Manpower Services Commission

Whether the Industrial Training Act should have been left to run as it was in spite of the criticisms directed against it is debatable. At any rate it was superseded, after a change in government, by the Employment and Training Act. This new Act purported to widen the terms of reference under which manpower issues were being considered. The Minister of State in the now renamed Department of Employment put it this way: 'There was a pretty strong feeling that what was needed was a national manpower commission bringing under one umbrella the two related functions of finding jobs for people and seeing that they were properly trained!' The Central Training Council was dissolved and the Manpower Services Commission was set up with wide-ranging powers including that of supervising the Industrial Training Boards.

The Employment and Training Act, like the Industrial Training Act before it, took some time to get into its stride. The Manpower Services Commission was formed at a time when the employment scenario was changing significantly. The older traditional industries, like shipbuilding, steel and coal were contracting. Even newer ones, like vehicle production, were under pressure. The Industrial Training Boards may have been well adapted to deal with the inflow of employees into an industry; they were not equipped to cope with the problems of an outflow. Unless effective mechanisms can be developed in particular locations to provide new employment for those about to be displaced from older industries, there is always a risk that large numbers of workers who lose their jobs will become permanently unemployed.

The MSC inaugurated a national approach to manpower issues. Its aims expressed concisely under its first Chairman, Sir Denis Barnes, were:

1 to enable the country's manpower resources to be developed and contribute fully to economic well-being;
2 to ensure that there is available to each worker the opportunities and services he or she needs in order to lead a satisfactory working life.

When Barnes was succeeded as Chairman by Richard O'Brien, shortly to become Sir Richard O'Brien, the numbers of people out of work had grown to exceed by far the numbers of unfilled vacancies awaiting suitable workers. In these circumstances problems of unemployment could no longer be explained as mismatches in the labour market, for which training could provide an effective answer. New means had to be found for countering unemployment.

Within a year of Richard O'Brien's appointment a new and extended set of aims was drawn up.

The aims were stated as being:

1 to contribute to efforts to raise employment and reduce unemployment;
2 to help assist manpower resources to be developed, and contribute fully to economic well-being;
3 to help secure for each worker the opportunities and services he or she needs in order to lead a more satisfying working life;

4   to improve the quality of decisions affecting manpower;
5   to improve the efficiency and effectiveness of the Commission.

The adoption of the first of these aims was a very significant move on the part of the MSC. It was one of which we needed to take account. And we were in a good position to do so. The Industrial Training Research Unit had by now become the largest supplier of research and development services to the MSC.

Growing has it disadvantages. Administrative burdens multiply with the increasing volume of work undertaken. This rule was broken in our case – I think we were especially privileged – when a new procedure was adopted for commissioning contracts. Instead of having to engage in lengthy negotiations on a contract-by-contract basis on R & D projects many of which were short-term, we met leading officials of the MSC once a year, presented our annual report for the previous year and outlined the work in which we were planning to engage. The MSC for its part outlined the problems with which they were concerned and we discussed how in principle they might be attacked. Agreement would then be reached in a modified programme for the coming year. A budget would be fixed and there would be follow-up paper work. Later we operated under a new arrangement based on a five-year rolling grant which allowed us to spend 10 per cent of our budget on research of our own choosing. So a system was introduced of singular simplicity. Its special advantage was that we could plan ahead and recruit high calibre staff for work in specific areas and offer them reasonably secure appointments. It might be thought that this generous arrangement which MSC operated with us would tempt us to coast. In fact this was not so. We were described by MSC as 'running a tight ship' and we were usually underspent on budget.

The 10 per cent discretionary grant enabled us to focus on issues that we judged to be important in the long term. Here we took account of the MSC's own special interests and aims. The field in which we chose to invest our discretionary resources was exactly that which was embodied in the first of the MSC's stated aims: *to contribute to efforts to raise employment and reduce unemployment.*

Training or work?

Our experience told us that the MSC's preoccupation with training had resulted in a whole range of policies that were in danger of becoming obsolete. As in other countries, regional disparities in economic activity and employment in the UK were becoming increasingly marked. Training might still be a matter of prime importance in thriving zones. But in depressed industrial areas many able trainees and skilled people were idle for want of work. The Skillcentres (Government Training Centres) we had visited showed a depressing picture. Technically, the training was proceeding well. But the human output from the Skillcentres was now adding to the queue for jobs and particular trades.

When we visited a number of Skillcentres in the industrial North, we found the morale of instructors to be very low. We were told that it was very difficult to teach trainees when they could see no hope of getting a job after their training had been completed. Some of the instructors were keen to go out into firms and negotiate with employers about job possibilities, to offer them trainees 'on trial' and to provide a back-up training service within the firm itself. We encountered a wealth of ideas and a zest to do something to improve the possibilities of getting trainees into real jobs.

What transpired was that the instructors were prevented by the system from putting any of their ideas into action. Their job was training. They would be trespassing into the province of the Ministry's employment section if they engaged in any of the initiatives they were contemplating. The managers of Skillcentres, being aware of what was going on and being more conversant with protocol than instructors, quickly put a stop to any attempt to step beyond standard duties. One manager prided himself on bending the rules as far as he dared. Yet even he recognized that there were limits to what a single sally could achieve without support from above.

The disillusionment with training as the prime instrument for regenerating employment in areas where major industries were in decline began to spread: certainly it spread from the trainees, to the instructors, to us. In contrast, public policy placed what we considered an undue emphasis on the value of training as a prescriptive remedy for unemployment in all areas.

Increasingly we found ourselves in an invidious position. Deservedly or undeservedly we had become part of the establishment. Eunice had been decorated at Buckingham Palace with the Order of the British Empire for her services to training and we had both been made Honorary Fellows of the Institute of Training and Development in a ceremony at Oxford. Yet here we were playing down the value of training as the spearhead for attacking unemployment in depressed areas and advocating instead a more comprehensive manpower approach to which we were now devoting the greater part of our energies. In our view training people for jobs that were no longer available in a depressed local labour market was an unrewarding activity.

Another era was opening and we wanted to be part of that even if it was not to be plain sailing.

5

Pioneering days

The limited but welcome amount of latitude allowed to us in the Industrial Training Research Unit during the period when Sir Richard O'Brien was Chairman of the Manpower Services Commission enabled us to focus on problems of our own choosing.

The number one aim of the MSC, as previously noted, was *to contribute to efforts to raise employment and reduce unemployment.* Since it seemed to us that new enterprises were urgently needed to replace those which had declined we chose to use our discretionary grant to tackle the problem of start-ups. If more bright ideas could result in flourishing enterprises, the cycle of economic decline in these localities could be arrested and reversed. The seeds of growth in a firm need to be implanted from the start, we argued. I had reached this view because my industrial consulting experience had convinced me that the deficiencies that beset firms can often be traced to imbalance at the top. The very small number of key personnel that run a company need to have an appropriate range of skills. The reality, however, is that many new companies have founders who are very strong in one field but deficient in others.

We also had some back-up research material to support us in formulating a new positive line of approach. For some years I had been running a research project at Henley Management College on the effectiveness of management groups. One central finding of this work was to bring to the fore the importance for successful performance of complementary relationships between the leading personalities in a team.

Team-role compatibility, as we were to describe it, could be assessed in a systematic way. Specific methods for generating the necessary information had been developed and tested, and hence definite steps could be taken to improve the balance and effectiveness of the management team. We had already tried out the approach amongst some leading companies where it had been well received.[1]

[1] Belbin, R. M. (1981). *Management Teams: Why they succeed or fail.* Oxford: Heinemann. A computerized personnel system called Interplace was subsequently developed from this work.

Launch-A-Firm

There now seemed good reason to believe that the experience gained in this field could be applicable to our new programme of research into special employment measures and in particular to a demonstration project called Launch-A-Firm. The idea was that we should identify embryo companies that were having difficulties in getting started and contribute to the initial design of their management structure. Once launched, these companies could then grow smoothly to produce an appreciable number of new jobs. That at least was the theory. The subsidiary aim was to try to locate them in areas of high unemployment.

To manage the project we were fortunate in recruiting Alan Randall, an old friend from our Cranfield days, who had recently taken early retirement when the Imperial Tobacco Company sold the subsidiary of which he was Managing Director. Alan, who was also well known nationally as the General Secretary of the Union of Independent Companies, had no difficulty in finding suitable embryo companies of promise. Nearly all of them were unbalanced!

The typical would-be entrepreneur was an inventor with a technical background who had designed a product while in a company of medium or large size, but had been thwarted when he had tried to develop it. These inventors tended to be loners. They were reluctant to enter into partnerships and had only primitive ideas about finance and marketing. We continually encountered the 'I want to do it all myself' syndrome. Most of these embryo companies never got off the ground or if they did they did not survive for long.

The better balanced embryo companies were associated with enterprising managers, but even so they were prone to treat their enterprises as private playthings. It was not uncommon to find them trying to set up a company in a favourite recreational area. We were nearly laughed out of court when we mooted the siting of a new firm in a declining area like Liverpool. We had to withdraw rapidly in order to maintain our credibility!

It is a well-known fact that Britain is good at inventing things but poor at turning them into commercial successes, which is an essential step in order to generate sustainable jobs. Why this should be so has always been something of a mystery.

Our project Launch-A-Firm gave us the chance to probe further into this area. Alan's brief was to look around for the project which offered most promise but which at the same time had run into seemingly insuperable difficulties. Our belief was that a human angle underlay many of these difficulties and that these would ultimately prove open to remedy.

In due course Alan found the ideal firm in which we could focus our efforts.

Jarrettjets

Jerry Jarrett was a well qualified and experienced design engineer who had created a unique set of turbine designs including a set of nozzles that could be fitted to existing turbines to improve performance and save fuel. One of his turbines had been commissioned by a rich luxury yacht owner not so much for its fuel economy as for the way in which it combined efficiency with the very minimum of vibration.

Encouraged by the success of his commission, Jerry left the engineering firm in which he was employed to go into business on his own account. During his first two years he attempted to obtain government funding for setting up on his own on the strength of his claim that the 'fuel economies achieved by his inventions had wide application and were in the national interest'. After a series of polite rebuffs and referrals to other departments, he set about building a prototype to convince companies of the validity of his claims. He invited inquiries from large turbine users and eventually won a firm overseas order for three. The following year he built a prototype in his small workshop which he demonstrated to over thirty potential users. There was universal agreement that it was cheaper, more versatile and more efficient than his competitors' models. In spite of the successful demonstration and general acclaim, Jerry received no further orders. The main reason was reluctance to place orders with a 'one-man band' with no organizational back-up.

The following year Jerry received an offer from a leading company in the USA to buy the patents and use his services as a consultant. This would have meant that Britain would have had to buy back the patent for use in the country of its invention. Jerry rejected the proposition on patriotic grounds.

The following year Jerry received an offer from a large British engineering company to take out a world licence on the patents, to pay Jerry royalties and at the same time to provide Jerry with employment within the firm. This proposition too proved unacceptable to Jerry on the grounds that it would involve forfeiting control over his own invention coupled with fear of 'being back in the system'. Alan found Jerry very active in getting in touch with potential users of his invention. He had been busy contacting manufacturers of pet foods, glue, potato crisps, frozen chips and so on. But he complained that their engineers knew little of steam turbines, and did not appreciate the potential savings in fuel economy which they offered. So it had all led nowhere.

Jerry's explanation of his failure to make progress included the 'not invented here' syndrome for the lack of reponse in big companies, the 'bureaucracy of government departments' and their failure to 'recognize the importance of the lone inventor' and the 'lack of entrepreneurial spirit and engineering literacy in the world of banking and finance houses'.

Alan conceived of a plan to help Jerry progress. In the first place he prepared the groundwork to enable him to register a new limited company Jarrettjets. Alan personally engaged in negotiations with the bank to fund the founding of the company. He then persuaded Jerry that his new firm should join forces with another company, Servojets, that already had an established business in the turbine maintenance field. Eventually the two firms combined to form a small viable business, which has survived in spite of a continuing succession of troubles.

Helping Jerry Jarrett took up a good deal of energy and time on the part of both Alan and myself. Alan formed the view that in spite of his energies and initiative Jerry was nursing a 'death' wish: he wanted the business to fail but in such a way that could justifiably transfer the blame to the ineptitude of banks, big firms and the govenment. He looked genuinely alarmed once Alan caused concrete progress to be made. Jerry was a poor negotiator. But he insisted until Alan's final intervention on doing all the negotiation himself. He expected others to respond positively to his invention. Yet he was loth to engage in any agreement that compromised his personal independence.

In the end we felt that results achieved with Launch-A-Firm were scarcely commensurate with the effort we had put into the exercise. From other similar experiences we concluded that the lone inventor who insists on remaining in total managerial control is not a good proposition for job promoters to back.

Alan and I were gradually coming round to the view that the legendary British failure to make the best of significant inventions could have something to do with a proneness towards personal insularity and a reluctance to work in unison with others. Without the establishment of a properly balanced team few projects can hope to fulfil their technical and commercial potential.

As our experiences with Launch-A-Firm were not too encouraging, Alan took the view that we would make faster progress by concentrating on existing small firms already located in depressed areas and grafting on to them the potential for expansion.

Expand-A-Firm

With this in mind we set up the project Expand-A-Firm. Alan worked with the Welsh Development Agency and Scottish Development Agency to find suitable companies in depressed areas. Although England lacked a comparable body, the Small Firms Division of the Department of Industry partially filled this role. At any rate with their help and the help of other bodies, including the Union of Independent Companies, Alan was able to find what we were after in various regions, especially in the more depressed towns of Lancashire.

The plan that we put into operation offered to selected firms the services of a full-time Development Fellow who possessed the special expertise needed to overcome the principal bottlenecks to expansion. The Development Fellow was recruited from the ranks of the executive unemployed and was very carefully selected with the aid of special personnel techniques and measures. Since the firms assisted were also carefully chosen, we hoped to achieve a good match between this key person and the firm. The aim of Expand-A-Firm was that if the Development Fellow was successful in his assignment he would create a job for himself and in doing so would generate jobs for others within the firm.

Create-Your-Own-Job

While helping firms to create jobs through growth was at the forefront of our strategy, we also realized that another approach was needed if we were to reach out directly to those who were unemployed. The industrial recession that followed the world oil crisis had caused the number of institutions catering for the needs of the unemployed to multiply. If the recession had been milder, the training and personal counselling they received would have helped them secure appointments. But, as it was, advertised vacancies became so few in some places that many participants of government-financed Training Centres began to dismiss their chances of finding any job in their own locality.

The idea of becoming an 'own account worker' was sometimes put forward by the trainee himself. At other times the suggestion came from the Centre Manager, especially in those cases where he had been in business himself. Even if the notion was entertained only lightheartedly at first, trainees began to take the subject seriously as they became aware of the commercial possibilities of the projects in which they were engaged. This awareness was reinforced whenever the Centre brought in contracts from the market both as a means of providing real experience for the trainees and as a source of supplementary income for the host establishment.

A prospective business capable of providing a livelihood for a trainee or unemployed person nearly always requires some initial investment. In particular special items of equipment or materials are likely to be needed to get things moving or even to test the market. This is where experience soon pointed up two financially restricting factors:

1   The trainees, being either too young or unemployed or both, seldom had any personal capital to invest in a project. A few trainees were

eventually able to find a little money of their own once a business was seen as under way. But at the outset of their projects these ventures were too speculative in nature, especially for the inexperienced, for even these small sums to have been forthcoming.

2   Training Workshops, Employment Trusts, Community Enterprises and similar bodies have funds of their own to meet needs seen as fully in line with their constitutions and general objectives. Unfortunately these seldom include helping trainees to create employment themselves by establishing their own businesses.

In setting up the project Create-Your-Own-Job (CYOJ) we took the view that prospective *own account workers* need not only training and guidance but also, in the case of the unemployed, a small amount of initial capital to enable the necessary bits and pieces to be bought. Certainly without a CYOJ grant the projects we set in being could not have been initiated. Nor could these bodies have touched the working capital sometimes available to them in governmentally funded operations since this can only be used for prescribed and approved purposes.

CYOJ was available to agencies that provided help for unemployed persons, with preference being given to those programmes that actively sought work projects from outside, contained personnel that could offer both counselling and business advice, and promised training in a variety of technical skills.

CYOJ also discriminated in favour of people who we thought had a fair chance of succeeding in a technical, business and even a human sense. We did not see self-employment as being the right choice for everyone.

Create-Your-Own-Job and Expand-A-Firm ran contemporaneously. Both programmes produced encouraging but varied results. CYOJ generated a certain amount of self-employment, which would not otherwise have taken place, at a very low cost. Most of the mini-enterprises however seemed to be precariously based. Only occasionally did there seem any prospect of the enterprise developing into, say, a limited company which would employ others and have real expansion potential. Where CYOJ operated in depressed localities the chances of any continued expansion were minimal. These small scale outfits depended on local contracts and local markets. In an area which is declining economically it is difficult, of course, to find opportunities for growth in the immediate environment. Even when a CYOJ enterprise flourished it was not easy to steer it into a position in which we could say with confidence that it had become entirely self-supporting.

CYOJ enterprises were mostly found within host organizations set up to provide training for the unemployed and as such the participants received training allowances or unemployment benefit. There were considerable advantages in developing an enterprise within a host organization: the special coaching needed was available and other facilities were at hand.

The problem arose once the umbilical cord was broken. The potential 'own account worker' would then lose unemployment benefit or training allowances and have to face up to the bleak realities of surviving in the business world without further financial assistance. Needless to say, at this particular point a considerable number of people backed away from the prospect. We were even accused of putting young people at risk: as self-employed people they would not be eligible for unemployment benefit. Clearly it was not fair to entice people away from the security of the welfare state unless they had at least a fair chance of achieving economic independence.

A new model project

By now we had gained considerable experience of the benefits and pitfalls associated with project CYOJ. The positive value of pilot programmes is to point the way to improvements. What emerged were clear guidelines for revising the rules so as to form a Mark II CYOJ with the likelihood of a higher survival rate.

The new model we proposed would offer a maximum of £1000 in capital equipment for a new business, irrespective of size. Each item of intended expenditure would have to be approved beforehand. The grant would be made to the support agency, preference being given to those that were run by people with some business experience or that offered a facility for imparting business guidance to intending starters.

In dispensing CYOJ funds we saw advantages in switching the emphasis from the ventures of the solo craftsmen, artist or other types of 'own account worker' (which tended to have a poor record) and to give preference to small groups capable of setting up partnerships or co-operatives. Young artisan entrepreneurs are inclined to lose heart easily and lack experience to guide them through difficulties. In this context we thought each assisted group should contain one experienced mature adult, even if that member had to be enrolled from outside the training establishment.

The Mark II model never really got off the ground because just as we were about to start it our experimental programme ran into funding difficulties. We were then forced into choosing between competing priorities.

Back to Expand-A-Firm

Meanwhile Alan had been making steady progress with Expand-A-Firm. With limited funds available it was not easy to lay down precisely which companies would be eligible for support without raising expectations and so creating a great deal of disappointment. In the end we decided that more was likely to be learned by taking a small cross-section of companies that had some special need for high level manpower but lacked the financial resources or personnel experience to introduce a key person without assistance.

The final decision was based on the following considerations:

Accessibility modified by the need for representative sample

Most of the companies chosen were located in Wales or the Midlands. The prime reason for this was that our Project Director lived in the West. It was easier – and cheaper – for him to keep an eye on what was happening there. The exception was one firm in Scotland. This was partly chosen because it seemed a good idea in principle that the scheme should cover the three countries that make up Great Britain.

Need

The firms selected were mostly in areas of very high unemployment. Some companies were well managed but lacked technical expertise or had sound businesses but needed good management. One company was facing the prospect of a visit from the Receiver before we decided to intervene. The companies in our sample had no common feature, therefore, other than being small and in urgent need of special manpower which they could not afford.

Singularity

In no case did we support a company that was in direct competition with another in the same locality. As a result we could be sure that any jobs created would be net employment gains for the area.

The following three examples show how Expand-A-Firm operated in practice.

An advance in metal bending

Metal Turnings is situated in a remote rural area of North Wales where employment opportunities are few. Bending steel tubes, their main business, is a labour-intensive operation which calls for little or no skill. It is the type of work which firms in the manufacture of cars and refrigerators are glad to sub-contract. The local Regional Agency had identified the company as sound, stable and well-managed and noted in particular an interest in a new process for producing aluminium tubes in complicated shapes for which there was a considerable market demand. The manager estimated that the process, involving critical temperature control and handling of components in a furnace, would take a year to develop and seemed to lie outside the company's current technical capability.

After some enquiries, we located an unemployed production engineer, who lived in the area and had relevant technical experience, and gave him a Development Fellowship. The work proceeded according to plan, and by the time the year was completed samples of the company's products were put on show at an engineering exhibition in Birmingham. These were well received and favourable reports of this new process appeared in the *Financial Times* and *Le Figaro*.

A company that has a production or research orientation often lacks commercial push. Certainly this company did not gain the hoped-for material benefits from its achievement as it sat back and waited for the orders to come in. The result was that by the end of the Development Fellow's first year the company doubted that it might be in a position to employ him on a permanent basis. At this point we began to realize that further progress would not be possible unless the company was able to reap some early financial benefits from the work already undertaken. The joint decision finally arrived at was: if a job was offered to our Development Fellow we would fund a new Fellow for a three-month period to overcome what seemed to be the critical manpower bottleneck on the commercial side.

This was duly done. New orders were gained, five additional employees were taken on and Metal Turnings set about building another factory to cope with the demand for the new product.

The company that nearly pulled down the blinds

Canvas Holdings has traded in tents, blinds and shop awnings for over 100 years and had always operated profitably until misfortune struck. A heart attack caused the sudden death of the Managing Director. His son who had worked on the production side took over the business. Very soon he began to feel the strain and to show signs of severe emotional disturbance.

It was not long before the company moved from being financially in the black to being in the red. A loan was arranged from the bank and the Regional Agency was called in to render assistance. However, the financial position continued to deteriorate. A point was finally reached when the bank decided to call in its loan and the company faced bankruptcy.

The Regional Agency now contacted our Project Director made a rapid audit of the company and pronounced it basically sound. The major problem was seen to be one of improving office organization and establishing a strong financial and commercial grip on the business. A decision was made to award a Development Fellowship. Due to the extent of the recession in the area there were many high calibre managers looking for jobs. Using the services of the Professional and Executive Register we were able to draw up a shortlist of well-qualified candidates. All completed certain psychometric tests and also underwent a searching interview.

Being unemployed the person finally appointed was able to make an immediate start. The Development Fellow expressed hopes that he might manage to save twelve of the sixteen threatened jobs.

One effect of the granting of the Development Fellowship was that the company was able to negotiate a new bank loan. Some months later we learned that all sixteen jobs had been saved, that Canvas Holdings had moved into the black and expanded to the point that it took on new labour.

The genius in need of help

Sensorgram Ltd was a company identified by the Regional Agency as one with great potential but it was facing an uncertain future. The manager was an inventor still in his twenties and worked with his mother in controlling the business. He had developed a high technology product that was geared to a luxury fashion market with good sales in the USA. It was one of a whole series of product inventions that the son had generated in his small research-based company.

When a depression in this fashion market caused a fall in the income of the company there was a serious risk that other developments in the pipeline would be threatened by the cash crisis.

We had been warned that he was something of an individualist, even by the standards of a young man. He did not dress like a businessman; he was inclined to be late for appointments; and he ran his business in a bohemian way. Nevertheless he could produce ideas and demonstrations that put him in a class of his own. Alan was impressed with his visions for the future and agreed with the Regional Agency that the company warranted support.

The manpower bottleneck in this instance was considered to be commercial skill in handling contracts, licences and franchises likely to bring in some ready cash before new products came on stream. In team-building terms the need was seen for a wise mature person who could put a steadying hand on the business while also affording every support for the creative spark who was the company's prime asset. The Development Fellow appointed was fifty-eight years of age. He had a technical background, but he had also gained much commercial experience in the USA where he had retained a large number of personal contacts. The intention was that he should spend the greater part of his time outside the firm.

The plan almost miscarried. So enthusiastic was the manager about the Development Fellow's entry into the company, that he arranged for him to take a flat locally and to receive a thorough grounding in the technical work of the company. A good deal of tact was needed to enable the Development Fellow to extricate himself and to get back on the selling road.

By increasing the income of the company through selling proven products, Sensorgram was able to make some measure of financial progress. This led to three new appointments. These however were all on the research side. The growth of Sensorgram was not exactly improving its manpower balance.

However, outstanding progress had been made on the R & D front. The company had succeeded in breaking into a new field, the production of scientific instruments, with a special concentration on the measurement of bulk liquids. Trials resulted in UK orders and there were good prospects for exports, but it was very much a touch-and-go matter whether the new products would be on the market before the company ran out of cash and credit. The danger point was passed and the outlook for new business and jobs continued to improve.

An evaluation of the work so far

Expand-A-Firm had been operating in eleven firms by the time we came to make our first evaluation. We had a favourable outcome in all but two firms: in both cases the project ceased when the Development Fellow left to take up a better paid position. After a period of a year from the start of each company scheme we were able to report the following:

- Three companies had developed new products with very favourable long-term business and employment prospects.
- Fifty-nine new jobs had been created and a further sixteen jobs were saved from extinction in Canvas Holdings.
- Five Development Fellows were offered and accepted positions in the companies they had joined once the programme ended.
- All the firms spoke well of the scheme and we had encountered no objections from any owner.

After reflecting on our experience of CYOJ and Expand-A-Firm we reached the conclusion that the latter was a better public investment than the former. CYOJ was cost effective and well received but we had to admit that the jobs 'created' in this way were of uncertain viability and in many instances few of the recipients, or intended recipients, saw them as an acceptable alternative to a 'proper job'. But it was better than being 'in training' or 'on the dole'.

Expand-A-Firm, however, was providing a sound basis for continued employment and was exercising a favourable economic influence in the localities in which the companies were based through buying in goods and services as well as stimulating local trade through increased personal spending.

Putting together our experiences of CYOJ and Expand-A-Firm we formed the view that an effective strategy for creating 'real' jobs for unemployed people would be to build up embryo firms within specially equipped Centres. There key personnel could receive supervision and coaching in needed skills, and assistance with the development work always desirable before launching any major enterprise.

Further, experience with Expand-A-Firm had taught us a lot about how to graft on high level expertise so as to enable an enterprise to grow in strength and to put on a reasonably secure footing its business and the jobs attached to it. We believed the appointment of a Development Fellow could do much to help a promising firm get off the ground.

Finally, we came to the reluctant conclusion that entrepreneurs, especially artisan entrepreneurs, are unlikely to progress very far on their own and to generate many jobs for others. A small group of people with complementary abilities and aptitudes is a far better bet for building an expanding firm. But favourable conditions need to be established for this to happen.

The next step

We began to look around for a Centre that met our purpose. We did not need to look far. Eunice had periodically travelled to Coventry in her role as a Trustee of the Community Education Development Centre which was now busy running major national projects. Through the connections she established, we gained an introduction to Coventry Top Shop, an education and training establishment that catered for the needs of both the unemployed and school-leavers unable to find jobs.

Coventry is a centre of the engineering industry, and much reliant for its prosperity on vehicle manufacture. The recession had fallen very heavily on the city and the City Council had taken vigorous steps to ensure that those affected by the recession should be helped as much as local resources would allow. The result was that the Coventry Top Shop had become, with the aid of much assistance from the MSC, one of the largest Centres of its kind in the country, eventually serving 1000 people. The Centre was professionally staffed and had a strong and able manager in John Temple.

Eunice, John and myself spent some time constructing a new proposal for developing jobs using Coventry Top Shop as the focus in a new pilot programme. We believed that the radical plans we had drawn up stood a very good chance of creating real employment opportunities for those leaving the Centre.

What we had failed to take into account in our plans, however, was that the political scenario in which we were operating was changing. The long era of training, based on a close mutually supportive relationship between the public and private sectors, was beginning to break down.

6

Public policy at the crossroads

Industry needs a range of special skills if it is to grow and prosper. It was with this in mind that the Industrial Training Boards had set out, as a first step, to assess the manpower requirements of the future. Once needs are foreseen, appropriate training and education programmes can be arranged and the economy as a whole gains.

The Boards could not have turned projections and plans into reality without the special powers they were given under the Industrial Training Act. As noted earlier, the provisions of the Act enabled them to raise levies on firms that failed to undertake their due share of training and, with this revenue, to issue grants to firms contributing to the training needs of the industry as a whole. Without these sanctions any firm investing heavily in training risked having labour 'poached' once training had been completed.

'Poaching' was a very common phenomenon. Whenever this happened employers reacted angrily. They would complain of a 'lack of gratitude' and make the almost inevitable deduction 'in future I'm going to let someone else do the training and concentrate on recruiting skilled and experienced people instead'.

Those who advocate leaving training to market forces argue that the fault lies with the employer for failing to pay the market value of a skill. Increasing the wages for skilled workers might provide one answer, but could well result in a general wage inflation. Without an increase in the supply of skilled workers the problem is not easily overcome. In any case there are some intrinsic difficulties about retaining young people over a period that bridges their learning and working life. The restlessness of youth builds up over a long apprenticeship. Eventual qualification becomes a passport to travel. We talked to many trainees about their experiences. 'I wanted the chance to see what other firms are like anyway,' was one typical comment. It was no accident that so many young people left the company that had trained them the moment their apprenticeships were completed.

Unless a way is found to break a cycle which may be described starkly as 'no training, no skills, no development', industrial economies will stagnate.

As it was, the United Kingdom had gone a long way towards developing an effective manpower programme and the Industrial Training Boards could point to a steady growth in the output of skilled manpower as a result.

Any long-term strategy requires continuity before the benefits become widely appreciated. A sophisticated programme also needs to be managed by sophisticated people. And finally the mood of the times should support what is being done. On all these counts events moved unfavourably for the strategy that had been adopted.

A new scenario

The Manpower Services Commission had survived through the reign of governments of contrasting political complexions more or less unscathed and had succeeded in adhering to the general line of policies that its board of independent commissioners had overseen. A break in this continuity came about when a new government was elected in 1979 belonging to the radical right and headed by Margaret Thatcher. This shift in the political spectrum took place in a number of developed countries over the same period and may well have had common origins. Public expenditure had risen inexorably in nearly all countries, not only absolutely but also in its share of the gross national product. With it taxation had risen too, bringing in its wake a direction of energies towards tax avoidance and evasion. An increasing proportion of those finishing higher education were drawn into accountancy rather than into engineering and other technical professions. As a result industry and commerce became less expansive and more cost and tax conscious. The public domain had grown steadily and was becoming unwieldy. Strikes had paralysed a number of industries and were impinging on the community as a whole.

The theme of the incoming administration was that the size of government had to be reduced, that tight control had to be placed on public expenditure, that private businesses needed more scope and encouragement, and ultimately that taxation levels would be brought down. The expansionist policies of John Maynard Keynes based on a skilful regulation of the economy were replaced with the strict monetarist approach of Milton Friedman and acceptance of the natural regulating forces of the market. The powers of trade unions were to be curtailed. The businessman, as the true producer of wealth, was to be given his head.

The role of the Manpower Services Commission did not fit comfortably into this scenario. First, the MSC was interventionist in its approach: it was attempting to ease the problems of the skilled labour supply to industry through positively managing the levy-grant system. Second, the MSC was also a good instance of a QUANGO (Quasi-national governmental organization) and QUANGOs were out of favour. The incoming administration preferred bodies it controlled directly rather than those which were semi-independent.

For a while there was no outwardly visible change in the way in which the MSC operated. The government was preoccupied in the employment field with its industrial relations bill governing the operations of trade unions. Manpower policy was temporarily pushed aside. The first step eventually was to review the statutory nature of the Training Boards and the powers they enjoyed. A process of consultation began. Industry was experiencing a recession at the time, the difficulties of which contributed to inflation and escalating costs. With fewer people being recruited, the value of training in the firm was being called into question, along with the provisions of the Industrial Training Act. Firms objected to paying the training levy when in fact they were not currently training staff.

The consultations produced their predictable outcome. The voices of those who wished to end the system were louder than those who saw merits in its retention. A government that viewed any intervention in the conduct of business with suspicion responded willingly. The mandatory levy-grant system which underpinned the Industrial Training Act was abolished. The life of each Training Board was made to depend on being voluntarily required by the firms that comprised the industry. Few Training Boards survived. The policy that had been devised to produce a continuous supply of skilled manpower for industry and commerce collapsed.

This now left a problem. Training had previously offered a means of absorbing the unemployed during periods of recession. That offered the advantage that industry could recover more quickly when the business climate improved. Not only would the skilled manpower be at hand but, in the intervening period, the labour force would have re-educated itself to deal with the technologies of tomorrow. This manpower strategy had worked especially well in Sweden. A recession can prompt a period of preparation, development and re-equipment. Failing that the personnel shed during a recession can do little more than languish in unemployment.

Britain's policies, however, did not follow the example of Sweden or build on the foundations already established by the Industrial Training Boards but veered in the opposite direction. During the developing recession, cost-cutting exercises were introduced into the public sector. Skillcentres, in which the unemployed were retrained, came under close scrutiny. Their effectiveness could be measured by relating the cost of running them to the throughput of trainees and the proportion of placements made in real jobs afterwards. Investigations showed that on these criteria Skillcentres were least cost-effective in the older declining industrial areas. The consequence was that training establishments were closed in locations where unemployment was highest and the need for new jobs was greatest.

The policy of the MSC had previously been controlled by independent commissioners. But as revenue from industry and the Training Boards declined, the focus of control began to change. The MSC became increasingly dependent on public funds supplied by the Government, and not unnaturally the Government wished to exert greater control over how those funds were spent. The decisions of the MSC depended on some sort of agreement being struck between Commissioners representing the separate interests of employers, trade unions and education. And it was in keeping with the style of government of the day that consensus politics was on the way out. When Sir Richard O'Brien's appointment was due to terminate, or be renewed, he was allowed to retire and his place as Chairman was taken by David Young.

It has always been my experience that policies are embodied by people. An understanding of the person in command offers an unrivalled insight into the lines and strategies likely to be adopted in the future.

The contrast between the retiring Chairman and the incoming Chairman of the MSC could hardly have been more striking.

Sir Richard had a wide-ranging background. His distinguished military service included a period as personal assistant to Field Marshal Montgomery. He had also acted as the manager of an engineering company and had held a number of leading positions in public life. I had once interviewed Sir Richard for an article in a journal. Then I had learned that his approach to management was rooted in an emphasis on two main factors: the quality of consultation and the quality of decision-making.

David Young, who was a close associate of the Prime Minister's Finchley constituency party, had been Chairman of a property company, had qualified as a barrister and, at the time of his appointment, was political adviser to Sir Keith Joseph, the then Minister of Education. Young had no industrial experience. In a technical sense his sole marginally relevant qualification for the job was as President of a Jewish charity with a special interest in training. When later, as Lord Young, he became Minister of Employment overseeing a Ministry with enlarged powers that embraced the MSC itself he produced the following self-description in an interview with *The Times*:

> I tend to be a doer rather than a thinker and I also see myself as a persuader. I am a conviction politician who believes that consensus is sometimes inevitable to win people over to your point of view.

The relation between doers and thinkers is crucial to the operations of government. Someone has to do the doing and someone has to do the thinking. The question is who does which and with what result.

Doers and thinkers

This was a subject that was soon to become a central topic for public discussion. The outcome was to exercise such an influence on public affairs and, as it happened, on my personal fortunes that a small digression seems permissible at this point about the person who was to play such a large part in changing the climate of public opinion.

The person in question was Tony Jay (later knighted for services to the Arts) and at the time of our first meeting well known to me as a writer of two brilliant books *Management and Machievelli* and *The Corporation Man*. The latter had become such a best seller in the USA that, with the royalties received, Tony felt secure enough to leave the British Broadcasting Company and set up a new company, Video Arts, which made films for television and for education in industry. In this enterprise he was joined by John Cleese, one of the great television comic actors of the day. As it happened Tony had just finished making a film about Henley Management College which was receiving its first showing at the Festival Hall in London. At the lunch that followed we were introduced as having a mutual interest in management education.

Our experimental work at Henley on differences in the composition of successful and unsuccessful teams was now nearing its conclusion. We had reached the point when, if given specified information about the members of a team, we could predict the likely outcome. Tony showed interest in some of the theoretical concepts that sprang from our studies and thought the subject needed popularizing. I was invited to his offices in Oxford Street to lunch with his own management team. Later Tony was to produce the first popular account of our work in the colour supplement of the British Sunday newspaper, *The Observer*. It appeared under the heading 'Nobody's perfect but a team can be'. The impact might have been great indeed had it not been for a strike amongst distribution workers which meant that most regular readers failed to get their copy! At any rate Tony's foreword to my book *Management Teams: why they succeed or fail* when it finally appeared gave it a considerable boost.

There was however one respect in which Tony, unwittingly, was to contribute to the difficulties which were soon to beset and almost overwhelm the nation's would-be job promoters. The problem was generated by what many would regard as Tony's greatest achievement in conceiving and writing the television programme *Yes, Minister*. The setting of this delightful satire was the Ministry of Administrative Affairs. The centrepiece of this award-winning comedy was the relationship between Jim Hacker, the cheery bumbling unknowing Minister, and the leading civil servants headed by the wily and highly manipulative Sir Humphrey. So convincing was this portrayal that many people regarded the characters in this Ministry as authentic.

One of the most enthusiastic followers of the programme was the Prime Minister herself. She not only wrote a special script for a successor episode called *Yes, Prime Minister* but insisted on playing the television part personally. The timing of this television programme was especially significant when seen against the political events of the day.

There are many in the business community who have little respect for those who work in the public sector and see them as people who seek security because they lack enterprise and personal effectiveness. The evident futility of the collective efforts of the Ministry of Administrative Affairs became gradually transformed in the public mind into a general indictment of those who ran the Civil Service. The lesson, as interpreted by many, was plain. To overcome bureaucracy you need businessmen. So it fitted well with the state of public opinion that a directive businessman, and close political adherent of the Prime Minister, was appointed to head the MSC.

With a self-declared doer now in charge of the MSC, some perplexing issues arose. Our own work on management teams had provided some good evidence that it is better for thinkers to command doers rather than for doers to command thinkers. If that was so, what would be the role of the officials, especially those who had merit as thinkers? And how could we contribute as research and development workers if we were all to report ultimately to a doer?

Changing objectives

The MSC gave an early indication of its change in policies by reviewing its aims and objectives. To some the distinction between aims and objectives might seem a mere semantic, even a trivial, point. It matters little unless the two differ. The MSC had not hitherto separated its objectives from its aims. The original aims of the MSC were headed by its declaration: 'to contribute to efforts to raise employment and reduce unemployment'. This bold aim was now downgraded to fourth position in the MSC's corresponding list of objectives where it read, more mildly, 'to do all that is practicable to place in permanent employment, in training or in temporary employment those unemployed jobseekers who most need help in returning to work'. This statement hardly encompassed 'raising employment', that is by job creation or by positive development policies of the type sorely needed in areas hit by major industrial closures.

The recasting of the MSC's terms of reference provided clues as to what was happening and the informal grapevine told us more. In practice, we were informed, the emphasis was to fall on cost-cutting exercises and an examination of each major item of expenditure. That is not to say that the MSC actually reduced its budget. Under the new Chairman public expenditure was to reach an all-time high as trainees now became a direct charge on the State and the self-financing arrangements for training under the levy-grant system were discontinued.

A change in the way in which the MSC conducted its business soon became apparent. Fewer decisions were made informally. The scope for consultation and negotiation became more limited. Letters from Moorfoot, the massive Sheffield headquarters resembling a red fort into which the MSC had recently moved, became more numerous, lengthy and directive. Eunice spent an increasing proportion of her time drafting correspondence that matched point by point the content of the letters received. Yet this energy was not repaid by evidence that anything was being accomplished.

The letters from Moorfoot introduced not only a change of style but in due course some alterations in basic intention. The new regime in the MSC began to make a major impact on our work. We heard that the MSC in reviewing its expenditure had decided to make economies in research. These were disproportionately bigger than in other areas. Since less than one per cent of the MSC budget was spent in the research field, there were clearly limitations in the savings that could be accomplished. The first casualty was research and development into cost-effective ways of creating new jobs. For the prospective job promoter this was a setback since this was a field which we had worked hard to open up. The next financial saving was to remove the 10 per cent discretionary grant which allowed us to work on what we considered important future needs.

Further news was that our block grant would be discontinued and in its place we would be allowed to compete for contracts on specific bits of work that MSC wanted done. At the time it was a matter of conjecture as to what that work might be.

Every organization that changes at the top retains a tier of middle management that provide an element of continuity, stability and experience. We knew that some members of the MSC believed that before any projected policies were finalized, account needed to be taken of some of the work in which the Industrial Training Research Unit was engaged. Even if the MSC had now steered away from its original aim of taking measures to 'raise employment and reduce unemployment', one of our research programmes had a direct bearing on the MSC's principal areas of interest.

ITRU and the MSC

During the previous two years we had been contributing to what was called the Youth Opportunity Programme (YOP), a forerunner of the Youth Training Scheme. The essence of YOP was to provide young people living in areas where it was difficult to obtain jobs with some experience of the demands of work in different skill fields. Many young people who make only limited progress at school are inclined to see no clear future for themselves, and do not even know what they want; the resulting disenchantment can lead to many problems for both themselves and society. YOP was a means of introducing them to the varieties of tasks that different jobs entail, giving them experience, and helping them to discover where their talents and aptitudes lay. Sometimes it was possible to set up for them actual work experience in a firm under supervised conditions.

Five YOP programmes set up in Skillcentres in different parts of Great Britain had been evaluated by us. A scientific evaluation is in fact a demanding time-consuming operation. It involves comparing clients and controls. Clients are those included in the experimental training group. Controls are an equivalent group not included in the programme. The two groups need to be carefully matched to avoid any differences in results appearing that might be attributable to a difference in initial aptitudes or to differences in what is termed the 'opportunity structure' of different areas. The employment histories of those falling into the client group had been followed up for five Skillcentres. We had information of what had happened, for instance, three months or six months after leaving YOP. To obtain this information our research workers had gone to a lot of trouble. It can take many foot-weary visits to the top flat of a Glasgow tenement before one interviewee of the sample is found to be at home.

At any rate the study showed that for two Skillcentres the job-holding record was better for clients in the client group than for the controls. But in the case of three Skillcentres the job records of the controls were actually better than for clients. The differences did not seem attributable to chance. There was, however, some good evidence to account for these contrasting results. The successful Skillcentres had taken the trouble to introduce their trainees to jobs through work experience in outside firms. Some of these trainees settled in well and so worked themselves into employment. In the other Skillcentres the trainees were not introduced to work experience. Their more intensive training had developed in them non-realistic expectations about jobs outside. Soon disillusioned, they engaged in less job-seeking behaviour than those who had been looking for jobs anyway and had not bothered about training.

This particular piece of research was published in a report entitled *Widening Employment Opportunities* and had been particularly well received by senior officials of the MSC. In essence the research showed how easy it is to waste public money by engaging in vast programmes that have been under-researched before they are launched.

An early visit to our Unit was arranged for the newly appointed Chairman, David Young. (Later, as Lord Young, he became a senior member of the Prime Minister's Cabinet.) The intention, we were told, was to bring to his attention the relevance of the work on which we were engaged.

Eunice had always been adept at organizing exhibitions of our work. In this case an extra special effort was made to translate complex research and development material into simple and straightforward messages and demonstrations of their utility. We also inwardly hoped that our programme into cost-effective methods of creating new employment might be restored. With this in mind, Alan Randall, our project leader in this field, travelled over to Cambridge from the West Country for the occasion.

The visit of the new Chairman plus a large retinue of officials was conducted with a mixture of pleasantry and formality. But the lesson from our painstaking study of the actual outcomes of training was received with evident scepticism by the new Chairman. He responded that 'too much reliance can be placed on research'. Our message may have perhaps had unwelcome implications for the Youth Training Scheme to which the nation was about to be committed on a national scale at great public cost. Nor was much favour shown to our suggestion that some of these resources might be better diverted to the training of skilled workers and tradesmen upon which industry is so dependent.

All in all the visit of the new Chairman might have yielded no positive outcome had it not been for his brief encounter with Alan Randall.

Alan's display material on the job-creation aspect of Expand-A-Firm was set up in one of the smaller rooms, so small in fact that not all members of the Chairman's party managed to enter. Those left outside peered through the half open door. Alan expounded his points emphatically, drew attention to the results achieved and received some appreciative nods.

But he was not leaving matters there. There were two new Expand-A-Firm projects that he had taken the trouble to develop. These firms could provide a considerable increase in jobs if the projects went ahead and might further illustrate the cost effectiveness of the strategy we had already pioneered. As back-up material Alan had in his hand letters from their Managing Directors stating that if the projects were cut they would take the matters up with their Members of Parliament. This threat however was not needed. The mere sight of Alan's looming, bulky and fiery presence may have been enough to win the point. The two extra projects were saved. A decision was taken on the spot. The necessary funds would be provided for a temporary extension of the programme. It was the only victory that we were to record that day!

In reality we knew that we now faced a curtailment of our comprehensive programme of research and development into ways of creating new jobs. But at least there remained, we supposed, one further avenue of work for the would-be job promoter in the Industrial Training Research Unit in the setting up of the Youth Training Scheme (YTS). A great deal of thought and energy had gone into questions of organization, training content and curriculum. Much less consideration had been given to the transition between training and employment once a YTS course had concluded. We devised therefore an Exit Options programme and proposed that we should set it up in Coventry Top Shop.

The large number of people entering training during the recession, especially school-leavers, inevitably raised an exit problem. If that exit problem was not foreseen and if measures were not taken in advance to find suitable outcomes for those finishing their training courses, there was a risk that training would become merely a holding reservoir. Unemployment would rise steeply again when the measures that apparently reduced it expired. We saw the options for those finishing their training as comprising one of only four desirable possibilities:

1   A job in the labour market.
2   Self-employment.
3   A further course of training and/or education.
4   Joining a start-up enterprise which could be brought into being by the training centre itself.

A strategies decision on which of these options was most realistic for each individual trainee needed to be made during the course of training so that part of training could comprise preparation for that end. If these four options were not actively pursued, the unemployed risked being recycled through training back into unemployment.

ITRU and Coventry Top Shop

As it happened we had worked closely with Coventry Top Shop to develop the fourth option for those finishing their training: a job in a newly launched firm. The professional work of Top Shop's marketing section, together with the high level of engineering expertise for which Coventry was renowned, had resulted in three prospective enterprises.

The most conspicuous of these was a rebuilt Spitfire. This was a sports car that had originally been manufactured in Coventry and was now mainly to be located in junk yards. Top Shop had bought all the old cars they could find, magnificently restored them and sent them out to a higher engineering specification than they had ever originally possessed. A second exciting possibility was presented by the Music Department. The combination of Coventry engineering and musical professionalism had produced a range of steel band instruments reputed to be the best in the country. A suitable enterprise was merely waiting to be launched. A third potential firm was waiting to be set up as a result of contracts, including export orders, secured by a garment-making section staffed mainly by unemployed sewing machinists. The design skills of Top Shop were usefully employed to produce an original range of products, including gloves for fruitpicking which enabled several fruits to be held before the hand was returned to the basket and which had been found to offer useful gains in productivity.

Eunice now began a new round of correspondence with the MSC about developing the employment opportunities latent in Coventry Top Shop. Although the MSC provided the bulk of the funds it became progressively apparent that this was seen *solely* as an education and training exercise. Employment issues could not be introduced at this stage. There was even an inspectorate busy ensuring that the resources of Top Shop were used only for training and *not* for commercial purposes. Motor enthusiasts from as far away as the USA were clamouring to buy the Spitfire. But it was to no avail. This vehicle could only be used for the non-commercial purpose of enabling Coventry schoolchildren to learn to drive in schools.

The correspondence on the Exit Options project ebbed and flowed for almost eighteen months before we were finally obliged to accept that the link between training and employment was not going to be forged through any comprehensive programme.

Writing subsequently in the journal of BACIE (The British Association for Commercial and Industrial Education) in an article entitled *The YTS: A Programme of Early Opportunity and Long-Term Uncertainty* I summed up the position as follows:

'YTS seems to have rigid elements built into it. Like traditional apprenticeships it is fashioned to run for a fixed term. Its goal seems to be a certification − a curiously academic concept − rather than a job. We have not yet persuaded the MSC that the transfer from YTS into employment is a problem that needs looking into.

I have indicated that I think the actual outcome of this programme is more uncertain than is generally credited. In this we have the added problem that different people are looking for different outcomes. Scheme organizers see YTS training as a vehicle for teaching general employment literacy, employability or lifemanship. Most trainees see it more, I believe, as job preparation. And I am wondering what their reaction will be if the jobs do not materialize. Clearly YTS with its assorted objectives will be difficult to evaluate. Yet with the public cost running at a billion pounds in the first year alone the subject can hardly be ignored. Will there be demonstrable evidence to support the deprivatization of training on so large a scale?

Looking on the bright side, we cannot exclude the possibility that YTS will generate unlooked for benefits. In view of the enterprising nature of some of the participating sponsors and managing agents there are at least some grounds for thinking this may happen. Time will tell. Personally I doubt whether adequate adjustments can be made without getting to grips with some of the counter-productive tendencies inherent in the design of YTS. The cornerstones of any reform, in my view, should be:

- to restore to school-leavers the prospects of taking up real jobs and training offered by employers by limiting the universality of YTS and undoing the likelihood of damage to the youth labour market,
- to take away the time-served element in YTS and to develop a more flexible programme in which job-search, preparation and placement are given a far greater emphasis,
- and finally to explore a range of methods for transferring less accomplished school-leavers from total state dependency on training schemes to partial support in real jobs.'

Once this final initiative of ours had been rejected by the MSC we had no recourse but to consider a series of contract projects in which they expressed interest in providing research funding. These were largely information gathering exercises or were related to very short-term issues. They did not seem to us to lead to practical developments that would have significant long-term consequences.

Our assessment and the end of MSC

For us the lesson was clear. The time had come to leave the Unit we had founded but to do so in a way that offered the best prospect of continued employment for the staff. To this end we arranged for ITRU to retain its independence but for the Industrial Training Service, with which we had long enjoyed a friendly association, to take over the management of what was to become a private research company dependent on individual contracts. The Manpower Services Commission gave support to this plan and provided generous interim funding. In the event none of our staff was made redundant: they remained in the Unit, found alternative employment in the academic world or in industry (mainly in the consulting field), or retired.

Experience in industry had always taught me that research is very prone to become a costly overhead, unless it leads to development and ultimately to some marketable product innovation. That continuous process is much in evidence in Japan but much less so in the United Kingdom. The difficulties of making research effective in the public sector, however, are vastly greater than they are in industry. If worthwhile outcomes are to be achieved a great deal of administrative and organizational skill is needed. The delegation of power and responsibility, consultation and informed decision-making are a necessary part of any effective system.

The importance which Tony Jay had originally attached to the subtlety of relationships between civil servants and their political overlords was well conceived. His television programme was very funny and vastly influential. But the conclusion that most people drew, that in the interests of effective action officials needed to be overridden and to have their powers greatly reduced, was fast becoming part of the political reality of the day.

Our concern now was that these changes were in danger of reducing efficiency of government. Top civil servants possess very high abilities and intelligence. They are commonly abused but have no means of answering back: they are made scapegoats when things go wrong and are deprived of credit by politicians when things go right. We knew that they had an important role to fulfil in helping to turn our empirical and exploratory research into innovations in policy. That possibility was being replaced almost entirely by direct Ministerial directive and by Ministers who had little knowledge of the field.

The new emphasis on a national programme of training of young people provided a valuable groundwork for some that could and did help them to gain jobs. But what was considered training became very diffuse. Public funds were made available for training young people in whatever occupational activities took their fancy, including football and snooker. The MSC also subsidized unemployed people, through the Enterprise Allowance Scheme, for engaging in almost any commercial venture, whether feasible or not. When in a court case a journalist discovered that the defendants on a prostitution charge had received public financial support for setting up a massage parlour, it was clear that an error of judgement had been made by a local MSC official. Still the episode brought to public attention the contrast with the policies previously developed by the Industrial Training Boards where future industrial needs had been treated as the focal priorities for public funding.

The new central control of manpower policies was soon to founder conspicuously. After spending billions of pounds on manpower programmes, Britain was to experience an acute shortage of skilled workers as soon as the economy moved out of recession. Eventually the Manpower Services Commission was abolished and most of its staff dispersed into Ministries from whence they had come in the first place. An experiment which began so promisingly had been driven into a cul-de-sac from which there was no option bar an expensive retreat.

7

Renewed operations

An era which had focused on training for skilled work was coming to an end. There seemed no good reason to address ourselves to what remained, including surveys on existing practice for which the MSC was now issuing contracts. The decisions to move out of the Industrial Training Research Unit in order to found the Employment Development Unit (later Employment Development Ltd) constituted a considerable risk. We had no assured income at the time. Nevertheless unemployment was rising very fast and there was a pressing need to deepen understanding on how counter-measures can be taken, whether nationally or at a local level. Besides which we wanted to finish the work we had started.

It is often surprising what people will do if they believe in something, even if it is against their apparent self-interest. The apostates from the new official line in manpower policy numbered six: Eunice, Jeanne, Hilary, Mary, Norman and myself. Somehow we had to do without the salaries we had received before. An initial solution was to work part-time in the EDU; Eunice, Jeanne and Hilary generously gave their services free; and I for my part intensified my other work as an industrial consultant in order to pay the bills.

It is not easy to work as a job promoter in an anti-jobmaking culture. Our experiences in this area were mirrored by other organizations engaged in local initiatives to fight unemployment through constructive measures. Very few received any help from government sources. By contrast there was a vast network of state-aided provisions to help programmes classified either as 'training' or 'small businesses'. This framework of policies suggested an underlying theme: that if a business culture was fostered and those out of work could apply themselves to training and were adequately motivated, specific measures to generate new employment in depressed areas were unnecessary other than in some exceptional blackspots.

Whenever a problem is seen as merely temporary, little in the way of resources tends to be forthcoming for research and development, for the creation of new types of needed professional expertise, and for the conduct of pilot and demonstration programmes. That climate of opinion was also hampering pioneering work by the appropriate international organizations. These included the International Labour Organization, a specialized agency of the United Nations in Geneva, and the Commission of the European Economic Community. The ILO and the EEC were both keen to further work on job creation but were restrained by some reluctant governments, including the government of the United Kingdom. This standpoint on the international arena was consistent with their general position on the domestic front.

The Employment Development Unit

It was against this unpromising background the EDU was inaugurated in Silver Street, Cambridge in the very building where we had started our researches years ago, although we now moved to the second floor suite. The top suite which we had first occupied reverted to College occupancy, while ITRU itself contracted so that all its employees were housed in Lloyds Bank Chambers. All work on measures to create new employment was transferred from ITRU to EDU.

With hindsight we may conclude that the Employment Development Unit set itself an ambitious programme for its resources, though one that is difficult to regret. What we decided to do was to publish the findings of our previous projects; to launch a new journal called *People and Jobs International* (which later we were obliged to suspend); to hold a conference on Community Based Employment Development (which was well attended and the results of which were published in the second edition of our journal); to focus our researches on some key issues, the results of which eventually led to formulation of the 'zero unemployment option' (see Chapter 14); and, finally, to put into operation outcomes of our job-creation researches under a brand new programme in Local Authority areas.

The first step of our new Unit was to publish a booklet *Countering Unemployment*, containing the results of the two projects Create-Your-Own-Job and Expand-A-Firm. The gist of this report was to show that both programmes provided cost-effective ways of generating new jobs. Nevertheless we considered that in the long run CYOJ presented the more limited prospects, especially in depressed areas. The report stated:

> Based on our experience with CYOJ it seems desirable that they should not be encouraged to operate as solo 'own account workers'. There seemed more point in steering these trainees into those activities of the training centre that had a commercial outlet. This is the area of the incipient firm. Here the staff of a training centre, if suitably qualified, can have a major role to play in getting an

enterprise launched. The projected conditions of a training centre provide an ideal environment for overcoming the development bugs of new products and services and for dealing with the many, once-only type, problems that beset the emergent company.

We had now learnt enough to realize that CYOJ requires a critical number of people, probably three or four, and that at least one person needed to be suitably experienced. The longer the firm remained in the womb of the training centre the more mature it was likely to become. The prospects of attracting into it other participants from outside, or even outside investment, can raise still further the chances of maintaining progress once the newborn company leaves home and fends for itself in the outside world. The ability to develop and launch new firms must count in the future as among the most valued skills of training staff.

An assessment of Expand-A-Firm

Project Expand-A-Firm seemed to offer faster and surer ways of generating new jobs and the jobs generated were less likely to be 'substitutions', that is formed at the expense of other jobs. Such initiatives can misfire and bring about what is termed the 'zero sum effect'. In contrast, one of the main objects of Expand-A-Firm was to produce 'job multipliers' with chosen firms generating indirect jobs amongst supplier and contract services in addition to those created directly. However our evaluation of Expand-A-Firm was based only on the jobs directly created. Here we could claim that 80 jobs were attributable to the programme in 16 projects set up in various parts of Great Britain. The net financial cost per job in these schemes compared favourably with that for new jobs under any other project that had been reported on. And the bottlenecks overcome meant that these firms had further growth potential.

Expand-A-Firm did however suffer from one snag. The only criticism voiced against the programme was that it was not 'administrable'. That constituted a prime objection, as a senior civil servant had explained to us, why Expand-A-Firm could never figure as a national programme. Expand-A-Firm depended on a judgement being made. Firms were *selected* for the scheme according to their growth potential and other characteristics. Similarly the Development Fellows, usually unemployed professionals and executives, were carefully *selected* for the firms into which they were placed. That element of discretion is unacceptable in national government schemes which need to operate, it was alleged, in a uniform and standard way. Differences in *discretion* between officials in different parts of the country could lead to *inconsistences* and the whole scheme would, on that account, expose itself to public criticism as operating unfairly and therefore unsatisfactorily.

The mechanisms of central government create rigidities which they share in common with all very large bureaucracies. To the extent that local authorities are smaller, they are less subject to rules and readier to negotiate about their own special requirements. It was not long before we were engaged in such discussions.

Study of Options for Unemployed People

Meanwhile, Norman was continuing with our one surviving research project SOUP. This nourishing title stood for Study of Options for Unemployed People and was one we had transferred from ITRU to EDU. The background of thought was an awareness of the trend in advanced countries for high levels of unemployment to co-exist side by side with high levels of unfilled job vacancies. Some of these vacancies were for specialist skills of which there was a scarcity. But other vacancies comprised low paid jobs that might have been deemed suitable for unskilled manual workers who figure so largely amongst the ranks of the unemployed. Why then did they not take up the jobs on offer? How did they see the options?

Norman's project was centred on three localities: Downham Market, a small town in an agricultural area: Kings Lynn, a port with a more mixed economy; and Corby, a steel town that recently lost its main industry.

The study was based on in-depth interviews with a sample of 300 unemployed people, controlled according to sex, age and length of unemployment. Sixty main questions, plus a number of subsidiary ones, were asked on incomes current and past, job-seeking behaviour and experiences, knowledge of and attitude towards current employment initiatives. Views on a number of projected possibilities that in effect would involve some modification in the current operating provisions of the Welfare State were also sought.

The results of these in-depth interviews began to influence the pattern-making of our thoughts. Their relevance will be considered in Chapter Eleven where we consider how unemployment might be better tackled in developed countries.

In general, when we looked at the preferred options of the unemployed, we found that they were more interested in having full-time work than temporary or part-time engagements. They were also more interested in a 'real' job than a community programme job. When the two issues were taken together a temporary 'real' job was preferred to a full-time job in a community programme.

Interviewees were broadly in favour of 'stop-gap' efforts in job creation, welcoming any alternative to unemployment; nevertheless such work was frequently thought to be offering something less than a real job. Although 'any job is better than none' was a recurring comment, it would subsequently transpire that 'any job' meant one at a 'realistic rate of pay'. The majority of those out of work were motivated towards obtaining work and getting more money. Those supposed higher alternatives to a 'real' job, which many of the comfortably-off middle class favour in terms of 'leisure', 'socially useful work' and 'gaining new skills' were not well received by those already on the dole.

Barely half the sample of interviewees gave a favourable assessment of the newly introduced Enterprise Allowance Scheme, for which they were eligible, which had similarities to but differed in a number of important respects from our own Create-Your-Own-Job. They did not like the entry bar which required them to have available a given amount of personal capital – 'Where am I going to get money like that?' They were however more favourably inclined to a flexible arrangement whereby an agency would match any capital they could contribute with an equal sum of money.

Near the conclusion of the interview the question was asked: 'Suppose the State *guaranteed* for everyone some kind of paid work, training in new skills or help in setting up a business. This would replace regular unemployment benefit. What would you think of such an idea?'

Here responses showed a high level of general approval:

Downham Market 87 per cent
King Lynn 84 per cent
Corby 80 per cent

The strong desire of the unemployed to get into regular work might seem on the face of it to have been out of line with the fact that some vacant jobs available in the labour market were not being taken up. This was a subject on which we had already gained some insight when in the ITRU. Then we had working with us, during one University vacation, Yung Kong, a gifted Chinese mathematical student. Yung Kong's studies brought two factors to the fore: one was the *job reservation wage* and the other *a rigidity factor*.

The job reservation wage referred to a certain level of wages below which unemployed workers were not prepared to accept a job offer.

Yung Kong established a positive relationship between the benefit level received by unemployed persons and the job reservation wage: that is to say, the higher the benefit level the higher the job reservation wage. Stronger still, however, was the relationship between the job reservation wage and the level of previous earnings when last in employment. Presumably people created an image of what they were worth. Those who had enjoyed higher incomes had further to fall than those with lower earnings and so they were less prepared to accept jobs readily open to them.

The other important element in the situation was what might be called the flexibility-rigidity factor. In our study we found some respondents with high previous earnings less insistent on waiting until a job at a similar pay level came along. In other words this group was prepared to lower the threshold at which they were prepared to consider job offers. The most likely explanation was that the failure to get a job at the level of previous earnings caused the once comfortably-off to reduce their demands and expectations as unemployment lengthened.

The picture was very different in the case of the long-term unemployed with previously low earnings. They were disinclined to lower still further their job reservation wage. In other words those on social security with a record of poor earnings resist coercion into jobs carrying very low wages.

While the job reservation wage had been studied before by research workers, the rigidity factor had been much neglected. Yung Kong had first shown that certain job vacancies received fewer applications than would have been expected having regard to the wage offered and the job reservation wages of job-seekers. The job of warehouseman or caretaker, for example, attracted fewer applicants than might have been supposed. One theory advanced for this labour market misfit was that unemployed workers develop a narrow view of their capabilities, relate their job expectations too closely to their past experience and have difficulty in envisaging a job that is unfamiliar. This problem underlines the importance of providing counselling in conjunction with training if unfilled vacancies are to be filled.

Yung Kong's exploratory researches were well supported by what Norman Walker found in his SOUP studies in East Anglia. The rigidity factor might be overcome through training. But, without associated counselling, training could harden the rigidity factor. The effect was that trainees would develop very specific expectations which were unlikely to be met.

Once the unemployed sense that they are failing in the job search and that their prospects are poor, they cease applying for jobs and begin to adjust to life as they find it. This was well illustrated in Downham Market.

The unemployed in this small Norfolk town enjoyed a stable relationship with the labour market which operated in a surprising way. The town had suffered a considerable loss in job opportunities with the decline in agricultural employment and the closure of several small enterprises, but the one bright spot was the flourishing sugar-beet industry. Good wages could be earned in the factory with plenty of overtime during the season. When the season closed most workers were laid off. However, they would be taken on the following year provided they were 'on the register'. Being 'on the register' meant being available to work when required in the sugar-beet factory. Elsewhere the phrase usually refers to the 'unemployment register'. In fact there was no real contradiction. Only by remaining on the unemployment register could a worker hope to remain eligible for his retention on the factory's register and so maintain a reasonable standard of living. Industry and the social security system had achieved a degree of mutual accommodation. What the town lacked however was any local agency capable of overcoming this formula for employment inertia at high public cost.

The case of Downham Market illustrates the duality of the problem that unemployment poses in many areas. Unemployment is bound to remain high unless some means are found to generate more jobs in target localities. This requires a policy of active intervention rather than reliance on administrative bureaucracy. The difficulty that has to be faced, however, is that a mindless national social security system can operate to the mutual advantage of local residents and industry but at the expense of the wider tax-paying public. Any change in the system would almost certainly encounter opposition from entrenched interests which have learned to exploit what is available.

Our work had raised the fundamental issue of how the Welfare State can best operate as a force for generating employment without making undue demands on public finance. We will give further attention to this subject in Chapter 11.

EDU in East Anglia

Having formed the view that changes in policy were needed at both national and local levels, we now turned our attention to what could be done locally. Was it possible to build on the proven track record of project Expand-A-Firm in order to halt the spiralling decline in those places that had lost their economic justification for existence? We lived in an area generally regarded as prosperous. But the county of Cambridgeshire still housed within it the problems of the obsolete community.

Far out in the Fens, for example, there is a village called Commercial End which, as the name implies, is on the road to nowhere but in which no commercial activity currently takes place. The few who reach this village, attracted by gardens open to the public on given days during the year, will discover the most lovely period houses, once the homes of rich merchants. At one time this habitation was the innermost destination of barges bringing into East Anglia from sea routes coal and heavy materials and taking out on the return journey corn and other agricultural produce. Legend has it that the village died overnight on the coming of the railways.

The modern equivalent of Commerical End is March. Only the scale is different, for March is a town rather than a village. Almost certainly the town would not have existed had it not been for the railways, for early in the century it became a major rail junction in the region. But just as barge traffic was overtaken by rail traffic, so road traffic has overtaken rail. Deprived of its strategic rail function, the town was left set amidst flat, featureless country with not a lot going for it. While the magnetic pull of the city of Cambridge with its colleges, historic buildings and hi-tech industries was creating an outward flowing zone of prosperity, its reach did not extend as far as March.

The Northern Fens of Cambridgeshire similarly contain villages that have lost their evident function. Once the school closes, followed by the post office and then the village shop, a pattern has set in that is very difficult to reverse. The only remedy is to bring new economic life back to the locality. This is not, of course, a proposition that central government can entertain. But it is a subject in which the County Council, always under pressure from its electors, is deeply interested.

Dr Peter Whitehead was the Economic Development Officer for Cambridgeshire at the time and much aware that the tools for fostering economic development in chosen locations are limited. Apart from improving the local infrastructure there are not many options left for a local authority unaided in this field or without the active interest of a private developer.

It was Peter who took the initiative of exploring the possibility of having a version of Expand-A-Firm tried in the parts of the county where remoteness was operating against the well-being of a number of villages and small towns and the continued survival of communities. The discretionary element, which could result in one firm being favoured more than another, did not concern him in the least. His main priority was to arrest and reverse the economic and social decline currently taking place.

The handicap was to find the funds. The County Council was under financial pressure and we were very unlikely to get backing from the Manpower Services Commission. In the end we thought of two possibilities and followed them both. The first step was to design a project that provided a regular visiting expert service to firms rather than stay with the more expensive resident Development Fellow which was one special feature of Expand-A-Firm. In this way the project costs could be reduced. The second step was to devise an operation jointly financed by the County Council and the Social Fund of the European Economic Commission.

For this purpose the project had to be given an appropriate slant. The simple reality was that the Fens were suffering a decline in employment due to the large-scale introduction of labour-saving machines into agriculture. There was an overwhelming requirement for job creation. Yet apparently that in itself did not constitute a case for support. Peter Whitehead had done his homework well and had discovered that a grant was more likely to be forthcoming if the purpose was seen as training.

The aim of publicly funded training is ostensibly to help people secure jobs. But enabling new jobs to be brought into being directly, so that the jobseekers could have them, was not acceptable unless training was put as the prime objective. It was all very reminiscent of our dealings with the

MSC. Anyway Peter and Eunice were expert drafters of grant applications. They made a good job of it and as a result we were rewarded with the additional EEC support for our project.

Setting up CEBEE

With so much experience of our earlier Expand-A-Firm project behind us we felt we knew how to proceed. The name chosen for our new project was CEBEE (Combined Employment and Business Expansion Enterprise). The aim of CEBEE was to identify promising indigenous firms in a locality where new jobs were urgently required, and to find ways of overcoming the main impediments to development.

We needed small firms, situated in Fenland towns and villages, that had the potential to grow bigger and create new jobs but were for some reason not doing so. Two members of our CEBEE working party knew many of the firms anyway; Dick Lawrie, the dynamic Fenland District Council Industrial Liaison Officer, and David Rigley, the thoughtful and dedicated Manager of the Fens Business Enterprise Trust.

FENBET was one of the Enterprise Agencies established throughout the country, some on the initiative of Business in the Community, although in this instance, it was claimed, the idea came entirely from Wisbech businessmen. Dick came up with a number of suggestions on suitable firms. David visited all these along with a number of others that he considered were possible runners. All the firms showed interest in the proposal. After much hard work, David arrived in our office with a wad of large brown envelopes each of which contained standardized information on the essential facts and figures of the candidate firms to be considered for inclusion in the project. The papers were laid out in a row on the table and we went through the merits of each in a now familiar fashion. Six firms were needed and six were selected. Project CEBEE had begun.

It was the first test of our formula for reviving business and employment in a specific local community area.

8

The Combined Employment and Business Expansion Enterprise

The sole aim of Project CEBEE was to assist enterprises with the potential for growth to create new jobs in target locations. In some respects the project could be likened to a talent spotting exercise with an award to be won in the face of competition.

The managing owners of small enterprises are usually very pleased to receive any free help available, and even more so when they feel it comes from a recognition of their merits. But while the prospect of engaging in a programme aimed at growth is exciting and challenging, many of those who run small enterprises find daunting the thought of doubling or trebling the size of their businesses. It is not easy for them to see a way past the usual problems: how to reach new markets, how to finance the period of development on which growth demands and, in a nutshell, how short-term issues can be reconciled with the long-term objectives.

Our experience with Expand-A-Firm had taught us much about the problems of developing family-run enterprises. To parody Tolstoy's famous dictum, one could say that all growing successful family firms are happy in the same way but unsuccessful family firms are unhappy in their own individual way. The need was to find and talk to firms that were not growing happily but had the potential to achieve fulfilment. Progress depended on getting to the heart of their individual problems and using professional skill and experience to find a way of lifting them into a larger league.

As our resources were limited, we had to focus them on the firms most likely to create and sustain new jobs.

The criteria we took as offering favourable pointers for inclusion in the programme were companies with:

- between six and twenty employees (the size which research has shown as being most susceptible to growth);
- a product or service with some unique or distinctive features;

75

- no effective competitors in the immediate neighbourhood (to avoid displacing jobs from one firm to another);
- one or two customers located well outside the region (a likely sign that market penetration had not been fully exploited);
- ambitions for the future;
- a readiness to work with other people (including advisers).

This last factor required very careful assessment. The Fenlander is usually wary of outsiders. Living in an environment characterized by isolated farms and communities, he is used to acting on his own. His self-reliance is both his strength and his weakness. Individualism can limit the growth process. I was glad that David Rigley, the manager of the local Enterprise Agency, came with me on the first six visits, for he had been to the firms before. David was given a fair welcome in most, mingled with a mixture of curiosity and reserve.

Lack of capital

Some firms in the Fens were so remote that merely to arrive was an event in itself. The directions one owner-manager passed to me did not resemble any I had met before: 'Drive into the centre of the village, go into the telephone booth, give us a call to tell us you are here and I will then pick you up in the Land Rover'.

I preferred to find my own way there. It meant crossing the bridge over the river, turning immediately left down a road by the river bank which evolved into a rough track and ended in a field. In summer my front wheel drive car negotiated two fields and ended up alongside a solitary former public house which in times gone by served the bargees with beer and victuals: in winter the car had to be left at the entrance of the first field while I struggled in galoshes and mud through a herd of inquisitive cows towards my far-off destination.

The former bargees' pub produced smoked eels and trout of such a high quality that it found a ready market amongst some of the most exclusive stores and restaurants in the country. A forgotten and almost inaccessible hostelry had evolved from a state of dereliction to becoming the mainstay of employment in the village. The trouble was that though big new orders loomed, the future of the business was imperilled by lending restrictions on the part of the bank. Many small developing companies are under-capitalized for the scale of operations in which they engage. In the short-term they cannot make enough money to repay the interest charge on their loans. Once they start to contract they are bound to lose money, for they do not have the income to support their fixed costs. It is a Catch 22 situation. The solution is to bring in outside capital which the true individualist is reluctant to do.

In this case the manager was persuaded to reduce his dependence on the bank manager. In due course a small source of new capital was found and introduced into the business. This in its turn attracted further capital and allowed the now expanding firm to move into more efficient purpose-built premises on the outskirts of a distant town. The work force doubled. Yet employees continued to commute to work from the village for which the firm still served as the mainstay of employment.

The ultimate DIY man

While the physical isolation of entrepreneurs in remote places is in danger of fostering the type of solo individualism that can restrict the growth of the firm, unrivalled technical virtuosity can have a similar effect. This poses probably a greater difficulty, since the problem is in the mind and is not a matter of circumstance.

Some miles away from the enterprise which started in a bargees' pub, was the firm of George Hardcastle.

Hardcastle was a brilliant engineering designer. His creations in specialist machinery are to be found in the far corners of the globe. He was the ultimate Do-It-Yourself man. We first met in what could only be described as an overcrowded cottage with an adjacent outhouse into which were packed four engineers and a mass of machines through which it was difficult to pick a path. Hardcastle had started by buying second-hand machinery, refurbishing it, adding attachments of his own and finally sending out a piece of equipment that was better designed for its purpose than the original. His improvements were even copied by the manufacturers themselves.

Hardcastle's firm needed space let alone expansion. He acquired a long disused co-op piggery, which must have been vast in its time, in a typical act of Fenland exchange by barter. Hardcastle himself worked twelve hours a day and generally seven days a week. Much of the work in converting the piggery he did himself including laying a new floor. When he moved into his new premises his effective machine shop area multiplied by a factor of seventeen. His work force increased three times and there was plenty of room to expand it further. The limitation, we warned, was likely to become the mounting undulations in cash flow resultant on such a substantial surge in his business. But even this problem he handled with consummate skill.

There was only one real obstacle that stood in the way of the firm and real business success – an organizational bottleneck that besets any one-man show. George Hardcastle was at the heart of every skilled job. Sooner or later he would have to delegate responsibility and this he showed no signs of doing. The situation became worse when Hardcastle's promising son, who had been working with him in the business and was beginning to act like a manager, left to start up on his own. They did not apparently see eye to eye. But Hardcastle would not speak about it.

Indeed it was difficult to converse with Hardcastle about any basic problem. He was also exceptionally difficult to reach on the telephone. 'He's up on the roof at present, trying to fix it,' I was told on one typical occasion. Appointments were difficult to make, but when I presented myself in person on his threshold it was a different matter. He would always find time. Indeed the first hour would be spent inspecting his latest machinery or drawings or some improvements to his premises. Only after this initiating procedure did the possibility arrive of getting down to essentials. Even then I gained the impression that he paid no heed to anything I said. But there I would be mistaken. On a subsequent visit I would be informed that such and such had already been done.

Whether anything about which we spoke would claim his attention was quite unpredictable. The only predictable thing was that maximum resistance would be shown towards any attempt to introduce some new well-qualified person who could act as a senior colleague, and he was equally adamant against promoting any of his employees. As a last resort I did bring Eunice along to meet his shy, much harassed wife, who played a key, but often unseen, part in the business. The initial object was to talk about holidays, all of which led on to discussion relating to the future of the business and the need for an organizational change. Hardcastle joined in and expressed grudging approval. We thought we had made some progress but it never actually happened. Instead complaints about staff who 'couldn't carry responsibility' increased. The business reached a certain level and there it stopped. 'I don't want it to grow any bigger,' said Hardcastle.

George Hardcastle was more difficult to deal with than any other of the owner-managers we encountered in the Fens project. But in one respect he was typical of other lone pioneers: he would never willingly attend a management educational course or seminar or actively seek advice. But he did respond in a disguised way to personal visits, especially on marketing issues. In a curious way I felt he was glad to see me, though he never expressed the slightest hint of gratitude. I doubt that he was the sort of person to acknowledge that an outsider's ideas were worth taking up.

Identifying bottlenecks

Our CEBEE visits enabled us to meet and assist several gifted entrepreneurs who were resistant to any criticism of their business plans and operations except in a crisis — when it was usually too late.

But in contrast there were other entrepreneurs who were ready to pick up any suggestion on how things might be improved. The most open and welcoming were found in well-managed small enterprises with few evident shortcomings. Even then it was sometimes possible to identify a bottleneck that restricted the growth of the business and the creation of new jobs.

Fenland Fabrics

A good example of a receptive and progressive company was Fenland Fabrics, which produced a range of designs and materials for which there was a steady demand from large stores. Two gifted partners ran the business, Mark Mathews and Henry Hull. Mathews was a connoisseur of designs with a good grasp of finance and a broad vision of where the company was heading. Hull had a great talent for making things, worked exceptionally hard and showed an aptitude for handling his staff. Both men, being creative in their separate ways, were prone to find issues on which they did not see eye to eye. But any proneness to conflict was reduced since their responsibilities were divided and complementary and Hull lived in the Fens and Mathews in London.

All went well until the volume of orders produced a strain on the productive capacity of the firm. Increasingly time was spent in progress chasing, dealing with indignant customers and pressing suppliers for materials that were holding up manufacture. One day when I entered the office I remarked on the sheer volume of paper that was stacked untidily on Henry Hull's desk. 'I know,' Henry said, 'and it allows me very little time to get down on the factory floor. We've even had for the first time labour difficulties as a consequence of my absence.' Continuing with my criticisms, I carried on, 'Nor on the office walls do I see a single production chart or trend graph'. 'The fact is,' said Henry, 'that even if you showed me a chart or a graph I wouldn't know what to make of it. I left school early and I'm not much good with figures'.

Mathews, Hull and I tried to find a solution that would allow Henry to spend more time on the factory floor where he had most to contribute. However Mathews showed a resistance to the idea of recruiting a full-time person to help with the paper work and the inquiries. The options, they felt, lay between having a full-time assistant, a half-time assistant and a retired experienced executive who would be able to 'sort it out'. Mathews and Hull took a different view on what could be afforded and each strongly argued his case.

Eventually I suggested that the company should buy a computer, enlarge the job and recruit a production controller to install and operate a new system. That approach was even more expensive. Henry was not familiar with 'production control' as a subject or profession, while Mark Mathews was apprehensive about increasing the cost of overheads. But eventually the plan was agreed. The salary on offer attracted only a limited field and the first appointee did not match the hopes that had been raised. A later replacement proved much more successful.

Once the bottleneck to growth was removed, orders and production expanded rapidly. The company acquired larger premises. The workforce increased from 26 to 85. Today Fenland Fabrics can point to one of the most efficient and highly computerized offices in the region and looks back with amusement to its chaotic old ways.

A firm and its manager

A personal weakness once identified need not act as the brake on an enterprise but may transform itself into a strength.

As our range of experience of firms in the Fens widened, we began to see how the characteristic of the firm was very much a reflection of the personal characteristics of their owner-managers. An expert engineer might possess the technical skills to enable a small firm to expand steadily in a locality and so provide a growing number of new jobs. But the prospect would be of no avail if some personal hang-up stood in the way of that development. Pessimism may be overcome by removing the ostensible reasons for its occurrence. On the other hand an outlook may be more deeply rooted. In this case the removal of one difficulty may result merely in the rise of another. Although an enterprise itself may look promising, it is a matter of judgement how far, given all the circumstances, any small firm is likely to expand.

Over-cautious

A good illustration occurred in the case of a small specialist firm operating in spark erosion engineering in a Fenland village. We had ascertained from independent sources that the firm had a high reputation for the quality of its products, and, in principle, looked ripe for growth.

But the two partners who ran the business saw themselves as engineers not managers. In spite of the full order book, they very much doubted their ability to compete with bigger enterprises. With that in mind they kept their prices low and paid their workers and themselves less than the market might bear. Even when they were overloaded with work they still charged standard prices. 'Next time that happens,' I said, 'do something just for me. Increase the next quotation by fifty per cent and let's see what happens'. 'I will,' said the senior partner. Some months later he greeted me in a cheerful mood. 'In spite of those increased quotations,' he said with a grin, 'we still got the orders'. 'Good,' I said, 'And in view of the fact that not all your machines are manned perhaps one might even think about taking on some new workers'. 'Impossible,' I was told. 'We have tried advertising for spark erosion engineers and got no replies.'

That isolated communities living in the Fens should be hidden repositories for unemployed spark erosion engineers seemed on the face of it unlikely. 'Who is the best of your current men?' I inquired. On being told I asked how he acquired his skill. 'It all came about by chance.' 'He used to work on a farm. When he applied for a job here, he showed good practical interest in engineering.' 'Well, let's see if we can find some more people with the right aptitude,' I suggested, and immediately thought of some methods whereby that type of aptitude can be detected.

We were due to meet again to put the plan into action. But when I next arrived I was greeted by a glum face. My friend had lost two of his best men attracted by a revival of engineering in Peterborough. 'They pay higher wages which we can't afford,' he explained. 'But if you can command higher prices you can also afford to pay the market wage for the job,' I protested. It was all to no avail. The other partner saw the venture as 'too risky'. The two principals announced that they would limit the firm to a size in which they themselves could supervise all the work. The consequence was that while we helped the firm to grow a little, it was clear that its job-creating potential was limited while the partners stuck to their cautious policy.

Give us the grants

The problem of helping firms to expand was becoming in many ways a person-centred business. The task was made easier in so far as entrepreneurs or owner-managers had received in the past some elements of management education. But for many there was a built-in resistance to being exposed as knowing less about 'how to run a firm' than they should. Periodically useful seminars took place within easy travelling distance. Yet there was nearly always a reason why they 'couldn't make it' whenever attention was drawn to a forthcoming management event.

There was, however, one function during the early days of our CEBEE project which proved an exception to the rule. The occasion was one which had been prepared by Dick Lawrie, who besides being the Industrial Liaison Officer of Fenland District Council was a member of our CEBEE Project Steering Group. A new Minister of State at the Department of Trade and Industry had been appointed with special responsibility for small firms: he was David Trippier, a man with a reputation for being an eloquent speaker and sympathetic handler of questions. Dick was keen to get the Minister down to the Fens and to invite employers and businessmen, on whom jobs in the Fens would ultimately depend. Upon the Minister's acceptance, a gala event was laid on. The large hall of a school next to the offices of the Fenland District Council was hired with a free buffet supper to precede the address. The turn-out for this well-serviced event was unexpectedly high!

In line with these plans Dick had duly written the speech to be delivered by the Chairman of the Council. The emphasis fell on the initiatives taken by the local Council of which some local people were justly proud. Project CEBEE was given considerable prominence – which is probably why we were given reserved seats in the front row. An additional aim in the Chairman's speech was to acquaint the Minister with the problems of the area.

Whatever the intention may have been, there was little sign that the visiting party took any note of what was being said. The Minister was there of course for a different purpose – to put over the Government's message. In it he drew attention to a 'a hundred measures' which the Government had introduced to help small businesses. Many of those attending were there to see what was on offer and were excited by what they heard. Much attention and interest centred on innovation grants. By the time the Minister left the expectations of the audience had been fully aroused.

Soon afterwards when visiting firms I found it difficult to keep discussion focused on the central problems of expanding the business. 'We want to make sure we get our full share of any grants that are going,' I was told.

Alas, when it came down to it the Fenland entrepreneurs found that there was little in it for them. As one of them put it, after pursuing an inquiry through the Ministry, 'There is always a good reason why it doesn't apply to us.'

The innovation grant rankled particularly in the mind of an enterprising managing director of an engineering company of which he was the founder. The company made standard conveyor equipment to suit a range of industrial needs but was also developing a major piece of sophisticated handling equipment that was reckoned to have potentially world-wide sales. The development costs were, however, very high and were considered beyond the reach of the firm. What our friend discovered to his dismay was that innovation grants could only be awarded for a project that

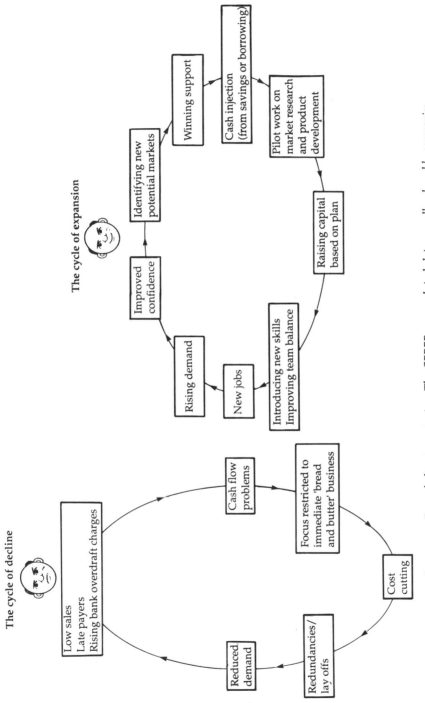

Figure 1   *From decline to expansion. The CEBEE approach in helping small vulnerable companies*

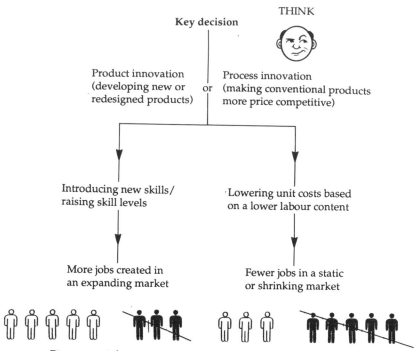

Figure 2   *Job outcomes based on alternative managerial strategies*

had not actually started. 'But if you don't start something,' he protested, 'you cannot tell whether it is really feasible'. Small firms seldom possess skilled executive courtiers capable of wheedling grants from legalistically minded civil servants.

How to chase grants

We discussed the matter in our CEBEE Working Party. Product development was the key to getting local firms moving. The way things were going we could not see any of them securing support for their endeavours. At the same time we knew that the Ministry dispensed substantial sums for particular projects, especially when project budgets were underspent. We knew several recipients in large companies who were quite surprised by what they had received. Such decisions were always taken by centrally placed officials. It might be better, we thought, if smaller firms were helped. That process could be assisted by those with local knowledge who could provide recommendations on deserving projects in the area.

We consulted the top Ministry man in the region who gave us his backing and advised how we might pursue the matter. The suggestion was

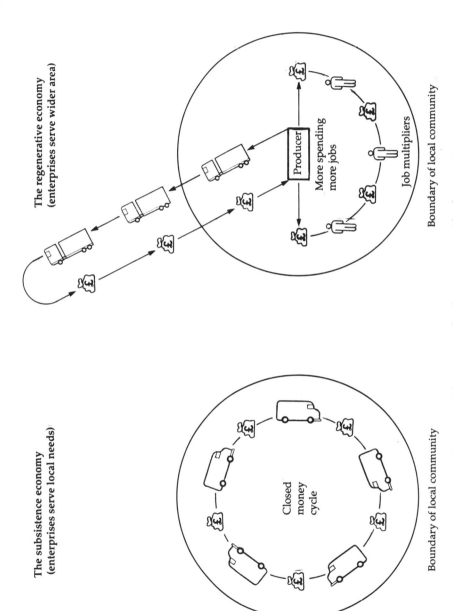

The subsistence economy
(enterprises serve local needs)

The regenerative economy
(enterprises serve wider area)

Closed money cycle

Producer
More spending more jobs

Job multipliers

Boundary of local community

Boundary of local community

Figure 3   *Job outcomes related to two types of local economy*

Michael P. Forbes
(UK) Ltd

156 Perne Road
Cambridge CB1 3NX
Telephone: 0223 211410

Being essentially a practical engineer and businessman I would not attempt to understand everything in this book. However I can testify that through Project CEBEE and with the personal help of Meredith Belbin and his colleagues, Jill Francis and Geoff Dale, my life and prospects have radically changed and many new jobs have been provided for others.

The small firm we used to run in Cambridge carried out contract work in engineering mainly for the farming and agricultural world. It was very difficult to run a steady business because you never knew what work you were going to get. Some customers took extended credit so that you were always up against problems with the bank. I was becoming tired of the hassle of running the business.

Forming the right management team I have learned is the key to running a successful company. Meredith Belbin's team role techniques showed us that some of us were doing things for which we were not fitted, while we were also failing to play our real strengths. My personal strength was shown to exist as a co-ordinator of others and less as a practical implementer, which was a surprise to me in view of my engineering background. I began to change the way in which I operated and to play a greater part in general liaison work, including overseas assignments, and in putting together new projects.

After producing a new business plan for our current company, we next looked for ways of financing it. With support from the Welsh Development Agency we were able to set up an establishment in South Wales in an area of high unemployment. We already have 18 new employees and have prospects of adding considerably to this number within the next two years.

But things did not end there. Meredith Belbin persuaded us to depend less on contracting and to develop a product of our own which we could make and market. We already had some experience of flour milling machinery and this helped us to devise a new system to meet the growing demand for wholemeal flour. The taste of stone ground flour is superb because of the slow speed of grinding. The speed of machinery used by large volume flour mills generates heat which drives off the volatile elements that carry the flavour of the grain. What together we succeeded in doing was to find a way of linking the traditional methods of grinding with modern machinery to yield efficient production in reasonable quantities without loss of flavour.

After producing a business plan we began to search for ways of financing it. Eventually the project attracted venture capital from a major European investor for an ambitious national programme. UK Stonemills will be creating 45 new jobs in Llanelli in two years rising to an estimated 110 in three years plus another 130 within the same period in other parts of the country.

There is a general message here that business can be helped to expand while creating real jobs at the same time if the problem is approached in the right way. I hope that those who read about CEBEE will find the approach as stimulating as we have found the experience of actually taking part in the Exercise itself.

Figure 4   *A CEBEE client writes ...*

that I should write a letter to the Minister. This I did and after referring to his recent Fenland visit gave an outline of our proposal and asked if it might be possible to meet to discuss the matter. After a long delay a courteously phrased letter came back. Its gist was to point out that the Ministry did already award innovation grants to small firms – defined as having under 200 staff (which by Fenland standards could mean a very big company) – and enclosed a brochure giving details of existing programmes, which we already had. The Minister went on to express satisfaction with the way in which the matter was currently being dealt with and, in diplomatic language, declined to discuss our suggestions further.

This episode served to highlight a basic division in outlook on how best to foster the growth of small enterprises and the creation of jobs in local areas. The centralist strategy is to devise a complex formula to take account of all possible circumstances and anomalies, and then to administer it dispassionately. By minimizing human discretion as far as possible, decisions in particular cases can only be challenged as defaulting on the rules. The price of this formula approach is that it is seldom cost-effective in achieving its purpose. The alternative is to award limited budgets to local groups of reputable people to use according to their discretion, to achieve a well-defined objective in a cost-effective fashion. The price of this delegation of responsibilities is some loss of control on the part of central government and with it the more serious risk of losing some of the credit for what is achieved.

Most governments prefer the former to the latter approach. Project CEBEE, however, was based on the latter strategy. This meant that while official projects were relatively rich, ours was relatively poor.

Nevertheless in terms of results, CEBEE was beginning to show a disproportionately handsome return for the resources employed. The CEBEE Project Steering Group became adept at identifying promising firms for the scheme and we gradually improved our ability to differentiate between the entrepreneurs who were worth helping and those who were not.

It was not long before we realized that the programme we were running was out of tune with the mainstream influence and pressures being exerted on small firms from other quarters. Our programme differed not only in form but in content. Experience led us to fashion a distinctive type of financial and manpower strategy that led some entrepreneurs to exclaim despairingly: 'But that runs counter to the advice we've been given by everybody else'.

The block to new ventures

The recurring problem of the developing small firm is its proneness to a cash flow crisis whenever its resources are diverted away from its current bread-and-butter business in the direction of new ventures. Following our visits to the more promising companies selected for the CEBEE project, David and I had formed the view that over half were undercapitalized and that is why the development of which they were capable did not take place.

Neither of us was professionally qualified to make a proper pronouncement on the matter. So on my next visit I took with me a senior partner of a leading firm of accountants who, though located in East Anglia, had spent a good many years in the City. He not only agreed with our reckoning but was able to explain to the leading person in each firm why that was so. In only one firm was the conclusion accepted on the spot. The others treated the advice with scepticism or wanted to refer the matter to their own accountant. On a later visit to one firm I found that the firm's external accountant had sided with the owner in rejecting the proposition. But at least the subject had got onto the agenda.

Leaving aside the restriction on its development, the more general effect of undercapitalization is that a company is liable to engage in what is called 'overtrading'. Its inflows and outflows of cash get bigger while its borrowing facility remains stationary. In time the firm exceeds its overdraft limit and is then in trouble. This often happens when a firm has big orders in hand and has stocked up on supplies. We heard many sad tales of enterprising Fenmen engaged on major contracts being summoned to their bank manager to explain why their company's figures were moving deeper into the red rather than towards the black. By waving letters from large companies and drawings of new engineering products they were convinced the bank manager 'would see reason'. Instead the bank manager did not want to see the drawings and was unimpressed with the letters.

Occasionally a firm's overdraft limit at the bank would be cut arbitrarily. This would occur when a new bank manager took over or when Head Office ordered a tightening of the reins on some overall view of the economy. The firms then had difficulty in paying bills of suppliers, often other small firms. The effects would then ripple through the region generating a local recession and sometimes closures.

The advice of a bank manager to 'cut back' on expenses tended to coincide with advice forthcoming from a firm's own accountants or from one of the advisers available to small firms through the Ministry. Often a firm ran several product lines. The old established ones were the most profitable, for these had benefited from the longest period of development. New lines or anything not fully developed could be isolated, on purely financial grounds, as loss-making. The net effect of this was a continuing pressure to abandon ventures of the type capable of creating and sustaining jobs.

It was an unwelcome surprise to discover that firms identified as having the best growth potential showed few signs of expanding employment New ventures were being eliminated on the recommendations of advisers and cash reserves were being earmarked for labour-saving machines, where savings could be precisely calculated, rather than on more speculative activities like marketing, market research and product design – functions that are the accepted harbingers of growth.

Where have all the skills gone?

While one of the main problems why firms were not expanding hinged on insufficient capital and investment, another major limiting factor was the shortage of skills. The change in government policy had, in our view, undermined the Industrial Training Act and more important still the basic provisions within it for safeguarding the long-term skill requirements of industry. In due course apprentice-trained engineers or college-educated technicians were treated like gold dust. Instead of being used to overcome this shortage, public money had been channelled into other directions which were less industrially significant, like the Youth Training Scheme which catered for lower level skills. One evident outcome of this latter programme in Fenland firms was the good supply of charming little girls who did some typing along with various odd jobs and making the cup of tea. 'They're YTS,' we would be told.

The problem of a shortfall in skills was compounded by the way in which firms reacted to the deficiency. The MSC was ready to offer to subsidize training. But the benefits of training are long-term. At junctures critical for expansion firms need experienced people rather than learners or, failing that, individuals of aptitude and ability with relevant skills capable of developing rapidly in the appropriate area. A recruitment and placement service was crucial. In this field public sector services had little to offer. The erstwhile Labour Exchanges, now renamed Jobcentres, had taken on a notably passive role. Jobcentres were built around the help yourself principle. Jobseekers looked primarily at the job for which they considered themselves best qualified and naturally ignored the other possibilities. And even if they had not, one doubts that without an intermediary their applications would have been seriously considered by employers.

Which way forward?

Somehow in our CEBEE programme we had to find a way round these two barriers to business and employment growth.

On the financial side we began to explain to companies the importance of the distinction between attracting capital investment and borrowing money. The overwhelming majority of the owner-managers of promising but under-capitalized small enterprises were initially opposed to the former possibility: 'Why should we give away any part of the company we've worked hard for?' And on the latter prospect they were far too optimistic about their ability to repay short-term loans at high interest rates. Our reply was to ask: 'Which would you rather have: the whole of a cupcake or two out of three tiers of a wedding cake?' For some, the amount of cake was less important than ownership of the whole. The attitude of the owner-manager to his business often bears comparison with the proud and possessive attitude of a peasant towards land long held in a family.

We were struck however by the number of owner-managers who failed to understand the nature of capital from an external investor. 'How much interest would I have to pay?' 'Is it cheaper than borrowing from a bank?' These astonishing questions arose because the thought of bringing in capital was hitherto inconceivable and therefore people knew almost nothing about the subject.

Our mission was to bring to the fore projects of potential merit within the company, especially those which had been devised to meet the requested needs of a customer. Usually there were several half-finished developments lying around. The aim was to select the best of these and to turn them into a marketable product. We would then reach the point when it became plain that further progress required money which the firm did not have. That was the stage when the claim for a capital injection would be pressed.

The line we took was that working capital needed for current revenue earning business could be financed through bank borrowing. But new developments were better financed by selling a share in the business, or potential business, to an outside investor. We undertook to help develop the product to suit the needs of the market, to find a way of projecting the image of the product, to help to write a business plan and to find a suitable investor. Of course what we were most interested in was the creation of sustainable jobs at the end of the process.

This process kept us so busy that we began to look for extra help. Here we were fortunate in being able to recruit two part-time consultants. Geoff Dale had spent much of his working life as the Education and Training Officer in a large company and as the treasurer of virtually every organization he had ever joined. With this combination of skills he was well placed to advise and develop managers who had no financial background and who were over-reliant on firms of external accountants. Since the accounts were usually late, owner-managers often had to guess at the financial decisions they should take. Geoff, who was patient and helpful by nature, proved quite successful in introducing computers to managers who were not computer-literate and steering them towards the crucial decisions upon which all future plans had to be based. We were also fortunate in benefitting from the services of Jill Francis, who was well qualified in marketing and had broad industrial experience. Jill was married to a farmer in the Fens and had a young family, but she had a great knack of using her time to maximum advantage. A number of managers tried to overwhelm Jill with abstruse engineering technicalities but they never succeeded. Her pleasant manner, firmness of purpose and knowledge of her subject always won their respect in the end. Together we succeeded in remodelling a number of companies, changing the products, the image and in some cases even the name of the firm.

The momentum of Project CEBEE increased once we had some results to show. Of the first six enterprises brought into the scheme only one remained with the same sized labour force at the end of one year. The other five that had between them 59 workers grew to provide 101 jobs between one year and eighteen months after the inception of the project. Some of these firms continued to grow steadily thereafter and to provide an increasing number of jobs to other 'feeder' firms. The renewal of our contracts with the Local Authority meant that the programme soon acquired a rolling character. As a project finished in one Fenland firm, it was replaced by the next firm on the waiting list.

A new stage

The news about Project CEBEE travelled around the region and beyond and in consequence we were invited to undertake similar projects elsewhere. New contracts were entered into in Peterborough, Cambridge City, Milton Keynes and the Isle of Wight.

Since our resources in key personnel to carry out these projects were slender, we kept a low profile. At one time we were running programmes in thirty enterprises simultaneously. This work-load was higher than we could comfortably manage but at least the pressures caused us to become faster-moving and more decisive. This style suited the more dynamic enterprises, where owner-managers were looking for leads on how to proceed, did not believe in wasting time and took appropriate actions with astonishing rapidity. Throughout our work we were told that firms preferred CEBEE to official programmes, though these were financially much better resourced than ours. A major reason appeared to be that we could act without referring back to higher authorities. Our greater degree of autonomy enabled us to switch the direction of the programme quickly if one avenue looked more rewarding than another. This condition made for productive discussions with managers, for there was no fear of running up against the bureaucratic constraints which they had experienced in the past.

Helping workers to work

Project CEBEE, being without the support of governmental agencies, had been designed to suit current circumstances which were a good way removed from what we would have wished. In particular the lack of liaison with the authorities who deal with the unemployed limited the way in which we operated. There were no facilities available comparable with those I had experienced in the USA during the earlier engagements in my career with Community Progress Incorporated. From time to time we encountered able individuals who were keenly seeking work but whose experience and qualifications had low credibility in the labour market. They applied to us because they thought, mistakenly, that the Employment Development Unit served some role in helping particular people to find work. To perform that function we would have needed a training and assessment centre. That would have provided the means to authenticate the specific skills and potentialities of jobseekers and so enable us to support the claims of certain candidates for particular positions. Without that information firms had no means of evaluating potential and looked instead at proven track record which seldom matched what was required.

Jobseeker Annie

Had we been adequately equipped we felt we could have done far more to support Annie. This sprightly widow of fifty had worked in her time as a laboratory assistant, had done well in science at school, possessed an arts degree from the Open University and had completed a secretarial course for mature women. She also had a broad experience of social and community work and held a certificate for the Institute of Advanced Drivers. At the time we had established a scarcity amongst our small firms of technical sales representatives who would have their own car, and could travel around the county to knock on the doors of engineering firms to discuss a range of goods and services. We felt Annie might conceivably fill the bill. She herself was keen on the idea. We gave her an intelligence test and a measure of mechanical aptitude and were impressed with her score. The problem was to build up her engineering credibility. Unfortunately we had no means of doing this. None of our small firms would risk taking her on. In the end after a prolonged job search the only job offered to her was as check-out woman in a supermarket.

If Project CEBEE was to reach out to the unemployed we had to approach the subject in some other way and this involved finding people with more immediate technical credibility than Annie who still had difficulty in finding a job. Firms commonly claimed, 'We cannot find the person we want,' because their candidate specification was too rigid. At the same time jobseekers lack the confidence to go after specialized jobs for which their general skills render them suitable. This bridging operation is very important if people are to secure jobs and firms are to find the people.

Bringing computer skills to a firm

Happily we had one notably successful experience in this field with one of our CEBEE projects in Peterborough. In this instance our work was made easier because we had a small sum of money available from an EEC social and regional fund that enabled us to make a secondment of our own choosing.

Getting into gear

Index Gear and Engineering was a small, newly established firm of specialist gear cutters which manufactured gears in small quantities from drawings supplied. There was usually something complicated about each order which was the reason why the work was won. A feature of the company which especially drew our attention was that it was trying to design and launch on the market a new gear of its own instead of operating merely as a contractor for other firms. This attempted development was straining the firm's financial resources, as such developments are always prone to do. The sticking point was that the cutting costs for the various components of the new gear were too high to make it marketable. The methods that served well for making a few special gears were unsuitable for standard operations.

Gear cutting as a trade involves a great deal of mathematical calculations. The whole procedure lends itself to computer operation using formulae, which, though complex, are readily available from published tables. Mike Eley, the owner-manager of Index Gear and Engineering, had accordingly bought a suitable computer. But he was now finding that the people who know all about computers are usually unable to cope with the engineering intricacies of gear cutting. Correspondingly his engineers could not programme computers. What was required was someone who could span both fields. This was a role for a firm of specialist consultants. But, with resources already stretched with the development cost of the new gear, the service was one that Mike knew he could not afford. The whole project was in danger of coming to a halt.

Our first step was to contact Peterborough Regional College. After consultations with the staff we had brought to our notice a bright, shy eighteen-year-old student who had done well in maths and science, was interested in computing, having a home computer of his own, and was conveniently in his third year of study for a Higher National Certificate in electronics. Graham Butler was a member of the registered unemployment and only a part-time student at the College. He had been actively seeking work where he could continue with training in day release. Graham seemed a good person to be tried out in the CEBEE project in the gear cutting firm.

Mike Eley was not sure quite what to expect from the secondment scheme at first and was naturally somewhat concerned about how it would work out. He anticipated problems with the acceptance of an outside 'expert', especially one so young, by a workforce that was very skilled and much sought after by other engineering firms in the area. There was also the problem of having to share the company's one and only office and a concern about the possible difficulties over the confidentiality of the company's affairs. However on balance he thought the benefits would be greater than the disadvantages and that a pair of expert hands on the computer might help to solve the company's production problem.

Mike tried to forestall any objections to Graham on the part of the workforce by briefing him thoroughly about the industry and its skill and introducing him carefully to each person in turn. He arranged for the gear cutters to teach Graham about their work and the calculation difficulties and for him to spend his first three weeks working on the shop-floor from 8:30 to 4:30.

In the first five or six weeks Graham found that to accomplish small tasks took a long time because he was having to absorb all the necessary background information. Also the gear cutters were inclined to give him difficult and perhaps unnecessarily complicated answers to his questions to demonstrate their own wide knowledge of the industry. The first two weeks of watching them working were a particularly strange and in some ways trying time for him, not actually doing much work of his own but asking as many questions as possible. At the end of each day he would spend as much time as he could on the computer, familiarizing himself with its functions. All in all Mike was 'very pleased and delighted' at the way things went, largely because Graham was so well accepted by the workforce.

During Graham's three months with the firm he designed computer programs to calculate and produce machining instructions for all types of gear cutting which the company might undertake. These programs reduced calculating time, for example, from six hours to half an hour and from one and a half hours to five minutes.

The computer was different from the ones he had been used to at college but, by his third week, he had taught himself how to use it with the aid of manuals and packages. There was no one in the company who could have helped him with this and although he could have phoned his college tutor to discuss problems he did not in fact need to do so.

When Graham took the job on he had not expected to be working solo or to have full responsibility for producing the programs. The work proved busier and more complex than he had expected. He found himself answering telephone inquiries from customers wanting quotations or progress reports and he had to find out the necessary information from the men in the workshop if Mike Eley was not available and pass it on. He also dealt with general administration such as sending out a change of address letter as Index Gear and Engineering was about to move into new premises.

The benefits of the CEBEE secondment scheme at the firm worked out to advantage for the three parties: for the Peterborough area and its employment prospects, for Mike Eley and the company itself, and for their temporary 'employee' Graham Butler.

The company benefited by having their highly skilled workforce fully engaged on production. The throughput increased and customer needs were met more quickly. Production also achieved a higher level of accuracy. New employees were taken on who did not need the ability or the special training to do calculations. Quicker and better quotations could be given to potential customers which resulted in an increased flow of orders. Because of Graham's programming work and his general involvement in the administrative side, Mike Eley was able to spend more time on research and development work for the future expansion of the business. He was delighted to be freed in this way and appreciated the immediate short-term benefit of having Graham there to deal with the telephone and visitors. Although this was difficult for Graham at first, he developed progressively from a rather shy person to one who could cope well with all kinds of people. The workforce seemed pleased with the whole idea of Graham's secondment for the computer programming and co-operated fully, once their initial scepticism had been overcome. Mike Eley described the long-term benefits to the company as 'massive' because the computer programs would deal with all types of work which the company was likely to undertake in the future.

Graham's contribution had much to do with the successful expansion of the firm which was, in due course, able to move into new premises over three times as large as the old factory. New semi-skilled engineers were taken on because the complicated mathematical calculations which could take three years to master were no longer hindrances to their employment.

This CEBEE project in Peterborough received considerable publicity in the press and on television. It was written up in the local paper under the eye-catching headlines WHIZ-KID BOOST FOR ENGINEERS with a photograph of Graham Butler and Mike Eley alongside a computer and some of the cutting machines in the production department. The human angle reinforced general interest in our work even if it distorted it in the process. Eventually Graham, the former shy, unemployed youth, was given a permanent position as the Assistant Factory Manager.

Looking back

As the CEBEE projects progressed we became quicker at recognizing critical bottlenecks in companies and marshalling the special resources needed to overcome the problem. We had a growing network of people who gave us special advice and so enabled us to widen our operations. However we began to develop some recurring lines of approach. We took a particular interest in small firms with good specialist skills that relied on subcontracting for orders or were feeling the pinch of intense competition in saturated markets. The aim in these cases was to develop a new product that lay within their capability but which had some 'unique selling potential'. This was the business that proved most likely to expand, to generate profits and to create new jobs.

Although we gained in applicable experience and technique in accomplishing our goals and we were pleased with the number of firms that succeeded in doubling or trebling their size, we made one mistake that in retrospect accounted for failures that ought to have been avoided. It was a matter of the strategy we decided to adopt towards a recurring problem.

Small firms are usually unbalanced in terms of their respective strengths in Design, Production, Marketing and Financial Control, being strong in one or more areas but weak in another. To improve the balance is a prime aim for the consultant who is striving to generate growth in the enterprise. That task is made much more difficult if the prime reason for any particular weakness is an insistence on the part of an owner-manager on retaining control and decision-making over a field in which he is incompetent. In these cases one of the conditions that we laid down before introducing new capital to support some new venture was that the company should widen its management base. To improve the composition we took account of both technical and personal factors in order to achieve a balanced management team in which the sum might prove stronger than the parts.

The problem, as always, was to apportion the allocation of shares. The original owner was usually loth to part with any shares but would consent under pressure to sell some minority of the shareholding to the incoming executive as this was the condition on which both we and the external investor insisted.

The mistake we made was to believe that this surrender of shares signified a corresponding surrender of power. The founders of small businesses in particular are reluctant to treat any fellow executives, however well qualified and able, on equal terms. Their decisions were overruled or, more menacingly, undermined behind their back. In one case a financial executive, who had been brought in to control a talented but profligate Chief Executive, found that additional signatories had been found for signing cheques so that the Chief Executive could still retain a free hand. In such circumstances these 'improved' management teams turned out to be a myth. The ventures which they were formed to supervise fell apart. Some were rescued only when the original entrepreneur had departed from the scene.

We learned one lesson from this experience: namely, that the distribution of share ownership is highly relevant to the future of each enterprise. If there is some doubt about the all-round capabilities of a majority shareholder, no real growth in the business and employment can be assured. A prime aim must be to bring about a reconstruction of the company, whenever necessary, so that no one individual can exercise total power.

Human factors turned out to be the most critical of all for the outcome of each new venture. By the later stages of Project CEBEE we had begun to use some of the more sophisticated techniques employed by large companies for assessing the personal characteristics and aptitudes of key personnel in the enterprises that were being considered for support. Creating new jobs is as much a people-centred operation as it is an exercise in raising finance.

9
The entrepreneur as a jobmaker

If new jobs are to come into being someone has to create them. We may have conceived ourselves in the role of job promoters. But there are other people who by their endeavours, if not their intention, create jobs directly. These prime movers, in line with how we have used the term before, we will christen 'jobmakers'.

We will here advance the thesis that the generation of employment is inseparable from the study of people. For successful jobmakers must inevitably be individuals with special aptitudes and characteristics. That is not to play down other essentials for jobmaking: the availability of financial capital, the propinquity of key materials and the suitability of conditions for the conduct of business. These may be important factors, yet they are primarily enabling mechanisms. They account for *why* new enterprises will flourish in one place rather than another. The enabling mechanisms on their own cannot create new jobs: enterprises will never flourish anywhere without the right people to set them up and run them.

Our work would have progressed more smoothly if that conclusion had been with us from the outset. Instead our attention had focused on the nature of the enterprise itself, that is to say on its technical merits rather than on the capacity of individuals within the enterprise to turn that potential into fulfilment. Once it transpired that human factors had virtually the biggest bearing on any outcome, we were faced with the perennial issue of nature versus nurture. Are entrepreneurs and good managers born with their potential there to be discovered from the outset of working life? Or can they be developed in the required way through education?

This point was brought sharply to our attention when we were commissioned by the Isle of Wight Development Board to apply our programme CEBEE (Combined Employment and Business Expansion Enterprise) to whole of the Isle.

The Chairman of the Board was then Sir John Nicholson, the possessor of a distinguished record of industrial and public service and now in his late seventies. Notwithstanding his years, Sir John was a man of robust character, as we were soon to learn, when at the commencement of the project we were taken to meet him at his Norman manor home on one of the bleakest days of winter. Without regard to the north wind as it howled and remorselessly penetrated our overcoats, Sir John emerged from the house to greet us in a sports jacket and, unruffled by the elements, proceeded to treat us to a prolonged conducted tour of the garden!

Clearly any views expressed by so sturdy a figure had to be taken seriously. As it happened, his understanding of our project differed somewhat from the way in which it had originally been presented both by us and by his staff. The project was interpreted not so much as providing the means of overcoming the identified bottlenecks to growth, as was our intention, but as being concerned with on-the-spot management education.

'Managers will not manage better unless they understand what they are doing,' he argued. Because of the demands on their time, entrepreneurs are commonly cut off from formal management education. This deficiency could become a real stumbling block to progress, expecially on the Isle of Wight where there was a greater risk than on the mainland of the population becoming a closed community.

Nature or nurture

It was this experience which prompted a different operational approach on our part. We had first of all to find out what sort of managers and entrepreneurs we were dealing with. And so we began to use some of the assessment materials with entrepreneurs that we had developed for executives for the purpose of normal work in management consulting. In other words we were now faced with the importance of scrutinizing the people as much as the enterprise, since assessment was a necessary precondition for providing an appropriate element of management education.

This was easier said than done. The reality was that those who resisted management education also resisted being assessed. Conversely those who welcomed the opportunity to learn something within their own premises also found the insights provided by assessments useful in cultivating an effective management style that could help them run their businesses better.

The crunch issue of nature versus nurture turned out to be difficult to disentangle even after review of a fair number of cases. That is because those with natural aptitude show a greater readiness to learn that to which they are fitted by ability. To parcel out which is the more important factor — nature or nurture — seems artificial and arbitrary. Aptitude and learning are multiplicative rather than additive in their effects. The mathematical and inevitable consequence of that condition is that a very small number of mega jobmakers are responsible for a disproportionately large number of the new jobs created. Conversely, many entrepreneurs, though collectively important to the employment scene, individually make only a limited contribution. And equally we had to admit, with the benefit of hindsight and after much agony, that even with worthwhile ventures some entrepreneurs were never going to make it. Entrepreneurs may share many things in common, but they are not a homogeneous body. Clearly if we wish to accentuate the positive there is much to be said for knowing more about the few who create so many new jobs.

In order to establish our bearings it seems desirable to make a global classification of each of the various sets of entrepreneurs according to their job-making potential. This analysis was made possible by examining the outcomes of the various projects for which we had been responsible to local authorities. There were eventually ten in the Isle of Wight and there were six, each running concurrently, in four other local authority areas. In the Fens in particular we had had a rotation of firms that had participated in CEBEE over a period of years, so that we were finally left with experiences in excess of fifty firms of which we had intimate knowledge and a further thirty firms that for some reason or another had been dropped from the programme but with which we were still well acquainted.

For the purpose of drawing lessons we could then make an overview of these firms arranged in descending order from mega jobmakers through meso jobmakers and marginal jobmakers to null jobmakers and failed jobmakers.

If the best way of creating new jobs is to focus on entrepreneurs, to find them, encourage them and help them, then, given that resources are limited, it follows that it is enormously important to discern who are potentially the mega jobmakers and who are the no-hopers.

The subject of no-hopers had figured very prominently in our discussions with managers of Enterprise Agencies. During the normal course of their work these managers spend much of their time advising individuals classified as 'new starts', Only a few of these were generally reckoned to hold promise as initiators of sustainable, growing enterprises. This view tended to be reached on the basis of the ventures in which they were engaged however rather than on their personal characteristics.

With all the wisdom that hindsight offered we eventually came to realize that we had spent an undue amount of time with some individuals who had been poor bets from the outset. There is a beguiling appeal about the would-be tycoon who combines inspiration with enthusiasm and energy but who is deficient in such qualities as numeracy and attention to detail. We should also have learned the lessons from one earlier experience with Project Expand-A-Firm about the difficulties of coping with inventors and technical specialists who showed very limited management ability combined with great resistance to influence.

The strongest warning sign in these cases was a tendency to indulge in self-congratulation and self-justification. The fact that their firms were in financial difficulties tended to be readily explained away. It was all due to an 'unimaginative bank manager', 'being exploited by accountants', 'being let down' by partners, poor staff and customers who couldn't pay or paid late. We also found a proneness to blame premises for misfortunes: 'our problems will be solved once we move'. The fact that the firm might not be doing well did not inhibit the confident claim 'If ever I come out of this business, I'd like to be a consultant like you'.

Null to mega jobmakers

Clearly there were some individuals who were not going to create jobs for others because they could scarcely create a viable job for themselves. Those who carry evident signs of impending failure must not, of course, be confused with the more stalwart self-employed and those typically classified in the census as 'own account workers'. By definition, these lack registered employees on their books. Yet in practice they usually generate some employment for part-time workers. One person will come in to type letters, another will handle the accounts or a third may clean the office. Outside the firm the marginal jobmaker will stimulate, or help at least to maintain, jobs in various local services such as printing and transport.

'Own account workers' are an industrial equivalent to peasants. Both place such a high store on independence as to be willing to eke out a living for an income below that which wage labourers would be prepared to accept. The lack of cash, rather than crippling their activities as it would with a larger concern, is overcome by other means. For example, they are ever ready to trade services with one another. It is not uncommon to find a market gardener supplying fruit and vegetables to a neighbouring builder who in return helps to rebuild a faulty roof. For many self employment is all about survival. Still, they make a living and they are not dependent on anyone else.

Marginal jobmakers are one step up the jobmaking ladder though they did not number among the target groups we set out to help. Still they did display some distinctive personal skills. Observations of their setbacks and the ways in which they tackled them suggested an aptitude for − even sometimes a delight in − hazard management. Their minds were occupied with the present and the immediate future. By wheeling and dealing, by 'horse trading' (a favourite word) and by 'making do' they earned their independence, usually a prime goal in itself. Set against these obvious merits was a strong disinclination to engage in any sort of planning other than for the immediate future. They were not very interested in making the transition from a cottage industry into a medium sized firm except in rare instances.

Our marginal jobmakers made their mark in helping to maintain subsistence employment in a locality. What they failed to do, except very rarely, was to provide the seeds of growth.

What we have to accept, as a result of the overview of the firms in our sample is that the bulk of the new jobs created came from a small number of enterprises. So it seems fitting to classify those entrepreneurs who were the key players as mega jobmakers.

This elite group contained individuals of varying abilities and personal qualities. Yet some common features could be observed. In comparison with marginal jobmakers, they had a better basic education and broader managerial or commercial experience. Fewer were professional or technical experts. Even where they had emerged from a technical background, they were hesitant about claiming technical skills: 'Others were better at it than I was'.

The mega jobmakers tended to be partners in an enterprise – though not necessarily equal partners – rather than sole proprietors. Typically they would have worked in a medium sized enterprise before spotting some unexploited niche in the market. They would see a spin-off enterprise as a new company venture involving the need for capital and some form of partnership between the key players, each bringing in valued experience. Of course the big break would seldom be made without an adequate period of preparation. Experimentation would often take place in primitive conditions, the garage or the shed at the bottom of the garden. But once the enterprise started, it was structured like a mini-company with its products or services carrying all the insignia of a new venture. As the venture progressed new jobs would come into being. In due course secondary jobs would be created outside the company in the search for local suppliers. And as the enterprise became more successful, more money would be spent in the district by those sharing in the fruits of success. In such a way does the mega jobmaker set in motion the continuing process of growth and job gains.

There is of course more than one road to success. Another notable pattern was for an employee to acquire skills within a company before embarking on a separate enterprise. The same trade now operates from a different base. If the given trade is a general demand, the new entrepreneur flourishes and by employing assistants becomes, in a direct sense, a jobmaker. However the departure of the tradesman operates to the detriment of the original employer. The new entrepreneur would characteristically take established customers with him, offering a better service at a lower price. As a result the older firm would tend to suffer a loss of business and employ fewer people, or, if the market is naturally expanding, employment would level off. The overall employment benefit resulting from the new venture was debatable in its effects.

Nevertheless, the generators of this second process were capable of bringing about some significant job gains that could not be ignored. They were hardly marginal jobmakers. Nor were they mega jobmakers. So we have chosen an intermediate title and called them 'meso jobmakers'.

The differences I have drawn between mega jobmakers and meso jobmakers are based on an observation of typical patterns. Of course in a minority of cases the typical tradesman becomes a mega jobmaker or rather has the potential to become one. These were the cases we were especially anxious to find and assist. The prospects of success depended on the entrepreneur being more interested in the nature of the business in which he was engaged and the characteristics of the market in which it was embedded than in the exercise of a trade or professional skill. That was what provided the scope for management education and personal development.

'So how do you see yourself?' one would ask. Any respondent who claimed to be a good engineer or carpenter or other form of craftsman was unlikely to have the makings of a mega jobmaker. The response of a 'a jack of all trades', said self-effacingly, was more encouraging. One light-hearted definition of a managing director is someone who does all the jobs that nobody else will do. If that is so there is quite a supply of potential managing directors to be found within small enterprises. Such individuals need to be discovered and helped and it is in the interests of society that this should happen.

If we now return to all our various types of entrepreneur, one could see in retrospect that few were fated to become mega jobmakers. Large firms do not arise out of marginal enterprises. All entrepreneurs do not start with an equal chance of progress. Occasionally we were misled by some entrepreneurs who showed the trappings of mega jobmakers and who we had eventually to admit were null jobmakers. These people had an expansive rather than an insular outlook. The vision and the energy would be there. But typically self discipline would be lacking. Their optimism would pivot on facts and figures which were thinly based or even illusory. Such people, though sometimes inspired, are capable of consuming a great deal of time and resources and of bringing about financial losses which have sad consequences for themselves and others.

Nature or nurture again

That problem need not be as serious as it sounds if more attention is given to how resources are best deployed in the first place. Fortunately a locality

	Mega jobmaker	*Meso jobmaker*	*Marginal jobmaker*	*Null jobmaker (no employees)*	*Failed jobmaker (jobs created and destroyed)*
Education and skills	Well-educated but in an unconventional way	Well-qualified as a tradesman or technical expert	Limited education but acquired special skills	Poor education, lacks any special skills	Of varied attainment but generally lacking in numeracy and financial understanding
Personal characteristics	A desire for instant learning. Quick to seize on ideas but strong in realism. Keen to use external resources. Prefers collaboration or a partner-ship to being a sole trader	Strives to keep total control over own business. Suspicious of 'encroachments'. Inspires loyalty in subordinates. Reluctant to part with any share of business	A 'Do it Yourself' approach. Sees job as a hobby. Needs people only as assistants	Introverted. Independent. Hard working. Desire to be self-supporting	Visionary, impulsive and optimistic. Prone to grandiose plans. Quick to blame others when things go wrong
Background	Broad manag-erial or commercial experience. Spotted niche in market while employed. Long period of preparation before making the break	Transfers trade from previous employment, often poaching customers from former employer	Pushed into self-employment by external pressures	A period of unemployment	An erratic career with several changes of occupation without any obvious sense of direction

Figure 5   *Varieties of jobmaker (typical patterns)*

needs only a small number of entrepreneurs to bring about much needed employment growth. Hence it is in the interests of many communities to maximize the number of mega jobmakers in their midst. To devise an action plan we have first to answer the question raised at the beginning of this chapter: can entrepreneurs be educated into fulfilling their mega potential or are they born and so have to be discovered?

The dichotomy is one that may be useful for purposes of analysis. In practice experience suggested that the two operations are best viewed as interconnected. Nobody becomes a mega jobmaker without engaging in rapid personal growth. Perhaps the constraints of time-served education are inimical to this development. Could that be the reason why so many intelligent and successful entrepreneurs transpire to have been dropouts from the system?

In the course of our on-the-spot education for selected entrepreneurs we did observe one striking personal quality in some of our clients. Mega jobmakers had a desire for instant learning.

The ambitious entrepreneur is on the look-out for any new tips on how to run the business better and on how to take advantage of any unexplored opportunity. For many people repetition is the prerequisite for learning. But the very opposite applies in the case of the true entrepreneur who belongs, it would almost seem, to a different species of being.

Our most successful entrepreneurs were adept at fishing for information. Once past the threshold of acceptance, a suggestion would be put to the test with awe-inspiring alacrity.

Business to industry

During the course of one of our programmes, we used to visit a small business that made and sold venetian blinds. The shop was in the front and the blinds were cut and assembled in a small area at the back. The business flourished in its urban neighbourhood until the question arose how best to expand into other localities. Such a step entailed securing a presence in departmental stores in the face of intense competition from other suppliers.

Rather than focusing our attention on the most advisable mode of entry into the retail business, we addressed ourselves to the matter of what made some blinds better than others and why and in what circumstances blinds were replacing curtains. It emerged that blinds were more effective light controllers. They had an advantage, for example, in admitting light to a room while minimizing reflection on a television screen. So we set ourselves the objective of searching for the best precision control mechanism on the market.

On my next visit I inquired without a great deal of expectation whether the search had revealed anything. 'Yes,' my respondent informed me, 'the best mechanism is made by a Swedish company'. 'It would be worthwhile getting in touch with them,' I suggested. 'I have already,' came the reply, 'they have visited us and we have been appointed regional distributing agents'.

The breathtaking pace of this development continued. We discussed the problem of the manufacturing facility of his enterprise which might now become obsolete. New equipment would be required. On the very next visit I learned that as a consequence of a satisfactory relationship established with the Swedish company, the enterprise was able to order advanced manufacturing equipment on favourable stage payment terms. Following market research, a new appropriate name and logo were invented for this expanded company and so in a short space of time the business was well on the way to becoming a small industry.

The salient point about our entrepreneur, typical of potential mega jobmakers, is the seizure of any relevant idea or possibility. Discussion of such topics as 'positioning in a market', 'unique selling points in products' and 'the role of market research' are valued only for their applicability. The general is rapidly related to the particular. The case for action and acceptance of the ideas that underlie them are inseparable. Results validate the principle. Whenever that happens a lesson is stored for future use. The whole process is highly economic in time and effort.

In this context it is worth noting how seldom the entrepreneurs with whom we came into contact availed themselves of any facilities for management education in the neighbourhood. The entrepreneur's son might be despatched for further education. But seldom would the entrepreneur himself attend a place of learning.

At the time we believed the explanation was straightforward: owners of business were too hard pressed to attend courses or seminars on management subjects. That was an evident price to be paid for success. The recipients of training and management education are more likely to be people with time available. The hope is that these people might one day grow into tomorrow's entrepreneurs.

On-the-spot education

The belief may well be mistaken. If mega jobmakers are by nature disinclined to suffer the passivity of structured learning in formal classes, the problem is how to reach them in another way. Sir John Nicholson's concept of the travelling management educator had a particular relevance to the needs of the active entrepreneur who has the potential of becoming a mega jobmaker. Such a person prefers to meet people on his territory and on his terms. Even so, it was rare to find that such a visit could last longer than two hours without a certain restlessness setting in. Perhaps there were other pressing demands on the time of the hard-pressed businessman, we supposed. But in the end we reckoned there was more to it than that.

The true limiting factor we finally concluded was something that might be called the learning/action conversion ratio. The true entrepreneur learns by turning all conceptual inputs into appropriate forms of action. Everthing is on trial until proven. And if something is worth testing, it needs to be done immediately. The conversion ratio is highest among entrepreneurs with the most evident natural flair. If that is the case, the travelling management educator is the only person likely to reach them.

There are many people running new businesses who were not like that at all. They were the most resistant to on-the-spot management education, being prone to congratulate themselves when things were going well, while adept at finding guilty culprits when things were not. Such people were not found to figure among our mega jobmakers.

Matching jobmakers and ventures

Much of the problem about creating jobs in key areas hinges on the shortage of mega jobmakers in the locality. Those with the potential need to be found and developed and matched with ventures of promise. That is in itself a complex operation. But it is an operation that can scarcely be attempted until we can with greater confidence spot the people who are worth backing. This needs to be done in advance rather than in retrospect on the basis of established track record. For unless this is attempted this potential career path may never come about.

Perhaps it was a stroke of good fortune that at a time of a developing personal interest in entrepreneurship, I should have been invited to become the external examiner for a doctoral dissertation at Brunel University for a thesis entitled 'Entrepreneurship and management practices among immigrants from Bangladesh in the United Kingdom'. The advantage of being invited to become an examiner is that one is usually presented with a comprehensive synopsis of the literature in the field plus some new and original material to add to what is already known. I was duly not disappointed but I was also pleased to find that an open-ended test called the Job Feature Questionnaire which my colleagues and I had developed had proved to be one of the best predictors of entrepreneurial potential. The author of the thesis, Dr Shahid Ahmed, was later to become the Head of the Management School at Dacca University.

The findings of Dr Ahmed's thesis prompted further interest on my part into the personal characteristics of potential entrepreneurs. We have since developed further test material in this area with particular attention to a role inventory developed for examining the contributions of the various individuals who play a key part in management teams. An open-ended management game designed to bring out traits in managerial behaviour has also been found to provide good leads into early entrepreneurial leanings. The foundations laid for progress in this area offer encouragement, in a technical sense, for the future. We must admit of course that more research and development in general needs to be done before early talent in this field can be confidently recognized. That is the pre-condition for making appropriate forms of further education available for those who show special aptitude.

The real problem, however, is not so much technical as one of changing current culture patterns. Entrepreneurship is clearly not a vocation that our educational institutions have fostered. All the pressures seem to operate towards other goals that are often linked together in a progressive sequence. Energetic, intelligent and enterprising boys and girls with superior all-round abilities tend to follow a well-worn path through the universities and into prospering firms, institutions and establishments. On completion of their education they are offered the most favoured junior jobs that can be found in well-structured organizations. All this stands in contrast to what is known about the typical background of the successful entrepreneur. He is one who starts his career in his early years, often enjoys or suffers a life marked by personal discontinuity (being a refugee is almost a qualification), and struggles through a sea of difficulties before reaching the foothills of achievement. That old formula for success — the combinations of hunger and talent — may be something that belongs to the past. If so, it may well be that another formula for sponsoring entrepreneurship must now be sought in the current conditions of society.

Large firms do, of course, launch new products and services and the way in which they do so in the most successful cases repays study. The spearhead is invariably a small team. The eccentric autocratic and often glamorous individualist who figures so prominently in the rags to riches story would hardly be acceptable today amongst the 'entrepreneurial' members of successful new product teams in large companies. Modern entrepreneurs, who tackle sophisticated projects, differ sharply from the traditional image. Foibles are still in evidence. But the distinguishing marks of the modern entrepreneur, in big enterprise settings at least, lie more in the way his or her creative qualities are tempered both by a sharp intellect and by a capacity for working effectively with others (when they so choose). In a highly competitive market the talented loner simply has not enough strings to his or her bow to cope with the complex ramifications of starting a new enterprise of any magnitude.

A number of lessons have come out of the study of teams engaged in creative ventures. Highly talented individuals with singular merits in one direction are often found to have counterbalancing shortcomings in another direction: it is as though real distinction in terms of one particular quality or ability is only achieved at some personal cost. What is sacrificed by the registration of one particular form of excellence varies from one individual to another so that the associations of strength and weakness do not necessarily follow given patterns.

Nevertheless there are one or two recurring combinations. For example people with outstanding mental ability and capacity for original thought are often poor at motivating others except where the adoption of their own ideas is concerned; similarly the drive to get things done is often most outstanding in people whose capacity for objective and impartial judgement is suspect. It is the same story in the field of professional achievement. The most brilliant engineer shows not infrequently a remarkable naivety when it comes to financial matters.

Collective working

The really effective teams seem to be composed of individuals with complementary strengths to which is added an accurate perception of these strengths and a willingness to use them to collective advantage. In that context human weaknesses and frailties are underpinned and handicaps may even be laughed at and enjoyed. If we capitalize on strengths we do not need superhumans to make up superteams.

The significance of this approach lies in its potential for developing new ventures and new employment in key areas where jobs are in very short supply. What seems to be needed is a Development Centre jointly funded by the public and private sectors in which new ventures can be established. The key to its success would be the selection of a small team capable of spawning a succession of new ventures. These initiators would also need to be adept in relating to prospective entrepreneurs, including the unemployed, whose potential is only likely to blossom under suitable conditions.

In other words, until we can be sure of funding and developing individual entrepreneurs in depressed areas we should rely on the strengths of creative teams to develop new enterprises that are both locally based and economically sustainable in the long run.

10

Jobs and regions

There are few countries where prosperity extends equally into all regions and where available jobs fall within the travelling reach of all who seek work. For those unfortunately situated, poorer opportunities for business and employment are taken for granted. People make the best of difficult circumstances. But once traditional enterprises cease to be viable, the human predicament demands some new solution.

The tendency for people to pack their belongings and set sail when local economic conditions declined and reserves were exhausted is a recurring pattern in history. The ensuing migration meant that loss of a livelihood was a temporary phenomenon. Pastoral people moved to undiscovered pastures. Agricultural communities tilled unclaimed fields. Miners in North America and Australia quickly deserted mining towns, with their wooden habitations, as soon as workable veins ran thin. Moving solved the problem. Land was cheap and people were content with shacks as housing. By resorting to travel, the displaced sought and found new opportunities.

That time has largely past. Migration no longer provides the instant solution for loss of employment. The jobs may disappear, but the people are left behind, locked in by the commitment of their capital to property that is difficult, sometimes impossible, to sell.

The most unsaleable of all is the social capital that maintains the fabric of their region with roads and schools and every form of amenity. In the modern world the city that has outlived the strategic significance of its location has no choice other than continued existence.

While new forces are operating, then, to restrict population movements, the erosion generated by slow persistent drifts still creates problems. Where migrations continue unchecked or are bound, as they often are, for the same destination, the net effect is to create new pressures on areas that already face overpopulation. Its counterpart is to add to the problems of those areas which the skilled and the enterprising forsake, for they leave behind the less skilled who ultimately depend on others for work. Neither of these conditions, though the product of individually chosen actions, operates in the public interest.

It follows that the regeneration of declining regions would be a general benefit and this presents a major challenge to the job promoter. Here the first goal must be to arrest the break-up of communities. Economics fortunes need to be revived in places where people feel the threat of impersonal but powerful forces operating against them and over which they have currently no control.

Reviving areas and regions

The key to making this recovery and bringing about population stability lies within the community itself. Community action programmes are to be found especially in North America where populations on a large land mass are separated by considerable distances. These communities cannot depend on central government but have to develop their own initiatives which they do with varying degrees of success. For some the emphasis lies on becoming self supporting with an aim that does not lie much beyond continued subsistence. In other cases there is a more positive intention to foster local industries. I was once told by a regional assistance organization, covering a large rural area, that when it came to coaxing people into engaging in some major initiative in which they had to invest some of their own savings, it was far easier to win acceptance in remotely situated habitations than in places well served by communications with urban centres. Commitment to local initiatives is greater when people see there is no other way.

To embark on a strategy for reviving a particular locality or region, a case has to be made out. Local Councils have to be addressed and minds have to be won. During our early work in the Fens we portrayed communities as mini-independent states each wrestling with a balance of payments problem. Imports are paid for by exports. Self-help in meeting local needs draws no money into an area, while there is at the same time a continuous outflow of cash as people purchase goods that can only come from major industrial areas. The inevitable result is that the area becomes poorer relative to other regions. The central question therefore is: what can be exported? The life of a community may depend on small job-multiplying enterprises that deserve to be found and encouraged.

The impact of this selective approach to enterprises is greatest in thinly populated areas where small changes have relatively big effects. A successful enterprise, that can export its goods and services, imports cash, much of which is immediately redistributed in the neighbourhood. Employees now have more disposable income. Formerly these same people were often either part-time workers or housewives with no income of their own. In the Fens some male workers had previously subsisted by running their own smallholdings. A job in an expanding enterprise provided additional income much of which was spent in pubs, cafés and shops, so regenerating marginal enterprises in the locality.

One of the most underrated effects of expanding small enterprises lies in the boost given to local sub-contractors. Success in landing a large 'export' order usually results in some significant off-loading of the work to other producers. These are nearly always located in the neighbourhood since the prime contractor in a rural area prefers personal contacts when passing on business. In the course of our CEBEE projects in each of the regions in which the programme was operating we noted that every expansion of an enterprise led to some degree of sub-contracting to local firms.

The job promoter in rural areas should concentrate on developing existing enterprises or drawing back sources of economic activity into remote and declining places. These form the foundation stone upon which all community life depends. Small, isolated communities rest on fragile economies, but if some means can be found to enable a small basic industry to flourish, with its local job-multiplier consequences, village life with all its dependent activities including school, post office and shops can continue to flourish. If not, the village languishes as a commuter outstation: it becomes in time a phantom community reliant for the breath of life on weekenders.

The question we have to ask is whether the process of autonomous regeneration to which our CEBEE programme was directed, which starts in a locality at the economic level and spreads to encompass all other aspects of the community, can be sufficient to provide the benefits needed for a region as a whole. With reluctance I came to realize that one was grappling with a problem of scale. Piecemeal action, however effective, cannot provide a fully adequate formula for the future of a region in danger of terminal decline.

The problem is that, in spite of the success of individual programmes, declining regions are being continually drained of better educated and more highly skilled manpower. The more conditions and opportunities deteriorate, the greater the tendency for the more gifted job-seeker to set out like Dick Whittington to London and perhaps become, if not the Mayor, then a well-paid executive providing a high standard of living for a demanding family. If people are the key to economic growth, a new strategy is needed to redress the demographic imbalance. In other words that strategy must be people-based in the first place for it to have any lasting chance of success.

Assessing regional strategies

Before the outlines of that strategy can be examined, it seems worthwhile to look at the regional strategies that have been tried and failed and to learn some lessons from that failure.

The strategy, long favoured by central government, has been to provide incentives for capital investment, and later, and more especially, for inward investment. One of the main recipients of government-sponsored industrial aid was the Teesside region of the North-East to which I used to travel regularly. The region is, or rather has been, dominated by large firms. It was the shedding of labour in the steel, chemical and shipbuilding industries, together with the subsequent ripple effects on dependent services and suppliers that caused unemployment to mount to almost unmanageable levels.

One firm I used to visit had gained in two ways from this shedding of labour.

In the first place the company's reduced labour costs produced favourable results on the balance sheet. But in the second place the unemployment which it had brought about prompted the Government to take corrective measures. These took the form of subsidizing much of the company's investment programme. Almost all of this programme was capital-intensive rather than labour-intensive. So few new jobs resulted. The executives were not only pleased about this surprise windfall, for an extension programme was already planned, but amused to think that this investment 'offer' had been made through the intervention of a Ministry official. Financial help had not actually been sought by the firm.

When the emphasis in government programmes of assistance shifted towards encouraging inward investment, at least it could not be said, 'It would have happened anyway'. Inward investment does represent a net economic gain for a Region, at least in the short run. On the other hand there are several disadvantages. The first is that inward investment is among the most expensive pieces of public spending over the full range of investment inducements. Overseas firms seeking investment inducements have potential sites scattered throughout the world from which to choose, each seeking to outbid the other. Only the most exorbitant offers gain takers. The second disadvantage is that distant firms that establish local subsidiaries have a habit of uprooting themselves to leave as suddenly as they arrive. Common reasons are that:

- Additional capacity is no longer required following improvements in production efficiency. All requirements can then be met at a company's main base.
- Products often have a life cycle. Extra capacity is often sought by firms around or during the phase of late maturity in that cycle. There is less point in staying once the investment benefits have been fully taken up.
- And finally there is a human angle. The key decision-makers in companies may tolerate a short spell overseas. But they usually prefer to return from whence they came, taking their firms back with them.

Inward investment involves a heavy financial outlay. A big risk is concentrated on a narrow front. The establishment of the De Lorean Motor

Company in Belfast required the most expensive single subsidy ever offered by a United Kingdom government to a foreign firm. It is a matter of contention whether the investment would have been justified had the company succeeded. In the event, the enterprise failed and its principal went to prison. The original decision to back the company so extravagantly has all the trappings of the folly that characterizes the away-from-it-all bureaucracy of central government. It is difficult to imagine that a regional government with similar resources could ever have made such a decision.

There is another, broader approach to the encouragement of relocating companies. This lies in the creation of Enterprise Zones and special areas that qualify for tax exemption and/or extra funding assistance from central government. These zones, which tend to be set up in areas formerly occupied by heavy industry, usually experience little trouble in attracting in new light industries. The common pattern is for firms to import their own skilled male labour but otherwise to employ female workers. This does little to assist those displaced by structural changes in old industries who are predominantly male. The transfer of employment from and between the sexes has major repercussions on family life and on interpersonal relations between man and wife. An area of high unemployment can soon find itself short of the special type of labour firms seek – young, female and nimble-fingered. That is another reason why incoming firms so often have only a short stay.

During my travel round the Regions I discovered that managers of local enterprises were often indignant about inward investment ventures and the operation of Enterprise Zones.

'If I moved three miles down the valley I would escape all sorts of taxes and charges that I have to pay here. There are firms there competing with ours that were never competitive before. It's like fighting with one hand tied behind one's back. I often ask: should we uproot ourselves and move down the valley? But what would be the sense in it? What good would it do to anybody.'

Another comment was: 'These zones disrupt companies. I know some firms that move fast to get the money. All that's being achieved is that jobs get shifted from one place to another at the taxpayer's expense.'

A much stronger note of indignation was reserved for inward investment schemes: 'These schemes deliberately discriminate against companies born in the area. Why should the Government hand out millions to overseas companies? We don't get a penny.' Or another view: 'Charity should begin at home. But the reverse is happening. The bigger and richer the firm, the more help it seems to get.'

Whether these comments were fully justified or not, people felt them to be true. A remote government does something – for and to – the Regions in what it presumes to be in their best interest. The Regions are not doing things for themselves because they lack the resources or the powers. What is created as a result is a 'them and us' situation.

The problem is accentuated by the contrast in the way in which officials behave. Redevelopment of an area can entail compulsory purchase in which both central government and Local Authorities have an interest. Farmers who were the owners of land in dispute have spoken of the 'arrogant officials from the Ministry' in contrast to the 'courteous local officials who asked if they could look round!'

Central government is not as responsive to local feelings as locally based organizations and authorities for it has less need to be. Unquestionably the 'men from the Ministry' have more to offer financially to developing small firms in the Regions than any other comparable body of people. Yet they received more criticism and fewer plaudits than others offering more modest forms of assistance.

From time to time I would hear appreciative words about a particular named individual who had helped a company to grow and develop. These individuals had fewer resources but enjoyed more personal discretion. This they owed to their membership of local and more informally organized branches of a national network, comprising Enterprise Agencies and Business in the Community. Occasionally one heard such statements as: 'I don't think we would have got to where we are today had it not been for So-and-So'. There is an important perceived difference between someone whose prime aim is to help another and someone whose prime aim is to establish whether or not a company qualifies for a financial entitlement. In other words it is not necessarily the person with the largest cheque book who can best influence the growth process in the small developing company.

Whither aid to Regions?

We now face a quandary on the most effective strategy for bringing jobs to the Regions. Should it be the responsibility of central government? Is it better handled by local government? Or should it depend on a partnership? In which case what form should that partnership take? Or should the subject be largely removed from the jurisdiction of government and left to private and voluntary organizations.

Small informal organizations may have a valuable role to play but it is one that is bound to be limited by slender resources and the small scale of their operations. In practice a Region that faces serious and sudden decline looks for big decisions. Central government is unmatched for the size and boldness of its potential intervention. On the other hand when issues transcend both the private and public sectors of the economy, they are better handled by local organizations that can draw on both public and private resources and which are more conversant with local facts and conditions than a distant bureaucracy.

These considerations led us to search for the type of institution to which job promoters should attach themselves in order to create viable jobs in Regions beset with serious problems of unemployment. Such institutions need to be of sufficient size and to have sufficient powers and resources to tackle problems of considerable complexity. But they should be subject to a stringent financial discipline to ensure that they are properly accountable for their performance. Every new job created can be assessed against a public cost involved if an appropriate measure can be found. In that way various institutions can be compared with one another on a common index and so the search for the most effective job-creating institutions can begin.

A way forward

Here I do not want to do more than suggest an outline of how to proceed and to suggest some pointers from an initial study.

A starting point needs a premise. So let us arbitrarily argue that a *job-creation programme justifies itself if the public cost of one net new job is equal to the annual total of social security payments plus the net loss of tax revenue that unemployment brings about for one average unemployed person.* We may call this the 'parity cost'. (I have taken a conservative estimate of this parity cost in the belief that only a proportion of new jobs will work through to the benefit of the unemployed.)

Then on this basis the cost of each job created through investment grants works out at eight times the parity cost, and in the case of inward investment grants about ten times. These are figures which we have calculated in the Employment Development Unit based on Ministry and Treasury figures.

By contrast under the Expand-A-Firm programme, described in Chapter 5, the cost per new job works out at less than 20 per cent of what is reckoned to be the parity figure. And under our CEBEE programme we think these figures have been well maintained.

We must also accept that on the basis of these calculations, the Enterprise Allowance Scheme operated by central government shows up particularly well. The recipients of this allowance are the registered unemployed who wish to become 'own account workers'. To be eligible for a year's partial support in self-employment, the recipient needs to have a certain sum of money in the bank and to have been a member of the registered unemployed for a specified period (that period has been subject to administrative change). The level of support offered has been calculated in such a way that the direct public support costs are offset by the savings made from not paying unemployment benefit. In fact there is no net cost at all.

While the merits of the Enterprise Allowance Scheme are undoubted, the reservation is that the programme offers only limited prospects for generating new businesses and jobs in the Regions. Most of the recipients work in the service trades where they are in direct competition with unsubsidized workers or are engaged in the arts and crafts. Those who survive and are successful provide employment for one or two co-workers or assistants. Research studies show that very few of these enterprises grow into flourishing firms.

The Enterprise Allowance Scheme can be cited as one of the most effective of the various government job-creation initiatives. But, as with so many other types of initiative operating on a national formula, it is at its least effective in the Regions. The reason is that the overwhelming mass of Enterprise Allowance businesses rely on local markets. And in depressed areas with falling incomes the prospects for such businesses are bleak.

We need to return then to how the Regions have been developing their own strategies for generating jobs for the unemployed. Whenever we have had the chance to examine minor *ad hoc* programmes run by local authorities we have found that they commonly exceed their parity costs by two or three times. What increases the cost of each new job is that few new jobs created are self-financing. Other jobs are in trades which exercise a substitution effect on existing jobs in the locality.

It is often difficult to arrive at cost effectiveness figures for community and training workshops and for Centres for the Unemployed when so much depends on the criteria taken and the assumptions made. Certainly the costs of staffing are high relative to the number of the placements that spring from them. Most of the unemployed are unskilled and training them to be semi-skilled does little to help them in a depressed labour market. When someone declares: 'I'll never get a job,' the real cost of getting that person into employment is bound to be heavy. A better educated and more skilled person is easily placed when conditions are favourable, so the cost will be relatively low. Naturally, once institutions are assessed on the cost-effectiveness of their operations, they start taking on good placement prospects and closing the door on no-hopers.

So any effective institution that sets out to create sustainable jobs in a Region needs to operate on a number of fronts. It should have:

- the standing to receive recognition and funds from central government,
- the powers and independence to negotiate business arrangements with private firms, and
- the will to address the employment needs of the unemployed including the most disadvantaged.

The last of these services calls for a full range of professional facilities in training, counselling and placement. If these facilities are not available, there is a danger that newly created jobs will go to migrants drawn in from outside and to those already in local employment rather than to those most in need of work.

Institutions that fulfil this comprehensive set of needs are rarely found. They may be finance-orientated, jobs-orientated or people-orientated but seldom all three together.

The way in which any regional institution operates depends on the way in which it is funded. He who pays the piper plays the tune. Where an institution is mainly funded by central government, it will reflect the particular policies of the government of the day, even if some concessions are made to local feelings and experience. Some governmental funding is supplemented by funding from supranational bodies, like the European Community, which produces additional considerations. Where the institution is funded entirely by Local Authorities, it will respond strongly to local pressures and concerns, especially with regard to unemployment. A further dimension is the part played by private finance. That will govern the emphasis given to the profitability of each and every venture.

Regional institutions at work

These forces combine in various ways in different institutions. So it is useful to take a brief look at how they work out.

Perhaps the best endowed of all regional institutions in Europe are those that serve localities adversely hit by the decline in the fortunes of coal, steel and docklands. The sums available for disposal are aggregates of what the industries themselves have allotted for the collective benefit of their displaced personnel, the contributions of national governments, and awards received under the auspices of the European Community. As coal and steel areas are characterized by densely-packed communities, a lot of jobs are needed in one place quickly. The only obvious way in which this can be done is through inward investment. These regional institutions are in a financial position to outbid other regional organizations seeking to attract firms in search of the most attractive financial package on offer. As a result many well-known companies have moved into these areas. A jobs count is what this exercise is all about. On these criterion these institutions can point to a high measure of success.

What is left out of account is that 'job creation' in these cases can be a misnomer. Most of the jobs have been transferred from one place to another at a high public cost. At the time when we were running project Expand-A-Firm, Alan Randall had inspected a former steel area to be shown the scale of jobs introduced into the trading estate that had been set up. 'What do you think?' he was asked. After seeing familiar jobs and noting the well-known names outside all the factories, Alan, as forthright as ever, shocked his hosts by declaring: 'I don't see a single new job on this estate'. Of course, new jobs mean different things to different people.

An organization which is not answerable to the local community may be more concerned with the number of jobs than with their quality and who gets them. Many of the introduced enterprises in former coal and steel areas are in light industry. The vacancies are for women rather than for men. The percentages I have seen of redundant coal and steel workers over the age of forty who have been successfully redeveloped is depressingly small, even in localities that have been economically revitalized.

What is plain to the job promoter is that different regional institutions cannot easily be compared with others, in any direct evaluative sense, because their objectives are not the same. They can be compared, however, in operational terms. To further that understanding one has to start with their terms of reference.

Development Agencies

The two largest institutions that serve regional needs in Great Britain are the Scottish Development Agency (SDA) and the Welsh Development Agency (WDA).

The titles of both these Development Agencies have a national rather than regional prefix: Wales and Scotland are countries within the United Kingdom rather than Regions. Nevertheless neither Agency embraces the whole country they purport to cover. For example, the Scottish Development Agency operates primarily in the Lowlands of Scotland leaving the greater part of Scotland to the care of the Highlands and Islands Development Board. So the SDA and the WDA are akin to regional bodies within Scotland and Wales, serving principally those areas which are more industrially developed. The bulk of the income of the Welsh Development Agency and the Scottish Development Agency comes from central government.

The WDA states its objectives as:

> 'The WDA aims to help regnerate the economy and improve the environment in Wales. It undertakes to provide finance and advisory services for industry, build and let factories, develop industrial estates, reclaim derelict land, improve the environment and co-ordinate efforts to promote Wales as a base for industrial growth.'

Wales was at one time renowned for its slagheaps and industrial waste. The WDA can claim much credit for the way in which these visual blemishes have been replaced by a combination of attractive landscapes and new buildings. The Agency has become the largest developer of industrial property in Wales. It has a wholly owned subsidiary undertaking venture capital investment in the field of new technology. It has a Seed Capital Fund to provide pump-priming cash to enable business entrepreneurs or innovators working in an academic environment to take working prototypes towards commercial production. The Welsh Development Agency has been a prime mover in inward investment projects with Japanese companies prominent among overseas firms relocating in Wales.

The Scottish Development Agency has similar terms of reference to the WDA. The Agency briefly states its aims as being to:

> 'further the economic development of Scotland, promote industrial efficiency and international competitiveness and further the improvement of the environment'.

Inward investment under its programme Locate in Scotland has been a major activity of the Scottish Development Agency as a result of which over 40,000 jobs are claimed to have been created in five years.

'Every company which comes to Scotland is a potential buyer of Scottish-produced goods and services. Every inward investment expands size of the Scottish marketplace.'

The Agency aims to further the economic development of Scotland and provides a wide range of advisory services for both large and small manufacturing and service industries. It builds factories, manages large estates, implements land renewal and environmental improvement schemes, co-ordinates and manages area projects, formulates specific industrial development programmes and provides financial assistance by means of loans and equity investment. Small capital investments are often difficult to secure. By developing a fund for smaller businesses, the Agency has exerted financial leverage by means of which larger private investments have been won for developing enterprises.

The Scottish Development Agency has played a key role in establishing Scotland's growing reputation as a centre for manufacture of electrical and electronic goods.

Almost all who are acquainted with the operations of the Scottish and Welsh Development Agencies are glad of their existence.

A common complaint is that no similar body operates at the time of writing in England. The SDA and WDA have both helped to bring about much needed new jobs. Each of these organizations contains a number of committed and effective job promoters. Yet it is notable that the terms of reference of the SDA and WDA both fail to mention employment. Had employment been a prime objective it would have been relevant to ask how far they achieved their objectives in terms of, for example, the job cost parity targets to which we referred earlier. Neither body needs to account for its activities in these terms because its overall operations are cast against a wider brief.

These Agencies may consult the community but they are not answerable to it. They are not required to bring about jobs in particular places. Those decisions are made primarily by investors. Nor as recipients of major government funding are they required to make a profit in their dealings with inward investors. We are therefore left with a form of organization that serves a number of worthwhile purposes but with undertakings that are difficult to evaluate in terms of the resources at their disposal.

The Highlands and Islands Development Board provides another example of a government-funded body that seeks to regenerate an area economically by using resources to best advantage. The distinction in this case is that the constraints are such as to propel the Board more strongly towards encouraging job-creating enterprises in local communities. That is because fewer options are available. Overseas investors may choose to establish a factory in the lowlands of Scotland, well served by docks, rail and road and with an ample supply of ready labour available. It is a different matter when it comes to towns and villages tucked away in out-of-the-way places. There the only resort is to build on what is already there. It was a Development Officer in the Highlands and Islands Development Board who once passed on to me the first lesson I ever received about how to generate new employment in an economically declining area: 'Always start by finding out who are the leaders in the community and encourage them to become the driving force behind any new initiative'.

Freezers from the north

Castletown is a village on the North-eastern tip of Scotland in the sparsely populated county of Caithness. The only town in the region is Wick, some sixteen miles away. Beyond that a mountainous wilderness, apart from a low lying strip adjacent to the coast, extends southwards towards the popular centres of Scotland. Glasgow is eight hours travelling time away for a lorry bound for the docks. Yet within the small Scottish village lies Norfrost, a private company which employs 210 people, produces 5000 freezers a week, of which 65 per cent are exported, and is the only freezer manufacturer that meets the stringent standards for importing into Japan.

Patricia and Alex Grant originally ran a television shop in the village. Their contacts with customers who travelled in from a wide area made them aware of the demand for freezer storage facilities amongst the scattered, small, remotely-situated farms and homesteads. Alex was an engineer and he believed he could develop something to meet local needs. The first freezer was built in the Grants' spare bedroom. Since then more than a million cabinet freezers have been manufactured. The Grants still own the business in its entirety. The success of the enterprise is therefore due to their own efforts. These efforts have been facilitated by grants and loans from the Highlands and Islands Development Board which in turn helped to generate substantial support from the Royal Bank of Scotland for a major programme of development and expansion.

Backing local talent

Some areas are likely to have very limited appeal to the prospective inward investor. In such instances regional policy demands a special skill in identifying and backing local native talent and providing the services that enable expansion to take place.

Smaller, locally-based organizations have in a number of instances acquired a deserved reputation for efficiency in helping to bring about new real self-sustaining jobs. The United Kingdom, like many other countries, is full of employment initiatives, many of which provide a commendable service for people living in a specific locality. Some of the most notable owe their standard of excellence to their sponsorship by a leading company, which compensates for any redundancies it may have created by offering well-conceived expertise and financial help.

Other companies direct their resources towards areas of need rather than to places adjacent to their own operation. The emphasis usually falls both on preparing the less employable for job vacancies for which they would not otherwise be considered eligible and encouraging self-employment and the formation of new enterprises where appropriate. One of the most impressive of these establishments was Project Fullemploy which directs much of its efforts towards ethnic minorities, unemployed youth and women seeking to re-enter the labour force. This enterprise received a grant from us when we ran the programme CYOJ (Create Your Own Job) described in Chapter 5. We were greatly impressed with the dedication of those who ran Project Fullemploy and with the results they achieved with only slender resources.

Other flourishing and independent organizations which have contributed to the generation of jobs in areas where they are in short supply are the Prince of Wales Youth Business Trust, Business in the Community, an organization set up by the Confederation of British Industry to contribute to the well-being of local communities, and Enterprise Agencies. Some Enterprise Agencies have been set up spontaneously by the interests and efforts of local businessmen, while in other cases the fostering of these Agencies has been one of the achievements and central objectives of Business in the Community itself.

Enterprise Agencies

Each Enterprise Agency is usually staffed by only two or three full-time people though others may give help on a part-time basis. The senior executives of the Agencies are often secondees from large firms, especially banks. Most of these secondees spend a year in their appoinment gaining experience which may later be useful in their careers. In the main, Enterprise

Agencies give help to would-be entrepreneurs and to small firms wrestling with a variety of problems and difficulties.

Enterprise Agencies do not necessarily have an interest in creating new jobs as such. When businessmen act as advisers the focus is on business and its viability rather than employment issues such as job-substitution or job multipliers and the problems of the hard-to-place. Nevertheless Enterprise Agencies do play an especially valuable role in helping new firms to survive during the first few difficult years of their life. Research has shown that firms receiving such help have only a third of the failure rate of firms that did not seek advice.

All these independent Initiatives contribute to the process of generating new employment and providing opportunities for those without work. But as with our own independent projects (Expand-A-Firm and CEBEE) we have to accept that their scale and scope are necessarily limited. Larger forces are operating on the economy to increase or decrease the number of jobs available and their efforts overwhelm anything that can be achieved by a few dedicated individuals.

Prize nominations

In seeking springboards for regional revival we must look beyond the range of what can be accomplished by local initiatives. An effective organization needs to embrace the powers, influence and esteem of a public authority along with the vigour, independence and resources of the private sector. Such an institution should be able to harmonize its concerns for the social needs of the community with the disciplines that are expected and demanded in the world of corporate finance.

After much search, and without prejudice to other enterprises with which I am less familiar, my choice for the job promoter's regional rosette would go to two organizations in the North of England, Lancashire Enterprise Ltd (LEL) and the West Yorkshire Enterprise Board (WYEB). Here it may be worth considering in detail how these two organizations operate.

The West Yorkshire Enterprise Board

The Board describes itself as 'a Local Authority funded investment company which provides finance for small- and medium-sized companies in the Yorkshire and Humberside Region'. It sees its objective as being to provide an additional source of finance for viable local businesses. It aims to meet the demand from small- or medium-sized companies, particularly those with insufficient collateral to gain further clearing bank finance and unable to offer a sufficiently rapid investment realization to interest the City.

The Board considers it vital that the private financial sector appreciates that it is market-orientated, supporting viable businesses which have good growth prospects. The advantage is that WYEB can then attract major funds which can be invested in local concerns and that the private sector can be encouraged to make joint investments with the Board in major projects.

On the face of it WYEB sounds like an orthodox financial institution. But it is only after reading the investment criteria that the wider purpose becomes apparent.

A business is eligible for support if:

- It is not retailing direct to the public.
- It is not a subsidiary of a larger business.
- The proprietors and shareholders are contributing a reasonable proportion of total capital.
- The investment will ensure good long-term prospects of profitability.
- The investment will be saving or creating jobs.
- It has 'good employer' policies.

WYEB is therefore an institution committed by its declared aims to job promotion. Still it has to act like a profit-orientated investment company. The seeming paradox is understandable because the Board is not commissioned by central government to create jobs. Unlike central government, it does not benefit from the savings achieved from lower social security costs and the additional revenue which an employed person brings to the Treasury as taxes.

An Enterprise Board, without the backing of central government, is obliged to generate income. It cannot offer grants to boost businesses and jobs without risking becoming unprofitable and losing the support of private sector finance in joint ventures.

The WYEB has therefore had to concentrate on making loans and equity investments. Its ventures in sixty companies have resulted in only five failures. The Board believes that its strengths in investment appraisal and aftercare result in lower losses than experienced by most other investment institutions.

The creation of jobs in the fulfilment of a broad set of social and economic objectives many believe runs counter to the ability to make a profit. From this assumption it is deduced that the needs of the jobless can only be achieved by a transference of resources from the employed through higher taxation.

This need not necessarily be so – as the West Yorkshire Enterprise Board proves. In a period of a little over three years from the Board's inception there had been no net cost to the public in creating new jobs. Investments in sixty-two companies have generated 4200 jobs with the investment per job being less than half its parity cost. But the investment itself has been profit-making. The former West Yorkshire County Council provided a capital grant of £10.5 million which has increased to £12.5 million through profits. The Board has also borrowed money to invest. Every £1 of Board money invested has been matched by £4 from the private sector. The Board seeks to provide funds to meet the 'funding' gap between the banks' need for security and the City's demand for high and rapid returns on investment. Because WYEB does not have to pay dividends, it can afford to spend more money on appraising and monitoring investments than can conventional institutions.

Among the Board's many achievements has been helping to save the former Leyland Bus factory in Leeds. It now specializes in producing a variety of new, own-design, small passenger vehicles known as mini-buses. Under an arrangement claimed to be unique in British industry, every employee has contributed a significant amount of the share capital to the new business. As the company expands, all new recruits have the opportunity to make a similar investment and commitment to their own futures.

Because the Board is self-financing and profit-making and able to demonstrate that it is investing and not just spending money it has won support from all sectors of the community and all main political parties. The Board is now registered as a fully independent investment company and as such believes it can survive any change of government or change of policy.

The Board has become in effect a hive of job promoters. But the hive differs from other hives because the bees are different. For example, the queen bee and Managing Director, Alan Pickering, joined the Enterprise Board after a career in investment and merchant banking. He is supported by an investment team of ten. The principal criterion in the selection of investment managers is that they have run their own business successfully already. Apart from anything else this gives them credibility with the Board's clients. Beyond this primary criterion they are held to have different qualities to contribute to the team. The emphasis however has been on personal calibre.

Pickering's general view is that the most effective measures to promote enterprise and employment are best made on a regional basis. It would not be appropriate to have a national system with regional sub-offices because 'central and local government don't communicate', 'civil servants can't or won't delegate from the centre'.

Pickering's words are worth quoting in full from our notes.

'All political parties should be aware of the need for a regional structure. This would make for a smaller, more manageable Board, instead of having an unworkable number of board members from all the various local government bodies in the region. WYEB has so far managed to avoid this unwieldy structure. Enterprise Boards need 'meaningful autonomy', rather than to be part of a national organization. WYEB holds itself to be accountable to the community as a whole, both in moral and political terms and this works through the Board members being people with local commitments as ex-members of the former Metropolitan Borough Councils or County Councils or County Councillors. There is at present no legal control over WYEB by local government but it may come in the future. What is vital is co-operation rather than control. Perhaps ideally there should be a local enterprise board to match the local government areas, operating jointly. In any case such a tie-up would only work if representatives from local government acted on the Board as businessmen and not as politicians. There must be no politics in an Enterprise Board's boardroom. In fact the politicians on the Board have not divided in voting on political issues.'

Lancashire Enterprise Ltd

A short journey across the Pennines takes one to another Enterprise Board. This is Lancashire Enterprise Ltd (LEL) which was set up by Lancashire County Council and is located in Preston.

Lancashire Enterprise Ltd is comparable in a number of ways with the West Yorkshire Enterprise Board. Both were started around the same time by local authorities, both have successfully combined the generation of economic activities with the creation of new jobs, both institutions have become independent companies operating in their own right, and both can point to a record of mounting profits which remain undistributed because there are no shareholders. LEL in the space of three years has had a direct involvement in 3176 jobs and 1346 training places and an indirect involvement is claimed in 'well over another thousand jobs'. In the course of this it accumulated a profit of £1.4 million.

The cost of each 'direct' job works out on our reckoning, at slightly more than half the parity cost so that LEL, like WYEB, can also claim to be producing 'jobs with profit'.

Our informant David Taylor, the Deputy Managing Director, plays a very active part in stimulating enterprise and employment in the Region being on the Boards of twelve client companies as a non-executive director.

In terms of its number of employees (seventy) and its scale of operations, LEL is larger than WYEB. Two thirds of its staff are professionally qualified but the proportion varies between LEL departments. In general staff are sought who have a breadth of experience and background within any particular field of expertise. They must be willing to work all hours. They must be happy to tackle a diversity of types of problem, small as well as large. This type of personality was held to be difficult to find, especially in conjunction with accountancy or banking expertise.

The LEL Board is accountable to the Policy and Resources Committee of Lancashire County Council to whom they report twice yearly. The first of these reports is generally putting in bids for proposals to be financed and the second is reporting on the outcome of proposals. The only sanction the County Council could exercise if they disapproved of LEL's activities would be to withhold funding for the future.

Initially there was a closer tie up with the Local Authorities. This had caused objections from the local press who felt that local government should not be having anything to do with business. However this opposition melted away in time. LEL believes its progress in winning support is due to the fact that it is engaged in 'sensible middle of the road work', is creating 'sustainable jobs', is not 'acting like a local authority' and succeeded in making a profit in its second, third and fourth years.

LEL in its earlier days was reactive to the problems in its area, intervening only to assist firms that were running into difficulties or threatened with closure. Increasingly, it claims, its strategy has changed to become proactive; it has set out to develop its own initiatives for reviving an area.

The unemployed, and more especially, the long-term unemployed, were found to be concentrated most heavily within a corridor stretching half a mile on either side of the Liverpool–Leeds canal throughout its length. This waterway had once served the textile and cotton mills of Lancashire, transporting goods to and from the great port of Liverpool. These mills now lay for the most part redundant, obsolete and crumbling into disrepair. Few alternative forms of employment sprang up in the canal corridor and the people living there found themselves locked into an area of dereliction.

In partnership with Lancashire County Council, district authorities and the British Waterways Board, LEL has engaged in a programme of major economic initiatives along the corridor on a scale that makes it one of the most ambitious to be drawn up in Europe. Wigan Pier, made famous by the writings of George Orwell, has been redeveloped into an imaginative commercial and leisure complex regarded as a model of its kind.

The strength of LEL as an enterprising organization was well illustrated at a time when the UK government was proposing to privatize and sell the Rover Car Company, including its most famous product the Land Rover. A deal was being worked out with General Motors, the United States giant. When this news became known Lancashire Enterprise Ltd put together a rival bid to acquire the Land Rover in a space of ten days. LEL was keen to protect jobs in Lancashire but also believed it was well placed to provide the investment. The bid only failed when the Government decided to reverse its plans following a wave of protest at the possibility that a famous nationalized company should be sold off to an overseas buyer.

LEL, along with the West Yorkshire Enterprise Board, provide evidence that, when the circumstances are right, public enterprise lacks nothing in comparison with private enterprise; that it can serve the public interest well while also meeting the standards by which success is judged in the private sector.

Enterprise Boards contain characteristics of both public sector organization and private sector companies without fitting into the typical mould of either. It is apt to compare them with the offspring of the combination of species in the botanical world. There is the same potential for hybrid vigour arising from the best features of both parents.

Does this mean that Enterprise Boards provide an ideal model for meeting the employment needs of the Regions? And if so why have not more people heard of them?

What future for Enterprise Boards?

To address ourselves to the first question, the model may be admirable but we also have to reflect on the constraints under which the Boards work. They are equipped to handle only manageable problems where the risks are limited. The reason is understandable enough. Enterprise Boards are not funded by central government and they dare not rely on the assured financial support of local authorities. In the circumstances they have chosen to become independent but with a 'reference accountability' to representatives of the local authorities that set them up in the first place.

The title 'Enterprise Board' is fitting: the importance attached to business orientation, especially in the field of property development, helps to make their activities lucrative. Were they to address themselves to the problem of getting the hardcore unemployed back into jobs they would be engaging in operations that had little chance of being viable. The rewards for success in a financial sense for the sponsoring body would be nil. While the benefits in savings accrue almost wholly to central government, there is no incentive for local institutions to act as its agents.

Now let us turn to our second question. If these Boards have distinguished themselves over a broad range of criteria, why have they not gained more public notice and attention outside their own regions? In my time I have talked to quite a few knowledgeable people who have never heard of Enterprise Boards.

I believe that the principal explanation lies in the fact that the philosophy implicit in the activity of the Boards does not yet accord with the ethos of the times. Their success has created an element of embarrassment for the main political parties. The origin of the Enterprise Boards lies with an initiative formally taken by the Labour Party. In the event the Boards became creatures of their own. The Greater London Enterprise Board became dominated by leftwingers and lost a great deal of money in an alleged scandal; continuity was largely lost when the GLC was abolished, though a successor organization Greater London Enterprise was able to carry on. In contrast LEL and WYEB were seen to owe their financial success to their property deals, aided by experts from the City. This was hardly an ideal model for a socialist organization.

At the same time the political origins of the Enterprise Boards were an embarrassment for the Conservative Party. There was disquiet too in some of the non-commercial objectives which the Boards espoused. The Conservatives have responded either by persuading current institutions to change their name, for example the Scottish Development Agency has now become Scottish Enterprise, or by setting up their own new organizations under the banner of regionally based Development Corporations. Exactly how these will operate and to what effect it is too early to say.

Conclusions

To sum up, the most intractable problem of the Regions is not just one of an overall insufficiency of economic activity but of being able to generate such activity where it is needed so as to provide jobs for those in danger of being deprived of opportunities for work. Unless this can be done, a continuing 'brain drain' is likely to result. The loss of skilled manpower will hasten imbalances in prospects and prosperity. The interests of the Regions demand that this decline should be halted and reversed. The mechanism most likely to make this happen is a regional body accountable to local government, but enjoying a wide measure of autonomy. That body will have a central interest in bringing into being self-financing sustainable jobs. Some of these jobs can be created without net cost to the public authority, as we have seen in the case of Enterprise Boards.

Much progress can be made in this field by using the skills of merchant bankers and property developers, specialists who may not conceive of themselves as job promoters and for whom the creation of jobs may be the consequence rather than the purpose of their endeavours.

The most employable people are the first to take up new jobs in an area that is being revived. Thereafter it becomes more difficult to reach out for and to draw in the under-employable, let alone that smaller group of people commonly but often mistakenly called 'unemployable'. To make progress in this important field a new breed of professionals will need to exercise their skills. There is bound to be some initial cost to the public authority, akin in many ways to the development costs that commercial organizations incur in launching new products. But in the same way these costs can be recovered in a longer-term pay off.

Central government and local authorities have not yet devised in most countries a satisfactory formula of breaking the log-jam that is the current barrier to progress. How this may be done is something to which we will later turn our attention.

11

Jobs and welfare in developed countries

As countries become richer and make more extensive use of technology jobs change in character. That much is well established; but what is more commonly debated is whether jobs become fewer, because less labour is needed, or more plentiful – or at least as plentiful – on the grounds that people with higher incomes spend freely and so create an increasing volume of employment.

A debate on this issue is hardly necessary, for unlike some undeveloped parts of the world for which data are scanty, developed countries make a point of accumulating routine statistical information. From any cursory examination of international statistics one observation stands out.

Some developed countries generate a plentiful supply of jobs, attract many important workers and have very low levels of unemployment (about one per cent of the working population). Other developed countries have rates of unemployment at least fifteen times as high. The liberalization of trade, the free flow of capital between developed countries and the growth of multinational companies might be supposed to have a strong equalizing influence on employment levels. Despite these factors developed countries evidently experience unemployment to an unequal extent. Why should this be?

Certainly welfare systems differ widely. Further, cultural factors impinge on this whole field and may be as important as the macro-economic environment in affecting employment outcomes. Even within a single country it can be observed that the cultural response to the challenge of unemployment has been changing over time.

Throughout much of my career industrial engagements took me regularly up the A1. The Great North Road, to use the old name by which it is known, is more attractive than most purpose-built motorways, for it incorporates sections of Roman road, curving bypasses round historic towns and innumerable lay-bys left behind during the process of road straightening. These provide ideal alighting and dropping off points for hitch-hikers. Being ever ready to learn 'how the other half live', as the saying goes, I have tended, if not in too much of a hurry, to pick up these opportunist travellers from time to time.

In due course it came to my notice that those journeying North were predominantly students, while those travelling South were a mixed group. Sometimes they were students but more often young men seeking work, and like Dick Whittington, seeking to find their fortune, in London. For all that, jobseekers had little idea of what they were going to. They were clearer about what they were leaving behind: the derelict North where there were few opportunities for young people and often ten other applicants for even the most limited types of job on offer.

Over the years the quality of unemployed hitch-hikers has varied. Jobseekers in the past would tell me of the problems of the neighbourhood, of industrial closures, of the insecurity affecting their own families and those of their friends; and they would express their hopes of what job they might find in the great Metropolis.

Nowadays the jobless still figure prominently among hitch-hikers, but many of them could not be described as jobseekers. Hitch-hikers on the Great North Road are becoming, I have discovered, barometers of the human response to the take up of jobs.

One typical case stands out of a young man travelling to his home town where he did some unpaid part-time counselling of unemployed people. This concern for the unemployed might be natural for one unemployed himself. I was duly impressed. But it transpired that his 'unemployment' was for social security purposes only. A university graduate, he had moved down from his home in the North, where jobs were scarce, to take up a well-paid appointment as a computer programmer in London. After two years he had found the work boring. So he decided to move back to his home town where he undertook paid engagements in the evenings as a member of a pop group. It was a more satisfying life-style as far as he was concerned.

Reporting the incident to a former secretary, who had once worked in the pop industry, I was berated for my apparent naivety. 'But don't you know,' she said, 'almost the whole industry lives off social security'.

Adaptations to unemployment

A leading national newspaper once assembled discussion groups of young people in three constituencies to give a deeper dimension to the gowing public debate over jobs. Unemployment was mentioned as the issue of most concern to young people on every occasion. This concern, however, remained unpoliticized because the new voters had 'come to accept unemployment with the resignation of a peasantry accommodating itself to a natural disaster. . . . This inertia visited upon a whole generation may be one of the most pernicious consequences of mass unemployment itself.'

People appear to have adapted themselves to the reality of unemployment in a way that compounds the problems. One respondent quoted in the report said:

'I know a lot of my friends who are on the dole and, I shouldn't really say this, but, you know, it's common knowledge they're all basically in the black economy and they're taking home £100 a week, quite good, and a few people have said to me, unless they were actually offered nine or ten thousand pounds a year they wouldn't go back to work. And all in the building trade, all sort of brickies, you know, that's sort of common knowledge, they all sort of take an hour off and sign on the dole and go back.'

The decision to 'sign on', meaning to register as unemployed for the purpose of gaining an unearned income, is an attractive alternative to the work option. In some well-developed countries contracting out of work is widespread, especially among young people.

Technically there are many loopholes to be exploited. At the time when I was visiting New York as an OECD consultant, New York State was claimed to offer on average the highest social security benefits in the world for the unemployed. These benefits operated on a sliding scale related to the income earned in the previous job with the proviso that there were no unfilled vacancies for a given occupation in the locality. All this information was handled by computer. The computer, however, could be easily fooled. The technique, apparently, was to describe a previous job in terms that missed the nearest computer job classification. A number of people I encountered were in fits of giggles about the ingenious job titles they had invented. It is small wonder that the jobless flocked to New York and that the City faced financial bankruptcy until it was obliged to put its house in order.

Technical loopholes in the law that have been exploited can be corrected. A more serious problem is the widening acceptance of illegalities. The most familiar of these is for someone registered as unemployed to take on undeclared work. This income is added to unemployment benefit and being 'unofficial' escapes taxation which earned income normally carries. Because 'unemployed' workers engaged in the black economy escape all deductions from their 'cash only' pay packets, they do not need to work all the time to end up with an income in excess of the net amount which a full-time 'official' job provides. Even when it is known that someone registered as unemployed has an income-generating sideline, that person may still claim that income was not derived from activities undertaken during normal working hours when he or she is expected to be unoccupied. That means they are available for work but are earning in the evenings and at week-ends. Members of the black economy can develop a cover which is very difficult to expose.

This problem of policing the grey area of unemployment is encountered in every developed country I have visited. Clearly unemployment, once viewed as a single entity, is dividing itself into two problems comprising voluntary and involuntary unemployment.

In their purest and typical forms the voluntary and involuntary unemployed have almost nothing in common. The former having made a strategic decision to become 'unemployed' are most resistant to re-entering the official economy. The latter, with little opportunity for adding to income on the side, and anxious, or even desperate, to find a job usually view the state of unemployment as 'the scrap-heap'.

Voluntary unemployment is an advancing phenomenon in developed countries, or so it would seem because this is not a condition that can be checked out at present. The two forms of unemployment are indistinguishable on paper. Official statistics deal only with what is measurable. Even when Ministry investigators are called in, cases are difficult to prove. Yet there is a growing awareness of the true facts because people when off their guard talk freely. Most of the unemployed known to me personally, I would classify as belonging to the 'voluntary unemployed'. This may be due to the fact that I live in a university environment where jobs are relatively plentiful and people are well educated and generally employable. In depressed areas, by contrast, one would expect to find that the voluntary unemployed constitute a lowish proportion of the total.

Yet even here one cannot be sure. When first we started our studies of cost-effective ways of generating new employment, I thought something might be learned by travelling to one designated locality of Great Britain which recorded the highest figure for unemployment in order to gain some insight into what was really happening. The journey took me considerable time because the place did not have good communications. I had taken the trouble to ensure that I talked to all the key people in the community who were likely to know anything about the problem and, if I am reluctant to name the locality, the reason is that the most important pieces of information imparted to me were preceded by phrases like . . . 'What I am telling you is in the strictest confidence.' The reason underlying this cloak of general secrecy is that these various officials and leaders of the community were caught in a cleft stick. On the one hand, they wanted to discuss the facts of the situation with someone who was interested: on the other hand, they were concerned that dissemination of the reality underlying the bad figures on unemployment might damage the community and expose them as betrayers of trust. In the circumstances I will refer to the situation in Farville.

Employment in Farville

The most salient fact that I learned was that while there were ample resources available from public funds for inward investment, that is to attract in foreign firms which could then create new jobs, the manager of the Labour Exchange confessed that he did not know where the labour would come from to man even a small factory. A large proportion of the registered unemployed had interests in fishing or agriculture or were permanently associated with seasonal work elsewhere. They had identified locations where well-paid contract jobs were available, especially in building and site construction, were willing to relocate for short periods while the work lasted and then returned home again to register as unemployed and carry on their private interests. Those in charge of the social security office had noted the close coincidence in time between temporary lay-offs of fisherman from the fishing fleet for 'technical reasons' and significant social events such as weddings!

It was true that there were not many job vacancies in Farville. But even for those that did exist there were few serious job applicants. This itself made it difficult to 'sell' Farville as a good place in which to establish new enterprises. The community in Farville had not only learned to play the system, but had also, it appeared, become mutually supportive in so doing. For this reason very few malpractices (that is, illicit behaviour not acceptable under current regulations) had been exposed.

Farville is not typical because in some depressed urban locations, with which I have had close contact, I know that any worthwhile job vacancy attracts a long queue of applicants.

What we can say for sure is that in developed countries where there is a scarcity of well-paid jobs there may be a range of responses to this pressing and sometimes chronic problem. One of these responses is that cultural adjustment results in a deliberate exploitation of welfare systems created by the State. Money earmarked for alleviating unemployment ends up by contributing to its consolidation.

Would-be workers

Developed countries have created bureaucratic mechanisms not only for supporting the work-shy but also for discriminating against and impeding job-seekers. Just as the registered unemployed are statistically over-represented in some respects, they are under-represented in other ways. A job-seeker, who has a working married partner, or a previously self-employed person who has lost his or her livelihood and now wishes to be employed, cannot be registered officially as unemployed and therefore does not enter the statistics of unemployment.

The largest group of would-be workers who cannot be counted as unemployed are those who reach an arbitrary chronological age. When a firm cuts its labour force by introducing early retirement, many workers find they cannot re-register as unemployed. Mandatory retirement in effect constitutes a form of involuntary unemployment. It has little in common with the origins of retirement in the last century. Then pensions were paid to soldiers unable to perform their duties due to the disabilities of old age. Both in military history and in the history of welfare-minded industrial firms, pensions were developed to compensate those with years of loyal service and suffering infirmities for loss of income due to inability to carry on working. The retired were in effect a subgroup of the involuntary unemployed.

The introduction of a statutory pensionable retirement age in developed countries and more especially the tendency to lower the age of retirement, has meant that more fit people, ready and available for work are withdrawn from it. This raises the question of whether those who are entering into the unemployment of retirement are doing so voluntarily or involuntarily. As with the official unemployed there are no statistics that bear on this distinction.

The subject is more than an interesting debating issue, because the conclusion reached has an important bearing on the allocation of resources. Should more public money be earmarked for pensions and supported ahead of the competitive claims of education, hospitals, housing and other services? It would be difficult to support such a proposal where the withdrawal from work was *involuntary* in the case of many retirees. But if retirement was the accepted and willing choice of nearly all people reaching a given age, the claim would be much stronger.

Research is needed to throw light on this matter and, as it happened, just the required information came my way in the fulfilment of those academic duties that I still retained after my departure into the world of industry. Periodically I was appointed an external examiner of doctoral dissertations. One such thesis, written by an Israeli psychologist called Jacobsohn, was entitled *Attitudes towards Work and Retirement among Older Industrial Workers in Three Firms*. This turned out to be an especially well-conducted piece of research in which a large number of variables were measured in relation to a pre-retirement industrial population drawn from three factories. Four post-retirement employment conditions were specified and respondents were asked which would suit them most. The most favoured condition was regular part-time employment (39.1 per cent), followed by occasional work (24.2 per cent), complete withdrawal from work (21.3 per cent) and full-time employment (15.4 per cent). The willingness or

of the general pattern of education and to establish a national system of training aimed at ensuring a steady supply of skilled people to meet the identified needs of a growing economy.

In essence there are four characteristic types of developed country:

- The tough interventionist (hard welfare plus active manpower policy).
- The soft interventionist (soft welfare plus active manpower policy).
- The devil take the hindmost (hard welfare plus laissez-faire).
- The feather bed (soft welfare plus laissez-faire).

The tough interventionist countries face the problem of selling policies that are devoid of any ready-made appeal to major pressure groups.

The soft interventionist countries face problems of living with inflation and of labour shortages in essential services.

The devil take the hindmost countries face disturbance from rising civil commotion, crime and violence.

The feather-bed countries face the likely problem of declining prosperity and rising unemployment.

Over the years a country may move from one characteristic set of policies towards another. During the interval between starting and completing this book, that is, between the middle and late 1980s, the United Kingdom moved from soft welfare to a harder system, at the same time disbanding much of the more sophisticated manpower policies it had adopted earlier.

As this happened several major changes took place: on the credit side, unemployment fell steadily and progressively for a record forty months preceding the end of the decade; the unemployed took up many lower paid jobs which had long been vacant; and an expanded labour force contributed to general economic growth: on the debit side, severe shortages were experienced at the top end of the skill spectrum; more sophisticated artefacts were imported and fewer exported; and the balance of payments worsened and brought in their wake higher interest rates with their aftermath of acute domestic pressures.

The example of the United Kingdom has been followed by a number of other countries and the effects have been similar.

Developed countries should always be on the lookout for new models, for otherwise one set of advantages and disadvantages will merely be replaced by another. The tough interventionist model looks on balance one of the best prospects for developed countries seeking to combine economic growth with a fitting spread of its overall benefits. But it is not a model that can be introduced without both a strong sense of commitment and the professional resources to make it work. We will look at some further aspects of this subject in Chapters 13 and 14.

12

The job promoter in the Third World

Anyone examining the international statistics of employment would imagine that unemployment posed a deeper problem in the developed countries than in the Third World. An international traveller, on the other hand, would form the opposite impression: in affluent countries the unemployed are scarcely recognizable, they blend in with and share in the standard of living of the high output society; in the Third World the destitute and the unoccupied appear to be everywhere, scratching, begging and eking out a subsistence existence.

Statistics are more misleading than impressions. Since in most Third World countries only a fraction of those participating in economic activity are registered as employed labour, the numbers registered as unemployed are also fractional when counted as a percentage of those of working age. The poor peasant can never be officially unemployed. Nor is he unemployed when drought, debt or civil commotion render him landless. The predicament of the destitute is disguised by the way in which official statistics are compiled. In some countries where 2 or 3 per cent unemployment is recorded, estimates by independent observers place the true figure at 45 per cent.

The inability of undeveloped countries to create and sustain jobs and incomes other than of the most marginal character opens up the question of why poor countries are so poor. Any strategy of economic help to the Third World demands an answer to that question if such help is to be fully effective or even effective at all.

In some cases a prime cause is natural disaster. The changing climate of the sub-Saharan region, known as the Sahel, has left some parts of once populous Africa barely inhabitable. There is no obvious strategic riposte to the large-scale onslaught of drought and sandstorm. Yet such natural afflictions cannot explain the conditions of the masses in most Third World countries. Many are rich in mineral resources and enjoy climates well suited to tourism. Their position gives them a substantial advantage over such richer countries as Iceland, Finland or Sweden. What then explains the widening chasm that separates North and South?

To answer that conundrum I feel that my personal experience has offered some insights. Over the years I have had the good fortune to travel widely both as a tourist and in a professional role on assignments to help with the development of vocational education. In relating what I have to tell I feel reluctant to name, and so embarrass, particular countries which have often extended to me warm hospitality. So in the circumstances I will approach the subject more abstractly by referring to the state and development of a typical Third World country, Turtia.

Patterns of employment in Turtia

Turtia is a country characterized by its rich cultural history and by its tribal diversity. Ironically it was colonialism which turned it into a nation, first by its struggle for independence and later by its determination to establish a proper measure of unity, identity and self-reliance.

Arriving at Turtia's main airport is a very different experience from what follows the touchdown at say, Stockholm, Brussels or Amsterdam. I had been warned in advance that procedures might be time-consuming and complicated. And so it proved. The entry forms to be completed on board the thinly laden flight of Turtia Airways proved more detailed and demanding than I had imagined. Who would read such complex documents? At each barrier at the airport dealing with passports, health and customs, a row of officials confronted passengers and each officer had some separate duty to perform. Here was evidence of employment being spread. One of the expected inoculations was not on my health document. The keen-eyed official noticed it and this led to prolonged argument. Clearly he was not persuaded that it was no longer a requirement as laid down by offices in London.

If the airport was fully served by officials it was even more fully served by baggage handlers. At least two handlers grabbed, or attempted to grab, each case that needed to be moved a few yards between one counter and the next. Fortunately the long and forbidding ordeal that most passengers faced was avoided by the arrival of Mohammed, a London educated Pakistani lecturer at the University. Mohammed has a special gift as an airport fixer. Obstacles vanished suddenly as we sped through the officialdom of the airport and on to our destination.

Just as the airport had become a means of dispensing jobs to more people, the University of Bussio, situated near a busy commercial city, followed a similar pattern except that in this instance it was to my advantage. There was always a boy to run errands and a full-time house boy was attached to each bungalow. Most remarkable, however, were the secretarial arrangements. Each typewriter had a male secretary — the job was regarded as too much sought after to be considered suitable for women — with the additional luxury of a boy who sat on the far side of the typewriter, whose job it was to take each typewritten paper to its appropriate destination.

Could it be that Turtia had formed an effective formula for distributing income and work from its principal earners to the broader section of the population? Was this an alternative to high taxation and the state provision of welfare?

Certainly it was an accepted practice to take advantage of every service that was provided. A boy in the market would look after the car, another would magically appear with string and paper to tie up purchases and carry them back. Contrary to my first supposition this instant porter was always honest and reliable. The morality of the market did not tolerate thieves. Each service was sanctioned by the stall holders. Benefits, however trivial they might seem by western standards, were being spread by the job-multiplier process through the community and with the consent of the community.

This network of services had — it gradually transpired — a rationale behind it that was unobserved by the casual visitor. Mohammed explained it to me. The head of the family was responsible not only for his wife and children but had economic obligations towards a much broader group of relatives including all those that he contracted through marriage. The relatively rich income earner would be expected to provide for the poorer members of his kin. The burden of that provision would be lifted wherever some new source of income could be identified. Every possible job that could be squeezed out of the economic system created an opportunity to relieve a personal and social problem. To approach the issues of a job in terms of efficiency and of the personal suitability of the infinitely large number of candidates for any position would be to introduce an entirely foreign notion. No family man could allow such an irresponsible consideration to interfere with his natural priorities.

The tenure in a job did not depend therefore on a person's competence. At the lower levels job-competence might not matter much. But at higher job levels the lack of suitable skills and aptitudes could have serious repercussions. This was well illustrated by the consequences of Turtia's policy of 'indigenizing' all expatriate jobs, and reserving them exclusively for the local population.

The customary procedure was to choose an understudy for every foreign manager. That understudy was of course appointed rather than made subject to open selection. The understudy would note exactly what his model did and attempt to follow the same pattern. Since expatriates had only contracts of limited duration the idea was that foreign firms would eventually be run entirely by Turtians. That was what came to pass. In the road-building industry, however, the policy proved counterproductive. A former British firm operating in Turtia had been completely indigenized so that all its key personnel were changed. Thereafter, following serious contractual mishaps, its public tenders had been rejected in favour of an Italian company which was seen as more reliable. This rival firm was not subject to the same domestic legal requirements and so was soon able to operate in Turtia with a management based entirely on expatriate nationals.

In the minds of some people the ill effects of indigenization registered most strongly in the field of cuisine. The most successful restaurant in Bussio had been foreign owned and managed. Armenians had played an especially prominent part in the culinary world, as in a number of other spheres of commercial life, and they had been hard hit by the indigenization policy. All this had led, it was said, to a great decline in culinary standards. I was in no position to judge, but before my final departure from Bussio I was taken out to a farewell dinner by my hosts at what was reputedly the best restaurant in town, a Chinese restaurant. 'But what happened about the Chinese management?' I inquired believing that the most competent people to cook Chinese food are the Chinese. 'Ah, in this case,' I was told, 'a Chinese was married to a Turtian so the indigenization issue did not arise'.

Where favouritism is exercised towards a relative, a tribal kinsman or a member of the same nationality, discrimination is bound to operate against competence. The competent are most liable to rejection whenever they are competing for key positions. There the only eligible candidates likely to be appointed are the protogées of the dominant social caste.

The low emphasis placed on individual merit means that in many underdeveloped countries latent talents are far more frequently found in unlikely places than in developed countries.

Mohammed, being a Pakistani living in Turtia, had no family to promote beyond his immediate circle of wife and two young children. He showed particular pride in having discovered and developed a waif whom he had first encountered in the large open-air market where he did his weekly shopping. Ali was one of the many young boys who volunteered to carry his parcels and, as Mohammed was a man of regular habits, he had made a point of awaiting him at the expected time in the expected place. Later Mohammed paid him to assist in the garden, then to act as nightwatchman and finally to assist in the house. Ali was co-operative, hardworking and honest but Mohammed later discovered he was intelligent too. Mohammed was teaching him English to good effect and now found that everything he taught him he had picked up quickly. Since Ali was one of many stray destitute children, the product of poor families who could not support them, Mohammed wondered how many undiscovered talents there must be amongst the landless and the workless in Turtia.

Aptitude versus nepotism

Promoting individuals with singular aptitudes works to the advantage of those discriminated against but runs into entrenched opposition from established job-holders as western firms in Turtia soon discovered. Companies keen to gain acceptance from the authorities were obliged to make compromises whenever issues of senior appointments arose. One large firm with whom I had dealings in the United Kingdom was an exception in this respect. Its experience showed that subsidiaries overseas, far from the active support of the home company, can lose money with unanticipated speed. And taking account of the way in which Turtia was pressing its indigenization programme, there seemed to be a strong case for promoting talented employees within existing Turtian enterprises into senior positions of responsibility.

This approach was followed in one enterprise in Turtia, which happened to be the company's largest overseas operation in an underdeveloped country. Sind had entered the firm as an accounts clerk. Not only did he pass his accountancy exams but he showed other talents too, all of which suggested that he possessed management potential. In due course he became in turn Deputy Chief of Accounts, Head of Accounts, Financial Director and Managing Director. The natural course of promotion, far from being welcomed, was opposed at every stage by very strong local pressures. The fact that Sind performed well in each appointment did not allay the antagonism shown towards his rise both by people within the firm and by local politicians. It transpired that Sind belonged to a minority tribe which had a low status within the social hierarchy.

Against such a background it became very difficult for him to operate effectively. The company believed it had chosen the right man. But the difficulties experienced in his promotion discouraged the company from engaging in any further talent spotting. Operations in Turtia began to be curtailed as confidence in local management fell. Turtia needed investment. But the extent of foreign investment in Turtia and the rate of economic progress generally were both influenced by the prevailing view of the reasons underlying the country's lack of development. Different interpretations made by differing regimes led to some fluctuation in policies and outcomes.

People and politics

The People's Action Party (PAP) the first party to govern since independence, had come to power by democractic means. But later it took steps to consolidate its position by banning political rivals. The official line of this leftist ruling party was to discount the importance of skills and enterprise and lay blame for the ills of the country on foreign exploitation and 'imperialism'. Overseas experts were replaced by local understudies. Strong measures were also taken to protect a weak financial position. The method chosen was to overvalue the local currency by rigidly controlling the exchange rate. In effect this made imports artificially cheap and so necessitated a counterbalancing operation involving import control through a complicated system of heavy duties and licensing. Financial restrictions made it difficult for foreign firms to remit profits earned from their Turtian operations.

All these measures affected the Turtian economy but not in the way that had been hoped. The price of protection was loss of interest by world markets. Turtia became not so much exploited as ignored by the great 'imperialist' powers. The remedies designed to overcome backwardness became the recipes for mounting inflation and hardship which bore most heavily on the poor. The leaders of the PAP become discredited and increasingly oppressive. Eventually they were overthrown by a military junta to the relief of the majority of the population.

The junta proclaimed a new set of messages. Turtia's hardships were due to betrayal by its political leaders and the corruption of the administration. An anti-corruption campaign began. The military took over political and administrative posts to an increasing extent. They soon found that these positions demanded skills they did not possess. Eventually the junta deemed it prudent to protect themselves from mounting criticisms of being too harsh and right wing by holding elections under a system of limited democracy.

The third phase of Turtia's history since independence began with the election of a government which in terms of the Turtia political spectrum belonged to the centre. The People's Democrats proclaimed a new theme which was that the advance of the country depended more on the spread of education than on any other factor. A crash educational programme began, compulsory primary school education was introduced and institutes of higher learning established.

Those who can't, teach

While it was difficult to predict at that stage how the educated upsurge would impinge on economic life, some pointers were already there. Two visits were arranged for me to important educational institutes. One was the college for training primary school teachers upon which the new educational system would depend. Examinations were rigorously conducted by an independent inspector, a Scotsman who was renowned as an unyielding upholder of standards, and whose accent was as uncomprisingly Scottish as the most fervent members of his clan. The level of examination set was so demanding that most students failed at the end of the year. That did not materially affect their prospects, for all were immediately engaged as primary school teachers. 'What happens to those who pass their exam?' I asked, expecting that they might become primary school Heads. 'Oh, they never become school teachers,' I was told. A teacher's certificate was the automatic passport to a good job in the business community of Bussio with a rate of pay appreciably better than that which could be earned by a school teacher.

With spreading education, certificated teachers began to fill the skilled manpower gap created by the upgrading of the technical grammar school, one of the educational institutions of which the City of Bussio had been justly proud. In the past the school had prepared boys for examinations in technical subjects and had by the standards of undeveloped countries unusually good laboratory and workshop facilities, most of which had been supplied by Western charities. The school also had a number of European staff, most being teachers of science and mathematics who had recently retired from practising their profession in Europe. It was reckoned that boys who passed their examinations would have an average of three job offers before leaving school. The technical grammar school was the source of supply of engineering apprentices in Bussio and so, ultimately, of competent technicians in the community.

All that was changing due to the new wave of educational enlightenment. The technical grammar school was now upgraded to become a staging post for the University. In so doing the school lost its technical character. Those going on to University preferred the Arts faculties with Law and Politics being the favoured subjects. This choice spelt escape from manual work with which technical subjects tended to be associated, and a significant gain in status.

So the City of Bussio, deprived of its source of technicians, turned to certificated teachers instead. The spread of education, while being treated as a paracea for the ills of the country was not perceptibly adding to the economic well-being of Turtia or providing a more viable base for new jobs. Some could argue that it was even detracting from progress by diverting resources from productive to non-productive activity. There is always an element of risk in the extension of education since it demands some deferment of benefit. Until that benefit materializes, the costs of higher education place a great strain on a weak economy.

Assessing the gains from education

The ultimate gains which society makes from its investment in education can be considered from various angles. One of the most useful and simple leads is to ask what happens to the educated élite, that small body of often gifted people who enjoy the best of the limited resources available. What job opportunities are open to them? How, through their work, do they return to society the debt incurred by its sacrifice on their behalf?

In Turtia I received information that, throughout much of its post-colonial history at least, the pick of the jobs was in Customs and that this government department attracted the most able candidates. Senior Customs officials became richer more rapidly than in normal industrial and commercial work. Others moved into lucrative fields in the banking world especially in exchange control where similar opportunities arose. Foreign currency was greatly in demand in Turtia but could be obtained, however, only through connections. Able graduates were aware of where the key positions of power lay and moved accordingly towards them. Higher education seemed unlikely to contribute in the way that had been hoped to raising the living standards in this developing country. Yet education had had a noticeable impact in other ways. The possession of an educational certificate, diploma or degree had become a new passport to success, a new means of unlocking doors for those who lacked family connections and social status.

The 'certificate' was becoming an end in itself, which made it difficult for me, engaged in vocational education in the University of Bussio, to work as effectively as I would have liked. In industry we tend to establish needs first and to work back from there, setting up the educational and training standards and the means by which the desired goals can be reached. When the certificate becomes the prime focus of attention the pressures and priorities are different. There is a general wish to ensure that every course member gains a certificate. All believe they are entitled to know precisely what is expected of them, compliance can be taken for granted. As a result all who study feel the certificate is their's by right. Whether the certificate holder has the skills to perform well in the intended vocation is seen by most people as a side issue. It can be politically unwise, without support from elsewhere, to make a stand on the matter.

Into what positions the educated people – or the certificate holders – end up is a touchstone in a developing country of the direction in which that society is heading. The same point can be made about Turtia's nearby neighbour, the State of Sunnia. And here the conclusions were saddening.

Patterns of employment in Sunnia

Sunnia is a poorer country than Turtia and known only for its tourism and groundnuts. It had already established a national system of primary education. This was a commendable achievement in view of the extreme poverty of the country and its dire lack of resources. Now with its growing population more and more semi-educated Sunnians were emerging from school to find that there were few jobs available.

One attraction of Sunnia is its excellent hotels, lovely beaches and attentive service. The bungalow in the hotel grounds was kept immaculately by a boy who spoke English fluently and responded intelligently to every line of conversation. One morning I returned to the bedroom to collect an item I had forgotten to take, and the houseboy to my surprise was standing by the bedside table. He was reading the substantial book I had brought with me, *Alexander the Great.* A sheepish, almost guilty face looked up. 'This is a very interesting book. Is it difficult to get hold of? The rise and fall of civilization is always interesting to follow.' That was not an utterance I would have expected from a hotel bedroom servant in London, Paris or New York.

The boy in the bedroom was one of the relatively few primary school-children who had proceeded into and through secondary education, had passed all his exams and had then to consider the next step. Sunnia had no university of its own. Its academically gifted progeny can only further their education by applying to a university in the USA or Europe or they are obliged to make a language switch to attend the university in a neighbouring country. Able secondary schoolchildren who did proceed into higher education – the underwhelming majority – took their pick of the best paying jobs in the labour market. And these were bedroom boys in the hotels. Once again one was prompted to ask: is this a country that is using its most able and educated people to best advantage?

Who makes good jobs?

In short, the most pressing question for those visiting Turtia and Sunnia is: how many new jobs are going to be created for those who are currently landless and jobless and for the great mass of young people who are proceeding through the school system? And where are the jobs to come from? Clearly major new projects, enterprises and economic activities are needed to absorb this ever-rising population.

The new projects most in evidence in Turtia and Sunnia were those which had been set up as assistance programmes sponsored by individual countries or by one of the specialized agencies of the United Nations.

The projects sponsored by individual countries varied greatly in their effectiveness. The least successful were those which appeared little more than an attempt to translate enterprises flourishing in metropolitan countries to a new setting in underdeveloped countries. The most successful projects in terms of job creation were those that had been tailored to meet the specific needs of the country.

As an impartial observer I would have presented the top award to Canada. Canada was one of the few countries that appeared to teach its personnel on overseas missions the rudiments of the native language and to educate them in an awareness of the culture of the country. The projects of Canadian origin were also well conceived. In a small but populous maritime town in Sunnia a fish processing plant had improved the incomes of fishermen and provided more job opportunities for local people. Fish was now being exported to other countries. This prospering but still very native town was one of the few in which the beggars were not instantly drawn by the arrival of tourists.

Another country offering well conceived aid to Turtia was the People's Republic of China. An irrigation and closely linked agricultural programme had been developed to assist one of the more backward regions of Turtia. The programme itself was not unlike those currently fostered by that specialized agency of the United Nations, the Food and Agricultural Organization. Perhaps it was the style of the Chinese rather than the content alone that impressed me most. One had heard much about *barefoot doctors*. Barefoot people are most likely to get to the people in need. That is what the Chinese seemed to be good at doing.

This point was brought home to me when my hosts in the University of Bussio drew my attention to a project which the Chinese were running in a town, a mean fifty kilometres away. They were helping to develop the local economy in a training school geared to the needs of local firms. My hosts maintained that some of the things I was advocating were comparable with an approach which the Chinese had already taken and that it was important therefore for us to meet. Politically and technically this proved more complex than I would have expected. The necessary negotiations might have been conducted on the telephone but this was ruled out. In the first place the telephone did not function satisfactorily, except for local calls: in the second place the delicacy of the visit was felt to demand that a senior member of the University should be sent on in advance as an envoy to prepare the way.

My eventual destination turned out to be a building which in its time had contained sophisticated equipment provided by the Americans but ill-suited to local needs. The Chinese newcomers had repaired what equipment they found but generally they were using more rudimentary materials. The centre had become a magnet of attraction in the region.

The Chinese mission received me with the greatest courtesy and explained their approach. The surprise was that their programme was focused not on unskilled workers but on the entrepreneurs themselves. Judging by the problems experienced by the English-speaking Chinese interpreter, *entrepreneur* must be amongst the most difficult English terms for a Chinese to master. It took me at least a quarter of an hour to comprehend the word so frequently on the interpreter's lips. Since these entrepreneurs were members of the local petit bourgeoisie, if not budding capitalists, I was hardly expecting to hear that these were the chosen few on whom so much attention should be lavished. The point of this strategy however was explained to me with unassailable logic.

The entrepreneurs are the key people in the community, the ones who will make change happen. They need to be convinced before all others that it is worthwhile to improve technology and introduce new products. The equipment they use must be affordable. That was why it was better to use sewing machines rather than to base teaching on machines that could not be bought locally and were too expensive to import.

One of the most important local resources in the area was leather. The Chinese proceeded to examine the practicability of making every leather object for which there was a conceivable market. After mastering the technique of manufacture, they then taught it to the entrepreneur and only later to such workers as he chose to send along. In this way local firms were given a boost and more jobs were created. The same strategy was used for other products. In each case the starting point lay with the entrepreneur and his existing trade and knowledge base.

Jobs and the International Labour Office

It was some years after my experiences with Chinese job promoters and with Turtia in general that I had occasion to reopen interest in how to create jobs in underdeveloped countries. That same about after we had set up the Employment Development Unit in Cambridge. Then it seemed to us that we should examine the employment problems in the Third World in an intensive way.

The first discovery was that there was already in existence a *World Employment Programme*. Indeed it had been running for ten years before we encountered it through library research. The WEP is run by the International Labour Organization, a specialized agency of the United Nations, with its headquarters in Geneva known as the International Labour Office. The ILO had produced one especially significant booklet by R. F. Plant.[1]

The size of the problem is summed up by Plant as follows:

472 million new jobs will have to be created in a 20-year period in Asia, 114 million in Africa and 80 million in Latin America, just to take care of the demographic factor. In addition, many millions of jobs are wanted for the existing unemployed . . . In the world as a whole, some 750 million new jobs will be required by the turn of the century

[1] ILO (1983). *A Short Guide to the ILO World Employment Programme.* Geneva: ILO Publications.

to provide for the growth of the number of workers. In the less developed regions, there will be 150 workers requiring employment for every 100 who were around in 1980.

We decided we would need to visit ILO in Geneva. We did so on two occasions, coming away with stacks of both published and unpublished material. It was clear that the ILO combined, to an extent unusual in public bodies, sophisticated research with practical programmes of development directed at key issues.

Several programmes stood out in our minds as having particular merit.

One programme was directed at helping poor people in rural areas with a leading project in Bangladesh. ILO had found that the gradual spread of prosperity in developing countries is usually localized. Development favours urban areas and the well-to-do, but often operates to the detriment of the poor in rural areas. This is a consequence of the inflation of prices for their necessary manufactured purchases and the depression of prices re-received for traditional rural commodities. Without capital and being denied credit, the poor are trapped.

A solution was to set up a special bank for the poor and to bring about a system whereby poor peasants were able to organize themselves to improve the level of guarantee offered to the bank. At the same time ILO organized teams to disseminate management skills in accountancy and to conduct market research as a means of ensuring that increased output would not lead eventually to saturation of a market. On the buying side, ILO project teams have taught the advantages to the poor of bulk purchases, assisted by bank loans, as a means of safeguarding them against exploitation by middle men.

Another comparable ILO programme aims at helping women to enter into economic activity and to improve their own position and that of their families. Many of the same principles of organization apply but in the case of women there is one added problem. In some countries married women are unable to have a bank account in their own name. Yet in these countries women, who have traditionally worked the land in conjunction with raising families, have shown remarkable entrepreneurial talents. The men by contrast drink beer and sit about, now that they have lost their role as hunters and defenders of tribal lands. Yet they enjoy to the full the fruits of female labour and enterprise. Not surprisingly ILO is viewed by some in traditional countries as a subversive force.

A third group to benefit from the special programmes run by ILO are refugees, many of whom live under pitiable conditions in countries adjacent to those from which they have fled. Here ILO is engaged in projects to find ways in which refugees may become economically self-supporting without undermining established enterprises in the host countries.

ILO is also engaged in programmes of reafforestation, notably in Nepal. The reliance of poor people on firewood for fuel is having a devastating effect on soil erosion in many parts of the world. The planting of trees and their husbandry will only be successful in its ultimate objectives if local people participate, give it their active support and learn to reap the benefits. Progress in this field is inherently slow. Nevertheless the impact of this work is beginning to spread as people appreciate its importance from direct experience.

The World Employment Programme is also tackling some complex issues that affect developed countries no less than the developing. These include the influence of internal migration on employment patterns within countries, whether job-creation schemes produce substitution or job-multiplier effects on employment, and what employment consequences result from the transfer of technology from one industry to another.

Why didn't we know?

We were soon asking ourselves why we had not heard of the World Employment Programme earlier. Was it due to an inexcusable oversight on our part? If it was, at least such unawareness is widespread. A number of leading figures in public affairs, including those conversant with manpower matters, had not heard of the WEP either.

Through talking to a number of officials at the ILO we learned at least part of the answer. In the first place, the WEP is funded so lightly that it is able to conduct only a small number of programmes, often no more than token projects, in various parts of the world. Apart from the finances necessary to support its own staff, additional projects can only be entered into by soliciting finance from the World Bank in Washington. In spite of the magnitude of the problem, the WEP receives only modest support from the wealthier countries of the United Nations. A most serious setback occurred when on policy grounds the USA left the ILO in 1977 and did not resume support until the next decade. This withdrawal meant that all ongoing functions of the ILO had to be maintained on a reduced overall budget.

The second point of note is that ILO limits itself in OECD countries to mere information gathering research projects. The difficulty here is political. There is in effect a demarcation issue between OECD and ILO, for ILO could easily impinge on what OECD sees as its own territory. The World Employment Programme has therefore a very low profile in Europe, North America, Australia and Japan. People have scarcely heard of it because it lacks a presence.

ILO and OECD are not in danger of overlapping to the extent that is sometimes feared. The programmes of OECD need to be sanctioned by the collective decisions of member governments to an extent that the programmes of ILO do not. ILO is therefore able to adopt a bolder and more radical approach than OECD which can be and is made subject to ministerial veto.

The prioneering job promoters of ILO are fighting an uphill battle. In this respect they are like their counterparts elsewhere. The problem will continue until job promoters are recognized as professionals who have a special contribution to make to world problems.

13

A profession in the making

That the job promoter belongs to an unrecognized occupation goes without saying. It is not merely a matter of title, for although the cause of unemployment extracts resources from society on a massive scale, very few in the public domain, if any, are set the direct goal of finding or generating jobs for others. Instead the massed ranks of public service workers address themselves to sub-goals of the problem: the provision of labour market information, training and issuing grants and allowances.

The larger the bureaucracy the more the State is subject to those same problems to which any other sizeable organization is prone: responsibility becomes departmentalized and fragmented. This is the condition which allows job creation to receive complex treatment from different groups of overlapping officials, but in the end to become nobody's prime concern.

In some parts of the private sector, the problem by contrast is treated more directly. Certain companies, including such notable firms in the UK as ICI and GEC, when faced with a need to reduce staff numbers, make a point of acting in an orderly and humane fashion that is both employee- and job-orientated. Redundant employees are helped in a personal way to find new positions or enter into new vocations or are assisted in starting their own businesses rather than left to their own devices in an often difficult labour market. This process is made possible by a combination of two factors. The first distinguishing mark is the existence of a special fund which is used in a flexible way and without reservation. The only proviso is that it should help an employee enter new employment.

The second salient factor is the appointment of 'job promoters' or that is what we shall call them. In fact these operational managers of the process we have described bear no consistent name, though some carry the title of Resettlement Officers. But in any case no special designation is necessary. Once their temporary engagement is over they will return to their normal duties in personnel or works management.

Such a fleeting function cannot be regarded as a profession however distinctive and refined are the methods employed. When assignments are brief, appointees act in an *ad hoc* fashion. They scarcely have time to find a forum where they can, on a national or regional basis (let alone internationally), compare their methods, exchange experiences and develop their skills.

Job promoters in efficient companies, which take their social responsibilities seriously, are chosen with care. They often have broad backgrounds and senior management experience. Their achievements are often remarkable, given their lack of familiarity with the subject. Yet they remain amateurs. It cannot be otherwise. Their appointments are only an interlude and a diversion from another career path. There is little doubt that if they stayed longer where they were, they would become professional both in consciousness and name.

There is no basic need of course to turn effective amateurs into effective professionals. Professionalism serves various marginal purposes like providing status and recognition for its members, protecting salaries and so forth. But the creation of a profession also acts as a protection from abuse and disservice and so operates in the interests of the public at large.

Watch out for do-gooders!

While there are some able amateurs carefully selected in large companies for challenging but sensitive assignments, there are other amateurs in the field of job promotion whose accomplishments are more debatable. These may include unpaid voluntary workers who will be appreciated for their sense of mission, since they recognize how important it is for their clients, economically, socially and spiritually to find new work.

The risk in some cases is that charity workers are grappling with a problem of which they have only a partial understanding. Their selfless inspiration passes directly on to their clients. But the benefits may have to be bought at a price that is initially unseen.

There are five characters in the general amateur world who merit admiration on personal grounds but of whom one might be advised to show a certain wariness.

The first is Fulfilment Fred. Fred sees unemployment as not only a challenge but also as an opportunity. In his view being unemployed gives a man a chance to discover his true identity, to find out what he really wants to do and have a go at it. Fred runs a training establishment that depends largely on voluntary contributions. Almost anyone who arrives there dispirited is given a spiritual lift by Fred. Fred finds ways of engaging people's interests in constructive activity and especially in the fabrication of such objects as wooden tool boxes, ceramic vases or soft toys. People become fulfilled in their new pursuits and, for a while, the future shines bright with the discovery of the message that a livelihood and a leisure interest are best welded together. Fred is always there to provide the spur. But the prospects of a livelihood fade from view when tool boxes, ceramic vases and soft toys pile up on the shelves. Occasionally, when some are sold, efforts are redoubled and new fuel is added to the engine engaged on this flight of fantasy.

For the occasional gifted individual the fusion of livelihood and a leisure interest is an economic possibility. For the others there is a long agonizing lesson to be learned: that work is seldom a matter of self-orientated fulfilment but more a matter of meeting the needs of others, through which the self achieves a secondary but often deeper satisfaction.

My second character is Educational Ernest. Ernest pursues his interests through study and by that route he has established considerable self-advancement. He believes that others can do the same. 'One can learn anything if one sets one's mind to it,' is Ernest's favourite saying. The Employment and Training Workshop to which Ernest, now retired, devotes much of his time contains a number of people being steered towards the creation of new enterprises. Ernest is keen to educate the prospective self-employed person into the skills needed to run a business or provide a technical service. Not only has he a voluminous knowledge of books and manuals he has personally found useful, but he is adept at researching into new sources of data. All this information is channelled towards Ernest's intended and somewhat mystified clients.

Somehow Ernest's educational efforts fall on stony ground. People do not respond to his material in the same way as he would. There are some gains in learning. But the gap between mere competence and real expertise is too large, for these learners, to make for success in a competitive environment. Ernest has educated his clients towards goals that lie beyond their reach. The resulting disillusionment overshadows any gains that individuals have made in personal development.

Subsistence Sam is a third character. Sam is a Do-It-Yourself man. He grows all his own vegetables, services his own car and decorates his own house. His wide range of personal skills are useful and he sees them as ideal for passing on to the unemployed, who, with idle time on their hands, can turn their position to positive advantage. Through his association with the Centre of the Unemployed, Sam has had a major influence in reactivating some who previously had been sinking into a slough of apathy.

Implicit in Sam's approach, though unstated, is the notion that DIY is an alternative to using money. And if you do not spend money you do not need to earn it. All seems well until there is an examination of outcomes. When the effectiveness of the Centre in helping the unemployed is put under scrutiny, it transpires that Sam's associates have a poorer record than others in landing jobs. Sam has encouraged the belief among the more receptive clients that an ability to turn one's hand to anything provides a formula for meeting their personal needs. In an industrial society this is a romantic vision and has a compelling appeal. In due course Sam's clients learn two things the hard way: that 'subsistence' is a euphemism for 'poverty', and that subsistence is also very time-consuming – there are very few hours left over for finding a route back into employment. Individualism detracts from learning about team interdependence, the recognition of complementary skills for the success of any enterprise and the need to draw on resources from outside.

My fourth character is Commune Charlie. Charlie comes from a well-to-do background but has 'dropped out'. The alternative society is for him immensely attractive and unemployment has no negative connotations. Charlie has something of a mission to find blue-collar unemployed young people and convert them to his enlightened views. It is not wealth or material possessions that matter but the social form that gives rise to the production of goods and services. Charlie plays an active part in developing the efforts of a work commune. Any rejection of outside values by the commune gives him special pleasure and seems in practice to cement the bonds between the members. Charlie helps to promote social organization, belongingness and the sense of a separate group identity. Yet the more that is achieved in this sphere, the more the group distances itself from the wider society in which it is embedded.

Charlie's limited interest in the realities of the outside world creates a situation in which the effective output of the work commune becomes secondary to social introspection. As it becomes increasingly apparent that their enterprise lacks economic viability, demoralization sets in. Although work and decision making are shared in principle, some individuals contribute far more than others. Once this issue is brought to the fore, dissension sets in and the ethos that binds the commune together comes under strain. Charlie's dislike of economic performance as a prime target has temporarily obscured, but not removed, the difficulties which both individuals and the commune have to face in earning a livelihood.

My final character, who provides a service to those out of work, is Businessman Brian. Brian spends as much time as he can afford voluntarily helping an Employment Trust. He has lived in the locality all his life, feels for the plight of those who have lost their job, and wants to do something to alleviate hardship. Brian has had a varied working life but has always succeeded in earning a good living for himself. Always quick to see and take advantage of new opportunities, Brian believes that, given a spirit of enterprise, others can follow the same path. Some can. But for most the path of self-employment is fraught with hazards.

Take the case of Ginger, a young man with a passion for cars who had never had a job and had achieved little at school. To add to the difficulties rendered by his bleak record he was a poor interviewee. So his job prospects looked distinctly unpromising.

Ginger responded with enthusiasm to Brian's mention of self-employment. Ginger had already serviced the cars of a few friends and he took it into his head that he might do this for a living. The idea was that service and simple repair work would be carried out at the customer's home. Brian considered there might be a sizeable market for such a service.

What had been over-estimated however was Ginger's competence. In due course unsatisfactory work was reported. More seriously, there was an objection from a local garage that the freelance service of an unqualified mechanic constituted a danger to the motoring public. Pressure was brought to bear on the Employment Trust and Ginger's attempt at self-employment had to be terminated. This had a shattering effect on Ginger's morale. Moreover the time Ginger had spent in the premises of the Trust had done little to improve his work credentials.

What had been left out of account was the essential difference between Brian and Ginger. Brian, as a man of entrepreneurial flair with an impressive range of personal skills, was likely to be a survivor in most circumstances and pressure situations. Ginger, on the other hand, was too immature an individual and too underdeveloped in his technical abilities to last long in the competitive world of motor repairs. How could it happen that the luckless Ginger was caught up in such an unfortunate episode?

Fred, Ernest, Sam, Charlie and Brian are all unqualified job promoters. Their efforts are directed at helping people out of work to secure a new form of livelihood. Yet it is questionable whether the positive benefits from their efforts outweigh their negative consequences.

A society that relies on amateurs offsets the need to develop professionalism. There is a parallel in the remoter parts of the world where the presence of witch doctors holds back the advance of modern medicine. So Fred, Ernest, Sam, Charlie and Brian are all witch doctors in their way. As non-professionals they are prone to have a limited understanding of the subject and rely instead on 'instinct' and incantation. A little knowledge is a dangerous thing but it gains a certain credibility when it is founded on valid experience.

Gifted amateurs are better placed to contribute useful skills when they belong to an organization that over time has built up sustained experience in the economic and social issues of an area. Examples of such organizations are Enterprise Agencies, Enterprise Boards and other special units set up by Local Authorities, and voluntary organizations to serve the needs of those out of work in some designated area.

The reputation of these bodies is often a reflection of the personal standing and achievement of the person in charge. So a means is found for dedicated job promoters to bring work to people or people to work because this is seen as the social and sometimes political priority of a particular locality. Skills have been developed because people have approached the task empirically and with common sense. They come from no single occupational background: they may be teachers, industrial managers, bankers, entrepreneurs. The job promoter's skills straddle a broad field. If there is no professional route into the subject it helps to have gained work experience in more than one field.

Yet however gifted the job promoter may be, the fact that he, or she, is an amateur puts him, or her, at a disadvantage. He may be aware of the specific outcome of some particular initiative, but it may be difficult for him to place in perspective all the ramifications of its impact on the local scene. After all, there may be significant issues with which he is unfamiliar or which lie outside the terms of reference of his appointment.

Why? Where? How? Who?

The public interest will create its own set of questions. If a firm is to be helped to expand, is it likely to do so at the expense of another local competing company in a market already near to saturation? If so, the net gain in jobs is nil. Would a firm that moves into special premises designed to create new jobs have generated an equal number elsewhere in the locality if it had been given planning permission to adapt its own buildings? Is a broadsheet that gives information on jobs issued to those out of work superfluous in a locality where there are ten applicants for every vacant job? Where the only issue is: who fills them? Without professionalism any well-meaning public-spirited action may turn out misdirected in the event.

One chairman of a working party on unemployment set up by a large County Council once detailed for me all the initiatives his committee had set up to tackle the problem. For the moment I was greatly impressed. He went on to say: 'Then we set up a mechanism for monitoring the effects of our actions. We had spent a substantial sum of money on doing all the things we could think of to relieve the problem. But after eighteen months we could detect no sign of any overall improvement. The problem remained much the same as when we started. Still we had done our best. We felt much better for it'.

Programmes can easily misfire when there is no solid core of people on whom to draw for knowledge and experience. Job creation has not hitherto been regarded as a field requiring professional intervention. In a healthy economy it has always been presumed that there would be sufficient new jobs springing up to replace those that were disappearing.

The job promoter

Now, however, there is a growing realization that areas hit by industrial and commercial closures will stagnate unless special measures are taken.

And so during the last few years Local Authorities have set up departments, or more usually, sections within a department charged with tackling the problem. The person in charge is called an Economic Development Officer, who is directly accountable in most cases to the Chief Planning Officer.

The Economic Development Officer is typically a university graduate who is likely to have studied Economics and Geography and who may additionally have spent a year in Planning. He or she starts with the advantage of knowing about the language that deals directly with job losses and job gains and will understand the processes that these terms embody. So they will know about the operation of job multipliers in a local economy, whether positive or negative; they will appreciate the economic advantages of improving the infrastructure and of engaging in selective pump-priming; but they will also be aware of the disadvantage of too naive an intervention in the local economy with the attendant disadvantages associated with substitution, labour displacement, deadweight and unfair competition. They will know something about these terms and the way in which the processes which surround them impinge on the overall functioning of a system.

Figure 6 on pages 160–4 (taken from the first number of *People & Jobs International*) sets out some of the relationships in this area which impinge, as I see it, on the issues of job promotion. The material content of the university courses which most EDOs receive facilitate their path to this new profession. Their starting advantage should not however exclude candidates with the right aptitude from other backgrounds.

All that can be said at this stage is that the foundation education of a job promoter must be comprehensive in nature and cover economic development, business studies, the growth of enterprises, the personal characteristics of entrepreneurs, the functioning of management and project teams, the psychology and characteristics of the underemployable, the training and education of underachievers, job, analysis, personnel assessment and techniques of placement in the labour market.

It is a complex and demanding programme. But so is the challenge of the problem.

Programme	Jobs outcome		Financial outcome	Avoids undesirable side effects of:			Programme advantage	
	Real jobs created	Job multiplier effects	Favourable cost/revenue balance	Unfair competition	Deadweight	Labour displacement /substitution	Targets on unemployed	Easy to administer
Make work	✗	✗	✗	✓	✓	✓	✓	✓
Work redistribution	✗	✗	✗	✓	✓	✗	✓	✓
Services to labour market	✗	✗	=	✓	✓	✓	=	✓
Services to new starts small firms/	✓	=	✓	=	✓	=	✗	✓
Investment grants/loans	✓	✓	✗	✗	✗	=	✗	✓
Job subsidies	=	✗	✓	✗	✗	✓	✓	=
Personal re-entry allowances	✓	=	✓	=	=	✗	✓	✓
Employment development based on combined public and private sector initiatives	✓	✓	✓	✓	✓	✓	✓	✗

KEY

✓	positive
✗	negative
=	mixed

OUTCOMES AND CHARACTERISTICS

Job-creation programmes are usually assessed in terms of whether or not they produce sustainable jobs or, more ambitiously, whether they set in motion a process which reverses the trend towards spiralling job decline. Account has also to be taken of cost. The most successful programmes have the potential of producing net savings in public expenditure which when taken together with the tax revenue from the additional income created outweigh the public costs of setting the programmes in being. On the debit side job-creation programmes are capable of negative effects that undermine their general acceptability in society; these include helping to put other firms out of business, adversely affecting the jobs of others within stable businesses and merely paying firms to proceed with plans, on which they were anyway engaged. Programmes may also be rejected because they fail to reach the right people, *i.e.* those out of work, or because their administrative characteristics are such that they are not easy to reproduce or to supervise.

Jobs outcome
Real jobs created

Real jobs refer to jobs that are financed by the income generated from the sale of goods or services in the free market, as distinct from jobs which depend on public revenue and produce no saleable output. Real jobs once created are less susceptible to cutbacks in public spending. By definition such programmes, if successful, place no continuing burden on the public exchequer.

Job multiplier effects

A new economic activity creates a demand for labour, but some economic activities also bring into being work outside the enterprise, both directly by creating a demand for local suppliers and services, and indirectly by boosting secondary employment as a result of the local spending by newly employed persons. Prosperity radiates prosperity and jobs. However, other forms of new economic activity fail to produce multiplier employment effects and merely redistribute jobs within the same static market. In this respect a distinction can be drawn between basic industries and dependent or service industries. The former tend to be associated with multiplier effects while the latter are susceptible to substitution.

Financial outcome
Favourable cost/revenue balance

Public sector initiatives to create jobs can be assessed on purely financial grounds. Generating jobs for those previously unemployed results in

Figure 6

savings in public expenditure on social security costs and an increase in revenue from a newly created tax-paying population. Where these two sums are greater than the setting-up costs (amortized over time) a favourable public cost/revenue balance is created. The balance, however, can be unfavourable where the setting-up costs are too high or the financial side-effects are too great or there is a failure to create real income-generating sustainable jobs.

Undesirable side effects
Unfair competition

Where enterprises compete directly with others for contracts and orders the use of public sector finance and other forms of assistance to one competing party is liable to run into objections on other economic and political grounds. It is unacceptable that the jobs gained by the more successful companies will imperil those in firms that fail to compete. Unfair competition also conflicts with business ethics. A current programme in the UK affords an example of the problem. Firms in Enterprise Zones, enjoying exemption from taxes and other benefits, are held to have an undue advantage over other firms sometimes only a short distance outside the Enterprise Zone and operating in the same market.

Unfair competition is observed to generate ill-will unless it can be shown that a programme has compensating advantages in raising regional prosperity and business and job opportunities.

Deadweight

Deadweight refers to the neutral effect of incentives on actions or decisions otherwise equally likely to take place without those incentives. In small-scale operations, deadweight is suppositional: there can usually be no certainty as to what would have happened if the inducements of a job-creating programme were absent. In large-scale programmes, however, the causal link is more easily observed. Much preliminary planning precedes the physical start of new investment in plant and equipment and during this interval a great deal can happen. Oil companies and producers of bulk chemicals have reported approaches by officials from government departments with the welcome news that their firms were eligible to receive payments of very large sums of money for the installations they were in the process of erecting.

Highly centralized programmes in the public sector are inclined to give rise to deadweight since decisions are more likely to depend on whether the rules apply rather than on consideration of the benefits to be gained as a result of particular decisions.

Labour displacement/substitution

Jobs are sometimes reserved or set up for particular disadvantaged individuals or groups of people (*e.g.* disabled workers or ethnic minorities.) No addition is made to the total stock of jobs. For each worker favoured by the system there is a corresponding worker who loses his job. Displacement may operate directly, an older worker may be encouraged to retire early so that a job may be created for a younger unemployed worker; or it may operate indirectly, a contract may be placed with a public agency where otherwise it would have become a commercial order undertaken in the private sector or vice versa.

Substitution in employment arises where the relationship between a new job created and an old job lost is not a matter of identity in the work content but of a replacement of function. A given market demand is satisfied in a different way through substitute materials or a substitute process. As with displacement the total stock of jobs remains the same.

Programme advantage
Targets on the Unemployed

Programmes devised to generate economic activity and hailed as likely to create jobs often fail to fulfil the expectations of their designers. Some programmes tend to be taken up mainly in localities where unemployment is already low and entrepreneurs prefer to live. Even in depressed areas, many programmes are found in the event to draw in housewives or persons already employed or those engaged in training or education. In some regional programmes most of the jobs created have gone to labour specially introduced into the region rather than to local people. For any of these reasons job-creation programmes may miss the registered unemployed.

Easy to administer

Since most job-creation programmes are funded by central government the essence of an attractive programme is one that operates through uniform procedures in a standard way. Such standardization has the added advantage of keeping administrative costs low. Easy to administer has, therefore, become a prime consideration in public sector decisions about job creation. Greater effectiveness may be more easily achieved with schemes that offer more local discretion and flexibility, but the price for this usually has to be balanced against higher administrative or managerial costs and the acceptance of some uncertainty as to how the programme may deviate from a core of centrally devised rules.

TYPES OF PROGRAMME

Each programme in each locality in the job-creation field has an individuality of its own. Yet the features which programmes share are usually more significant than their incidental differences in portending common outcomes and common problems.

continued

For the purpose of analysis, the various approaches to the generation of employment can be placed into eight types. The types suggested here carry unfamiliar titles. A title which any programme bears can, of course, mislead: it is the strategy that underlies the programme together with its content that matters. The titles of the types in Figure 1 embrace programmes that bear a wide variety of names not only as inevitably occurs between countries, but also within a single country. The reasons for the generalities chosen may become evident to the reader as each type is described.

Make work

Make-work programmes comprise temporary employment activities of low economic utility but usually of some limited benefit to the community. Their main value lies less in terms of their output - they seldom compete with paid public services - than in meeting the needs of those without work, especially the long-term unemployed and the unskilled. Make-work programmes can impart useful skills involved in basic work practices, especially in the areas of construction, repair, decorating, and environmental improvement. They can arrest the downward spiral of human decline and despair through the social education of re-engagement in work. Make-work programmes also marginally increase a person's chance of getting a real job since it is easier for a job applicant to secure a job offer if he is usefully occupied rather than if he is doing nothing.

Work redistribution

Programmes aimed at redistributing existing work operate as an alternative to programmes aimed at generating additional jobs. The strategy underlying these programmes is to spread existing employment in the direction of those who cannot find work by restricting the work opportunities of those already working. This can be achieved in several different ways.

The approach which enjoys most favour is through making a shorter working week available or even allowable to each worker. There are four forms of this approach. The first is through reducing the number of hours worked each day. the second reduces the number of weeks worked per year. The third is through banning overtime. And the fourth is through job-splitting, *i.e.* a full-time worker is replaced by two part-time workers.

Work may also be redistributed by reducing the length of working life. One method is to postpone the age of entry into employment through the extension of further education or through the introduction of vocational and preparatory training. Making the employment of juveniles illegal is also another common practice. The second main method of achieving a shortening of working life is by lowering the age of exit. Mandating retirement at a given age removes

would-be workers and early retirement increases the flow of other retirees before that critical age is reached. The length of working life can therefore be reduced at both ends.

In addition, however, working life can be shortened through planned interruptions. The sabbatical year offers time-off in the academic community. Some large industrial organizations also arrange long leaves every few years. During these long leaves other workers need to be hired to fill the vacant places.

Work redistribution can be brought about in several ways. One is as a result of agreements made between trade unions and employers or between groups of employers wishing to avoid any loss of competitive edge by entering into such arrangements on their own. Another approach is through governmental legislation (*e.g.* the French Government, shortly after the election of President Mitterand, introduced a ban on overtime). A further way is through the provision of financial inducement (*e.g.* the British Government offer employers a cash incentive to introduce job-splitting).

Services to the labour market

Nearly all countries possess some form of public employment office with a range of services that assist or lubricate the processes of labour market. These services include the publication of labour market data, training in skills which the labour market needs, advertising job vacancies and advising job-seekers.

Manpower Services can be seen as creating jobs only in a marginal sense: they do not increase the number of jobs available, but they do increase the availability of jobs. Even in times of so-called full employment some frictional unemployment exists because workers need to change jobs as old industries and firms are replaced by new ones. Under full employment, or near full employment, some workers cannot find suitable jobs and some firms cannot find suitable, adequately skilled workers. Efficient Manpower Services reduce the duration time of jobs awaiting workers. In that sense they create more job-time by filling jobs more rapidly.

Services to the labour market are a more questionable means of assisting jobs during a recession. This is because job vacancies tend no longer to remain unfilled through mismatches in the labour market. But benefits may occur later. The stock of skills built up during a recession can accelerate the process of economic recovery through increasing the supply of trained manpower upon which recovery depends. If, however, the presumption of an early recovery proves false this strategy does not have much to offer. Workers can lose the skills they have

Figure 6

acquired through lack of opportunity to exercise them. There is also the danger of producing the needs of unrest. Unemployed workers can hardly be enrolled in training programmes without increasing their expectations about the benefits that training will confer on them in career terms. There are bound to be repercussions if these expectations are not met.

Services to small firms/new starts

A belief that small firms will provide most of the new jobs to be created in the future is widely held in developed countries. The services most commonly made available to small firms and new starts are advisory. Small firms, striving to expand their businesses, often lack specialist skills and knowledge especially in marketing and financial matters. Various types of advisory centres have been developed to meet these needs. For prospective entrepreneurs in particular, there has been a marked growth in opportunities in recent years with provision of specially designed training and education courses available at very low cost Other services to small firms and new starts are specially built or adapted premises at low rents, some with group facilities, including typing and book-keeping, that can serve the needs of several small businesses. Small firms and new starts are also gaining an increasing share of special advantages through some limited exemption from rates, taxes and building and planning restrictions in designated areas (*e.g.* Local Enterprise Zones).

Investment grants and loans

Public investment has been one of the most time-honoured ways - at least since Franklin D. Roosevelt's New Deal - of boosting economic activity through concentrating on key projects with the potential of creating both direct and indirect jobs. The most generously funded programmes involve capital grants (sometimes 100% grants) and government funded contracts. Other forms of assistance include subsidies, loans and tax remission, all of which are channelled towards job-creating investment.

The high costs associated with this approach have operated against setting up comprehensive national programmes. Instead, programmes of this type have tended to focus on special regions where unemployment is high.

Programmes broadly fall into two types. The first type is usually an emergency programme designed to introduce or to raise the output of manufactured goods as a means of boosting regional income to compensate for the loss of traditional basic industry. The financial incentives tend to be very attractive to capital-intensive industries and to firms with high-cost investment problems.

The second type of programme is directed towards improving the infrastructure of a depressed region. Better roads, a modernized rail service, a new airport or an improvement of a port will generate a first round of jobs through construction activities. A second round of jobs is expected to follow from the attraction of new industries ready to take advantage of the upgraded facilities.

Job-creating State Investment Programmes have found less favour in recent years due to their unwelcome effects in adding to inflationary pressure and the high cost borne for each new job created.

Job subsidies

Job subsidies are financial inducements to employers to give employment to an unemployed worker or an unqualified school-leaver or to retain in employment a worker who would otherwise be discharged due to trade recession. The degree of subsidy offered to an employer can be calculated to make it profitable to the State, that is to say the subsidy costs are lower than the alternative public support costs of an unemployed worker. These calculations depend on a number of assumptions. An estimation has to be made *inter alia* of how likely it is that unemployed workers will find jobs in the labour market without any form of special assis-tance. The financial advantages to the State are less debatable in the case of the long-term unemployment since in all countries, from which studies are reported, the probability of finding a job falls as the duration of unemployment increases.

The attempt to use job subsidies to induce employers to retain workers, who might otherwise be discharged, is much more difficult to evaluate, and more difficult to administer since complex negotiations with employers are required. Much preliminary negotiating is also involved in schemes to take on school-leavers ostensibly for training, especially in small firms where no training facilities exist and where the attractions of the programme are essentially those of a job subsidy. Job subsidies are usually welcomed by employers who benefit financially by this job-creation approach, but are ill-received by other employers who see them as constituting unfair competition. Job subsidies also impinge on the labour market as a whole and reduce the job prospects of other job seekers. It has been questioned whether job subsidies do really add to the overall job stock. They do, however, recommend themselves as a cost-effective measure for reducing the public support costs of hard-to-place unemployed workers.

Personal re-entry allowances

A job-subsidy programme provides an incentive for an employer to take on a hard-to-place unemployed worker. A complementary approach

continued

is to offer an incentive to the unemployed worker himself to re-engage in economic acitivity and to forsake continuing dependence on social security.

There are no programmes, as far as the author is aware, which offer an incentive to unemployed workers to take up a job in the local labour market. There may be a case for introducing trial measures in this field (*e.g.* free travel to work for the hitherto long-term unemployed). However. a variety of programmes exist for entrepreneurs who emerge out of the ranks of unemployed, ranging from government grants in Singapore to the Enterprise Allowance Scheme in the U.K., under which applicants receive £40 per week for a year to assist them in setting up their business. For public funds this approaches a zero-cost scheme, since the £40 approximates to the unemployment and other social security benefits the particiants would otherwise have been receiving. For any business that survives beyond the year there is an immediate net gain for public funds, which is greater still if the business takes on other employees.

Relocation allowances are used to enable unemployed workers to move to areas where jobs are offered. Many different types of personal training grants are available to the unemployed, including managers, wishing to acquire the skills needed for working in small firms. These provisions are variants of personal re-entry allowances and facilitate transfer into economic activity. Re-entry inducements, together with the costs of re-entry assistance including training, can be calculated and programmes devised in such a way that measures to promote employment need produce no net increase in public sector borrowing. In other words, programmes of this type have a good opportunity of becoming self-financing.

So far, however, personal re-entry allowances are operating in a way that benefits entrepreneurial, managerial and skilled workers rather than semi-skilled and unskilled workers (who mainly feel the brunt of unemployment). The benefits are also more evident in prosperous areas, where the jobs are and where entrepreneurs prefer to live, than in depressed and declining conurbations.

Employment development based on combined public and private sector initiatives

These programmes contain a special blend of common features: they are locally based and managed; they have as their central objective a need to create jobs locally and to place in them those who are currently without work; and they have a pragmatic approach to the way in which they are run. Hence jobs are created in the community, new jobs are fostered in existing local businesses and small businesses are developed, including solo businesses, partnerships and co-operatives. The titles under which these programmes operate are various. In the UK they appear as Employment Trusts, in Canada as Local Initiatives Programmes. The Netherlands can cite The Hague Enterprise Centre. The USA contains many Community Action Programmes, in one of which - Community Progress Inc of New Haven, Connecticut - the author worked some fifteen years ago. Some of the most interesting examples are found in Sweden. All these locally based programmes are characterized by their flexibility of approach, whereas nationally directed programmes have more limited objectives that accord with the terms of reference of the particular government departments that fund a given activity (*e.g.* training).

Figure 6   *Outcomes and characteristics of job-creation programming: some suggested relationships*

reluctance of Jacobsohn's respondents to retire was influenced by their state of health, the extent to which they were eligible for an occupational pension and other factors. Yet overall the conclusion is that only a minority of workers facing pensionable retirement wish to give up work completely. For them retirement is a form of enforced unemployment.

Jacobsohn's results are in line with a good deal of American research material. The Americans have taken this work seriously. To 'retire' a person involuntarily, before the age of seventy is now legally akin in the USA to a form of discrimination, comparable with its racial and sexual counterparts.

Naturally I approved of this avant-garde American legislation. As an expert witness, I had contributed written testimony to the preceding Senate Investigating Commission. This invitation had arisen as I had helped on behalf of the National Council on Aging to set up the National Institute of Gerontology in the USA. What I hoped to find from subsequent census statistics was that workers in their sixties would begin to make a more significant contribution to the American economy. In a fair and just society work, like wealth, needs to be spread. But, as with OECD recommendations on abolishing mandatory retirement and substituting flexible retirement, the actions taken do not always result in the effects intended. One suspects that overriding any legislative measures are a great number of devices from financial inducement to subtle pressures. Those so ousted find difficulty in gaining new jobs. In practice they have little alternative but to reconcile themselves to becoming dependants.

A dilemma and how to face it

Developed countries are beginning to face a special type of dilemma. The provision of welfare, whether in the form of the dole or State pensions, to able-bodied citizens creates an alternative life-style to work and provides the economic basis by means of which it can be pursued. For demographic reasons this dependent segment of the population is liable to increase. Conversely the proportion of the population engaged in producing goods and services shrinks. As this happens the strain in carrying the full economic burden grows and gives rise in the economically active population to a sense of being 'overworked and overtaxed'. The problem now posed is whether the State should respond more to the demands of producers or those of dependants (the needy). The more people are withdrawn from participation in work to the alternative life-style the sharper the dilemma becomes.

Developed countries vary in terms of whether they have *hard* or *soft* systems of welfare and whether they pursue an active manpower policy or prefer laissez-faire economic doctrines. An active manpower policy seeks to provide high level skills – business, professional and technological – as part

14

The zero unemployment option

Some countries have high unemployment; some have low unemployment. There are even those that claim no unemployment, including member states of the Communist bloc, though this may be a statistical illusion and in any case is rapidly changing. What we have to ask is whether zero unemployment is even theoretically feasible, let alone desirable.

It was Beveridge's contention that there was some irreducible minimum level of unemployment in any free, progressive and expanding economy. He put the figure at 3 per cent which mainly comprised frictional unemployment, that is to say the loss of jobs that inevitably occurs as declining firms and industries are overtaken by the advance of others. People between jobs are, technically speaking, unemployed unless they fill in their time with training or temporary work. Some unemployed people are needed to fill vacancies. Further, when more people are chasing jobs than there are jobs available, there is less risk, economists tell us, of wage push inflation. Hence a small amount of employment can be a factor making for stability, provided those out of work are true job-seekers. This general argument is not of course very comforting for those out of work.

How far society should acquiesce in some minimum level of unemployment depends on one's values and to some extent on how the term is defined. Should unemployment refer to those who are not gainfully occupied within the population of normal working age (which definition necessarily includes the work shy)? Or is there a case for adopting the more person-centred approach by referring to the employment status of those who want paid work but for whom such work is not available (which inevitably includes some of the retired)? This last point has been brought to public attention by several recent cases in a number of countries where individuals, acknowledged by their firms as satisfactory workers, have made legal objections to being compulsorily retired on grounds of age alone. This is the dilemma being posed increasingly by the growing numbers of fit and healthy individuals now moving into the upper age groups.

Who are the unemployed?

So at the heart of the matter, any policy that aims to tackle unemployment must turn the spotlight on those whom the term should cover. The unemployed, when loosely used, can comprise contrasting population sub-groups. On the one hand they can include individuals of normal working age who avoid set work, if at all possible, either because they have their own unearned income or would prefer unemployment benefit, in other words the 'voluntary unemployed'. On the other hand we could be referring to the involuntary unemployed, that reservoir of labour that gushes into activity whenever an economy picks up, and which includes those who do not normally figure in any headcount of the unemployed. The flexibility of the labour market actually depends on the composition of the economically inactive population made up as it is of two distinct groups: job-seekers and non job-seekers.

Clearly unemployment can be defined in a number of different ways according to one's starting point. So what we have to ask is: which is the best working definition from the point of view of the job promoter, who strives to balance the fullest extension of job opportunities with prudent public finance?

We need some solid ground on which to build. Let us respond then with a working definition of unemployment as:

> 'the absence of gainful employment in respect of a person in search of work who is not in receipt of any regular income from the public sector'. (Examples of a regular income would be an educational grant or a disability allowance or a retirement pension.)

It follows from this definition that it is in the public interest, on material grounds alone, to find employment for all who seek it and otherwise have no adequate means of support nor alternative income. In some areas this would be a tall order. But equally it is plain that in some favourable localities, with problems limited enough to make them manageable, a zero unemployment policy would be a feasible proposition. In other words all job-seekers could be offered something, including a choice of opportunities. These would include a community job, a programme of preparatory training and trial work placement in the private sector, a programme preparatory to self employment and a programme aimed at creating spin-off enterprises from a development and training centre. By adding to the supply side in the labour market, this approach to full employment would be unlikely to set in motion the wage-push inflationary pressures which low unemployment normally brings in its wake.

Whether it would be economic or not to put so bold a plan into operation would hinge on the success of the venture in meeting its aims. That in turn depends on how expertly it was conducted. The dilemma that has to be faced is that it is more costly to process the unemployed through programmes manned by qualified staff than it is to send a social security cheque through the post to the unemployed. The former strategy could also be expensive to set up but thereafter it would become an economic proposition in so far as it achieved a better record than its rival programme in enabling job-seekers to transfer from public sector support into private sector gainful employment. For that to happen therefore a high level of professional skill and accumulated experience on the part of the facilitators is an essential requirement.

It is my personal view that, in a sophisticated society and with the appropriate means, we have every prospect of making a success of this radically different strategy given time. What is lacking is the will.

There is a common conviction in the 'value' of having a pool of unemployed although the theory is hardly borne out in practice. Some of the most enterprising societies in developed countries enjoy low unemployment rates. Switzerland has continued to strengthen its economy and increase its share of the world market in, for example, sophisticated engineering while long maintaining levels of unemployment of only 1 per cent or less. Singapore with unemployment around 2 per cent is a byword for enterprise in the Far East. Sweden has amanaged to maintain its industrial vigour in spite of being a country with a small population outside the EEC trade bloc; its unemployment has seldom risen above 3 per cent.

Evidently enterprise can flourish without needing a reserve pool of labour. What happens in those industries is that labour migrates upwards through the skill (and pay) spectrum. People leave poorly paid jobs for better ones. By this means there is always room for growth in higher value added enterprises. The labour needed is drawn in from less profitable, lower wage industries and is assisted by training. If lack of a reserve pool of labour restricts some economic activity, any problems experienced are likely to be felt in the less advanced businesses. These have poorer prospects anyway for generating stable new jobs.

Abolishing unemployment

There are reasonable grounds then for believing that assured employment can be offered to the unemployed without jeopardizing economic stability generally. For this to happen a new type of contract would have to be set up between the State and those who lose their jobs. The prospect is that unemployment, in the sense in which it has been defined earlier, could be abolished under an appropriate set of conditions. One of the key facilitating means would be the removal of Unemployment Benefit.

This proposal is not as far-fetched as it sounds either philosophically or technically. Unemployment Benefit is a curious type of contract between the State and the beneficiary which is difficult to justify in principle. Under it, someone is promised an income on the express condition of making in return a nil contribution in goods and services to society. If this agreement is breached by engaging in work for which payment is received the benefit is removed and prosecution could follow.

However well it is administered Unemployment Benefit entails the consolidation of contractual dependency. Payments tend to increase in line with the generally improved standards of living and this makes dependency more attractive. If the trend were to continue, human society could one day be divided along the lines of a beehive into two streams, workers and drones: the busy workers contribute to the nest through tax and the drones draw on the proceeds of the workers' busyness (its spelling being significantly close into the word business).

Few would wish to see the social rigidities of the beehive in contemporary society. It is not a fear that strikes people during a period of bustling change when a person may be working at one moment, unemployed at another and re-engaged in work shortly after. Yet the possibility that we are moving towards the beehive model is there before our eyes. In many chronically depressed areas there is a growing population of second and third generation unemployed. This inactive group contrasts sharply with workaholics who abound whenever commerce and industry thrive.

Employment insurance

If unemployment is to be tackled in a proactive way, the size of the problem needs to be reduced to manageable proportions. Those who are between jobs should not be counted as part of a primary problem. Most workers are destined during their working life to lose their jobs from time to time for one reason or another. The intervals out of work may be small. The more able displaced worker may have no wish to apply for an assured job or training under a public sector programme but to spend the time instead applying for another position. New mechanisms for helping to bring this about can be encouraged.

Active job search can be a time-consuming business and adequate provision must be made for the income of the worker to be maintained during this period. This is the area in which private insurance companies should play their proper part. A statutory requirement should oblige employers to take out insurance to cover their employees against compulsory lay-offs. The funds released would in effect finance frictional unemployment.

Someone who had not yet entered the labour market would not of course be covered against frictional unemployment under this scheme of things but would be expected to apply for the public sector guarantee of work and/or training.

A radical systems change of this type would introduce a new pattern of incentives for employers. While conventional social security purports to offer insurance cover in the event of unemployment, it does so in a way that does little to lessen and may even aggravate the problem. Because the foundations of social security are not based on insurance principles – where the premiums are in keeping with the risks entailed – employers are free from the pressures that would otherwise operate. Hence few firms bother to find alternative employment for redundant staff in spite of being in a good position to do so by virtue of close familiarity with the skills and general abilities of their employees. A proclivity to fire workers and leave them to sort out the consequences does not affect a firm's contribution to insurance. The problem created is merely transferred to the public sector.

By changing the insurance code, responsibility would be transferred back again. Naturally hire-and-fire employers would pay higher insurance premiums than employers offering employment security. The level of benefits for which insurance cover was taken out could well be a matter of keen interest to trade unions. Nevertheless there would have to be a statutory minimum level of cover for which all employers would be liable.

Public responsibility for unemployment should begin at the frontier where responsibility from the private sector ends. But by moving back the frontiers, as we have suggested, the zero unemployment option begins to look a more feasible and attractive proposition.

To make it more feasible still, two other basic changes would also have to be made. One involves accountancy; the other would require greater devolution on the part of government.

Combining unemployment and employment

At present there is no incentive for any Ministry to engage in placement or job creation activities as a means of reducing the bills it incurs in social security payments to the unemployed. The two sides of the ledger do not relate to one another because in almost every country those responsibilities are divided between different organizations. Each organization is intent on meeting its statutory objectives in a consistent fashion that no one can criticise.

For example, when working in the United States, I observed how the Manpower Development and Training Act was impinging on the unemployed whom it had been designed to help. Many excellent establishments had opened up to provide training and placement services for eligible clients. The effectiveness of these establishments was assessed from their record in subsequent job placements. That being so, the most employable people began to form the major intake into training and the hard core unemployed was screened out. 'We don't want to take in unemployables,' became an accepted axiom.

Organizations that strive to meet the needs of the least employable are open to the criticism of not being cost effective. That may be because the true costs are not being measured. These costs are best assessed by a single organization that meets their financial and other needs when they are unemployed and makes financial savings whenever they are placed in jobs. Such conditions allow equations to be made.

But it is not just a matter of economics. Society needs a very special infrastructure, and one more professionally equipped than we have seen before, in order to re-engage the underclass. Without that provision the productive members of the community will continue to support through their taxes those who assert their right to be unemployed. And the poor will be permanently with us.

An integrated system of responsibility by removing the usual boundaries of bureaucracy offers the prospect of dealing with problems of unemployment that have often been seen as intractable. But at the same time we are drawn inevitably towards a choice point; for that there are only two basic ways in which integrated responsibility can be achieved.

One route could end up in the creation of a mega Ministry. The advantage which this would offer in its scale of approach is however offset by some conspicuous obstacles. A large unwieldy body would have difficulty in co-ordinating its huge limbs. More serious still is the problem that besets any centrally-based organization in dealing with politically sensitive issues in the provinces. A well administered programme requires a multiplicity of decisions taken on their merits rather than on a set of standard rules blindly and obediently applied. Almost certainly there are few decisions that would go uncontested in the provinces unless local representatives were actively involved in the decision-making process.

Relinquishing power from the centre

There is however a second and, I would claim, preferable path to progress. It is one familiar to all serious students of management. Devolution is the acknowledged means by which large conglomerate industrial enterprises are able to flourish efficiently. Devolution and the delegation of decision-making is commonly practised in industry. It is far rarer in government — with Switzerland as the only notable exception. A great deal of government has to do with power which is not as a rule willingly relinquished either by ambitious politicians or by the mandarins of a central civil service. To be willing to delegate requires a humility and a realization that certain decisions are better taken by others nearer the scene of action. Good delegation flourishes primarily in a democratic culture. *The ability to retain responsibility but to delegate well marks out managers of distinction.*

Neighbourhood development

The highly complex nature of the problems that need to be tackled underlines the point that the decision to operate a zero unemployment programme can only be operated effectively by neighbourhood administrations. Whatever institutions are set up to achieve that purpose need to have a local mandate and the resources with which to operate. As Sir Adrian Cadbury, the distinguished industrialist, once said to a conference on local government: 'A body needs to be elected, for otherwise it has no authority, and to have money, for otherwise it has no power'.

Regional development bodies, backed by Local Authorities, with funds made available both by central and local government, would be well placed to find the best way of combining economic development, the provision of welfare benefits and job creation. Such a body would have no departmental boundaries to overcome. If there were fixed funds available, efficiency in getting people back into work would produce an immediate benefit to the local community through either lower taxes or improved services.

For a zero unemployment policy to be adopted, the key decision would have to be taken in the light of local circumstances and the presence or otherwise of the appropriate resources for setting it in motion.

The price to be paid for this freedom would be a likely disparity in social and economic practices between different regions. This is something that nearly all central governments shun or appear to shun. Uniformity is preferred as less likely to create political embarrassments.

The prospect of regional variation might, one could argue, be better regarded as a potential opportunity rather than a problem. The varying practices that separate regions would bring about would invite competition and comparison. Such a route would open up the road to excellence.

How we got here and get there

These general conclusions on how a zero employment policy might operate were the products of a zigzag personal journey.

It was the research started in the ITRU and finished in the EDU that convinced us that the registered unemployed would in the main rather have an assured job without the assurance of unemployment benefit than unemployment benefit without the assurance of a job; it was working with CPI in the USA that provided testimony that the underemployables could be placed in 'real jobs' if a high enough level of professional expertise was available to train and assess them and to find jobs in the labour market suited to their abilities; it was through working with others in training centres that we came to appreciate their potential value as creators of spin-off job-multiplying enterprises; and it was as a result of collaboration with institutions at the local level that we were persuaded that this was the best place at which to make devolved decisions on how limited financial resources could be used to best advantage. These elements of experience, when put together and interpreted, have played their part in helping to construct the framework of a zero unemployment programme.

Let us recognize however that a certain momentum is already gathering towards the goal of zero unemployment. The established forces in this case are not so much professional practitioners with a message as political thinkers commonly identified with the Left and Right.

Workfare

Our first stop should be at Workfare as it is applied in the United States. This approach to zero unemployment has gained its impetus by withholding unemployment benefit and substituting a public service job instead. Workfare has fitted the mood of many Americans. As one grain farmer from the Mid-West put it to me: 'Why should we work hard and pay taxes to support other people for doing nothing?'

This reluctance to support the unemployed is common, I have found, among blue-collar workers holding stable but poorly paid jobs. Whenever a low paid worker discovers an unemployed next door neighbour with a large family leading a settled life on unearned income and enjoying an allegedly equal or better standard of living, resentment is commonly felt. The objection to this state of affairs is voiced on moral grounds, just as their natural adversaries, those who act as watch-dogs on behalf of general welfare, do so on moral grounds also.

Almost half the States in the USA adopt versions of Workfare. These vary both in the stringency of the conditions that affect enrollees and in the quality of services they provide. At its best Workfare assists those genuinely wishing to escape from public assistance and secure better paid and more attractive jobs in the world outside.

Workfare is steadily becoming a system with a proven track record. Society has registered gains by enjoying the benefits of projects that would not otherwise have been undertaken. Several of the Centres into which the client population of Workfare is received have done much to help those who previously had little prospect of employment. The provision of preparatory training of its client intake and good contacts with local enterprises have often combined to enable those offered 'work or training' to find a *real job* outside. The success rate claimed by some centres (65 per cent or more) shows that positive responsibility for the unemployed can serve to raise their employment prospects and at the same time reduce the escalating public cost of underwriting chronic unemployment.

There is a further gain that arises out of the mandatory element of attendance for work or training. Sources in these Centres indicate that between 15 and 20 per cent of prospective clients turn out to be 'not available for work'. This figure is far too big to imply medical disability where that has not been already notified. Workfare has a built in safeguard against fraudulence. Claimants of Unemployment Benefit may take a job on the side and, with their double income, live better than many regular members of the working population. Social security snoopers have great difficulty in detecting them and their attempts to do so may antagonize other innocent people. Snoopers are unnecessary when attendance or non-attendance at a Centre for clients without regular jobs is treated in the same way as in any normal place of employment. A self-regulating system would undermine only the jobs of social security snoopers themselves.

Since Workfare began in the USA American industry has lost some of its competitive edge in world markets and the economy has developed a large balance of payments deficit. Yet unemployment has fallen at a time when it was rising in other developed countries. It would be ironic if the USA, long the front runner of the free enterprise system, lost its lead only to regain it in another field: a new way of reconciling the public and private interest.

Workfare has great potential for development because it is so young. Yet as it stands there are problems about transferring this model from the USA unchanged. It is not merely the not-invented-here objection which people outside the USA are bound to raise. The greater problem is the Rightish and almost punitive image that Workfare has acquired. The poorly trained and poorly educated may be pushed into marginal jobs. But that on its own does very little to help a declining area recover its lost vitality. Vocational education, the upgrading of skills, enterprise formation and area redevelopment have not as yet become adjuncts of the programme. A truly effective zero unemployment strategy must address itself to more than the unemployed and their programme supervisors. The basic thrust of any major initiative in a depressed area needs to be spearheaded by a small number of entrepreneurs, area enthusiasts and professional job promoters. And it must extend a positive vision of the future it if is to broaden its base and appeal to a wider section of the community.

The Right to Work

One must concede that an example of inspiration from the opposite end of the political spectrum is to be found in the slogan associated with the campaign for the 'Right to Work'. A programme aimed at a furtherance of human rights becomes a rallying point and gives a sense of mission to participants at all levels. Unfortunately, what the campaign lacks is not image but substance. The underlying presumption of its advocates is that the State through ownership of the means of production can create jobs and enterprises and disregard costs and commercial considerations. That is because, in the eyes of its missionaries, the interests of the unemployed are paramount.

So we have two approaches that have one aim in common – the prospect of zero unemployment. Yet each approach is the antithesis of the other. The essence of Workfare is of obligation without entitlement. The essence of the Right to Work is of entitlement without obligation. A programme that embraced both rights and entitlements would command far wider support than one that is prone to make friends and enemies at the same time.

A Social Dividend

Finally there is one other initiative on the Left which deserves mention, which has figured in the travels of a job promoter, and which in its own enticing, but peculiar, way points a beckoning finger on a competitive path towards zero unemployment. I refer to the mention of a Social Dividend and its many derivatives. The case for this 'socialistic' measure was put to me once in an elegant way in the luxurious surroundings of the Savoy Hotel in London by an old colleague with a national reputation as an industrial consultant and a strong interest in the public sector of the economy.

The idea is that the State guarantees a subsistence income to every citizen through unifying taxation and welfare payments into a single system. If income is low, it is automatically supplemented and, as it rises to high levels, it is taxed progressively. The incentive to take on marginal jobs is increased as such work provides real additional income. The poverty trap is avoided because there is no loss of entitlements as happens under the present system, divided as it is into workers who pay tax and the unemployed who receive benefits. Everyone would be busy doing the things for which he or she was best suited. No one would suffer from the stigma of being unemployed. Such a system would be attuned to the great productive capacity and low-labour requirements of modern industry. New possibilities would open up for a person to lead a fuller life and make better use of leisure.

'It does seem to me', I said, 'that, human nature being what it is, large numbers of people would be tempted to disengage from regular work and avail themselves of the Social Dividend. Given a decline in the wealth creation process how would the money be raised to maintain such a costly system?'

'What is money?' said my friend, as he tucked into his smoked salmon sandwiches. 'Little more than printed paper in a highly productive society where the only serious problem is not the creation of wealth but its distribution throughout the whole of society.'

I did not wish to argue the point in the light of the animation being expressed. But we did feel prompted to explore the proposition further in the Employment Development Unit. The financial outcome of the Social Dividend and its variants was difficult to calculate – let alone its social outcome. But whichever reasonable assumptions we made, we calculated the scheme as an expensive operation. What that meant in effect was that in order to finance it, the most productive members of society would need to be more heavily taxed than at present. The advantages of the change would be felt most by those who treated work casually. Certainly my friend was not amongst their number. Still he had a point. The Social Dividend might encourage inertia, but it would also be a formula for zero unemployment, if we accept the definitions of unemployment given earlier.

It is inescapable then that the zero unemployment option, whether in a theoretical or in a rudimentary operational form, is already part of the political agenda.

Conclusions

To sum up, the abolition of unemployment benefit is feasible, some would say desirable, provided there is something else to take its place. What that something else should be is of course a matter of debate.

As the old saying reminds us, 'an ounce of experience is worth a pound of theory'. Pilot experiments with new, bold and comprehensive programmes, administered on a small scale in well defined localities, are just what is needed to provide the necessary experience on acceptable models. Judgements could then be made on the merits of various types of zero unemployment options.

Job promoters would of course take such a strategy to heart. But politically such radical ventures are difficult to bring about. That is because the intention of engaging in such experiments denotes commitment to a path leading in that direction. The resistance comes from competing voices proclaiming the desirability of alternative paths. What those voices are and their importance in shaping future global patterns, we will consider a little further in my last chapter.

---------------------------------- 15 ----------------------------------

The end of an apprenticeship

Long journeys provide the time and opportunity for learning something new. Many years had passed since jobs first seized my attention as a subject of study and since that day we first occupied the garret premises overlooking the far end of King's College Chapel and the busy bicycle-laden streets of Cambridge. Now within these same offices paper-crammed packing cases announced our impending departure. Such moves are not made easily and without upheaval. Every office dweller whether unwittingly or intentionally becomes an archivist. The penalty for hoarding paper is delayed until one fateful day. Then every document that needs to shift its position poses the question: should it be retained, refiled or consigned to the shredder? This repeated challenge to instant decision making is a tiring but not entirely fruitless business. For the compensation, if there is one, is to offer an historical overview of events previously disconnected in the mind.

So it was for us when, prompted by the overriding need of our College landlords to find more space for student accommodation, we were obliged to start the arduous undertaking of moving ourselves and our possessions. And as we dug with archaeological zeal into long forgotten layers of letters and reports, a new meaning began to emerge from the relics we were uncovering. It soon became apparent that we could classify our papers as belonging to different periods. Certainly one could identify two distinct eras in the past through which our small band of job promoters had worked and survived. And now we could detect signs – or was too much resting on hopeful imagination? – of a third era opening up before us.

The manpower policy era

The first era was an attempt at developing and managing a sophisticated manpower policy. Nationally, Industrial Training Boards had been established each with a governing body comprising employers, trade unions and educational representatives. The Boards had been asked to address

176

themselves both to the immediate and long term needs of their industries and to take necessary measures to ensure that there would be a continuous and adequate supply of skilled manpower. What gave the Boards their powers was their statutory right to raise levies and award grants. Armed in this way they were able to take what measures they saw fit in order to reach their goals. The Manpower Services Commission, which in due course supervised the Boards, acted largely in a co-ordinating role, addressed itself in particular to those fields in which the Board did not operate and maintained a certain independence from government. During this period of attempted industrial regeneration, independent research and development had been given every encouragement both in providing a general service to help the Boards and in formulating policies to help those out of work. How fortunate we seemed on reflection, as we examined the papers of that era, that we had been able to flourish, to acquire techniques and build up our experience in an age imbued, albeit temporarily, with a sense of industrial purpose.

The era of centralization

That age was brought to an end by the onset of new political thinking, which largely did away with the independent Training Boards. Power now centred on the MSC itself which in turn came under the direct control of government. This was the era of standardized and highly centralized policies conceived on a far narrower front than formerly. The rise of the new hegemony was associated with – and may have contributed to – mounting unemployment. It was a period that had generated in our files massive correspondence in dealing with, or attempting to deal with, the non-negotiable directives of central government.

What struck us particularly as we perused the content of the correspondence of this era was one anomaly, as it now seemed. Strange to relate, the more remote our research activities had been from actual application the easier it had been to secure public funding. Difficulties had been encountered as soon as our researches and demonstration projects were found to have a direct bearing on public manpower policy and in particular on practical methods for the promotion of employment.

It was interesting to speculate why this should be. Perhaps innovation does not sit comfortably alongside orthodoxy when power is being wielded from the centre. Then deviance can cause more concern than ineffectiveness. Job promotion, we were beginning to find, was becoming an increasingly difficult activity in which to engage.

This was the era when mounting impediments had prompted us to establish an independent EDU. Then it had proved easier to work with local authorities, in conjunction with other local bodies, perhaps due to their simpler structures and the greater scope offered for more direct relationships. But they were also closer to the problems and more subject to local pressures. Local electors and communities demand a positive and visible answer to the problem of declining job opportunities in their immediate localities and are not content to wait for national, fiscal and monetary policies to work themselves through.

The dilemma for local authorities, as it turned out, was that while they were well placed to use intimate area knowledge to set in motion economic development and job-creation programmes, powerful disincentives debarred such enterprising ventures. All initiatives cost money and have to be evaluated in terms of outcomes. But the financial rewards of any success under the regime of the period went primarily to central government through lower unemployment benefit and reduced social security costs. Local authorities received little of the pay back from finding real jobs for those out of work. And it was a feature of this period in the United Kingdom that local authorities could be penalised by central government for 'overspending' as a result of engaging in employment initiatives.

The era of local enterprise

The third period we detected in sifting through our papers was one suggesting a new sort of cultural trend. It might be described as an awakening interest in particular sets of people. These comprised primarily two diverse and contrasting groups: the unemployed and entrepreneurs, especially those classified as 'New Starts'. The latter had received a great deal of attention. With the help in many instances of Business in the Community and with small financial contributions from local firms, local authorities and central government, a network of Enterprise Agencies had been established nationally. Records showed that those prospective entrepreneurs who used the services available had approximately a third of the failure rate of those ignoring the services. At the same time the Department of Trade and Industry provided subsidized consultancy to small firms so that help should become available in a personalized way for small businesses. A Business Expansion Scheme added to the picture by allowing tax deductible investments to be made by outsiders in unquoted companies so that financial risk-taking would be encouraged in the formation of developing enterprises.

The unemployed themselves have been treated less in the aggregate. They have been individually called to interview, enlisted in new programmes or encouraged to join Job Clubs. There are now more people available than hitherto to provide them with personal assistance. New forms of local co-ordination between the unemployed and the business community are being set up through the establishment of Training and Enterprise Councils (TECS).

All this lends credence to the view that a new more enterprising spirit is detectable in relation to job promotion. The period in question has been associated with — and has almost certainly been a factor in — a continuing decline in the headcount of the unemployed. Exactly how much weight should be attached to the effects of this virtually covert policy in job promotion, it is of course impossible to say.

So these layers of documents could be conceived as an historical trend that offer grounds for optimism for the natural optimist. On the other hand our unearthed documents could equally provide substance for the views of pessimists when we examined the official position taken up by the major institutions that form the fabric of society. The literature dealing with formal responsibility for job promotion is sparse. This contrasts with the vast literature dealing with the facts and figures of unemployment as we were persuaded by the sheer effort involved in coping with our files. Bulky reports and sheaves of statistical data about people in work and out of it were available from a seeming infinity of sources. The dedicated compilers were those whose responsibilities began and ended with the provision of information. Figures about jobs and analysis of trends may be of interest to many. But job promotion was evidently nobody's prime concern.

Where does responsibility lie?

Whose business should it properly be? That is the crunch question which must be settled before there can be any reasonable faith in the belief that progress is likely to be sustained in the future.

The current position is clear: when times are bad, there is a general scramble to disclaim responsibility. It is the publicly stated position of the present Government that 'real', that is, self-financing, jobs are created by the private sector of the economy. Public sector jobs, which government can bring about, are burdens on the taxpayer since they are financed only by reducing the standard of living of the working population. For their part, the business community rejects the notion that responsibility for employment lies within the realm of business objectives. That is because the pressures operate in the opposite direction. By setting out to reduce the labour content of its goods and services, business becomes more efficient, competitive and profitable. That is where the priorities must lie. Only in this way, the business world claims, can enterprises survive and provide the low cost goods and services from which the public benefits.

The final contenders in the public mind for responsibility for the supply of jobs are economists.

In a corporate sense it is not a responsibility that economists themselves are ready to accept. They prefer to interpret their own role as charters, forecasters and explainers of the economic process. The subject offers possibilities for endless debate. As the well known jibe of George Bernard Shaw reminds us, if all the economists were laid end to end they would not reach a conclusion. True, there is often a consensus on how problems are aggravated. There is less agreement on how they are solved. Which is understandable, for many economists would not accept 'solutions' as being part of their remit.

So, if these three parties – government, business and economists – disclaim their power to bring about jobs in the numbers desired, what other options are left? Is the matter to be left to fate and to the silent forces of evolutionary progress? Should the individual then be left to struggle for him or herself? That option creates a vacuum that someone, almost certainly, will attempt to fill. So which voices will contend for the ears of ordinary people who wish to develop some reasonable expectations about jobs and the future?

These questions brought us to the final – and perhaps the most important – theme that interrupted our packing. The subject was brought to our notice by a collection of largely unread documents about jobs in relation to society and the part they play or need not play in our lives.

Jobs and society

Job philosophers may seem even more removed than job statisticians from the lives of everyday people. That is because philosophers write largely for one another. Unlike statisticians, they provide a service of no presumed value. Yet, in so far as a few philosophers seek to influence the wider world and their themes may be taken up by persuasive politicians, their potential influence is far greater.

From a cursory reading of these collected documents we soon reached the view that there are only four distinctive schools likely to make their mark in this century and perhaps even the next. They belong to the anarchic libertarians, the welfarers, the worksharers and, now new on the scene, the job promoters.

The *anarchic libertarians* – or advocates of laissez-faire – consider major intervention in the 'natural' workings of society as morally objectionable. Mass unemployment may still be seen as a blight, for their numbers include many convinced humanitarians. But what is conceived as 'social engineering', or even a commitment towards any agreed social goal, is interpreted as an affront to freedom. In a free society people go about their daily lives in their own individual way. The fewer the constraints placed upon them, the freer they are held to be. Community planning inevitably limits the liberties of a minority.

Should the sum total of individual choices work out to the maximum public good, giving rise to the hope that people and the social units to which they belong are naturally perfectible, the anarchic libertarians would be well placed to extend their influence. In so far as that proposition is acceptable or is doubted, public opinion is likely to be drawn instead towards other schools of thought.

The *welfarers* have something in common with the anarchic libertarians in that neither school accepts that there is any intrinsic merit in every able-bodied person in society having a job. The productive capacity of industrialized society in the eyes of the welfarers is so vast that the equitable distribution of wealth is seen as the primary problem rather than its production. Those who wish to opt out of work in favour of leisure should be free to do so. A guaranteed minimum income based on some redistribution of accumulated wealth would assure them of the basic necessities of life. The choice of whether or not to opt in to work in order to enjoy desired luxuries then becomes a personal matter.

In affluent societies, welfarers exercise a powerful voice because the financial means exist to turn their aspirations into reality. That possibility has been fully exploited politically. Largesse has been widely distributed in a number of states, from the oil rich to those that have established their supremacy on commerce and enterprise.

The repercussions, in Western countries at least, have however produced a backlash against this whole school of thought. One undoubted factor has been the reaction of people to the conduct of the jobless when set alongside those engaged in work. The comparison has caused concern. The unoccupied, especially in the younger age groups, all too frequently fail to live up to an acceptable standard of civic behaviour. 'The Devil makes work for idle hands' is an old saying that has not lost its ring of truth.

In defence of their standpoint, the welfarers would argue that until recently people have only been educated for eventual participation in a working society. To be fully prepared for the leisure society requires a new approach, to which education must be redirected. Once people know how to use leisure, they will handle it better.

The welfarers accept implicitly a division between workers and non-workers, even though these groups are not absolute since any one person may move between one group and another at different stages in life. Whether that movement actually takes place in an equitable way and how far 'education for leisure' succeeds in embracing the general population are issues crucial to the prospects of welfarers in being able to claim public attention and support.

Worksharers differ from welfarers in that they see the provision of a job and the income that goes with it as a desirable objective. The issue of responsibility is important in their eyes for they are concerned that there will not be enough available work in the long run. The industrial revolution removed vast numbers of people from agriculture, replacing jobs on the land with jobs in manufacturing industry. Post-industrial society will create service jobs in considerable numbers. But many of these, it is claimed, will eventually be transformed into self service operations or computerized, so leaving an overall shortfall. The sum total of available work is therefore fixed. The social interest, therefore, requires that available work should be shared so that personal incomes can be assured. Work will play a less important role, so it is claimed, in people's lives and there will be widening opportunities for leisure.

Some worksharing schemes have already been tried out but have not on the whole met the response that was hoped for. Part of the difficulty is that individuals have been reluctant to relax their full-time grip on a job. Job ownership has had a deeper grip on the human mind than had been supposed. People fear to lose their indispensability or spoil their chances of promotion. Employers too have been less than enthusiastic. The legal ban on overtime introduced by the French Government as a means of spreading work and reducing unemployment was eventually rescinded after widespread protests and objections.

It is difficult to see that worksharing can operate other than as a voluntary activity. And if it does so, the scale of its practice may be too small to exert much overall effect in reducing employment. Where jobs are scarce, sharing will have less appeal to those who have the good fortune to be already placed in work. There is a very real possibility that worksharing will founder on the rocks that have sunk many ships before — the nature of the human psyche.

We come lastly to *job promoters* whose basic message is that work provides the essential link for a reciprocally beneficial relationship between the individual and the community. In the eyes of the job promoter full employment [the condition] and the 'right to work' [the entitlement] are compatible and desirable. Job promoters can claim to be an emerging force with the experience upon which to build.

Yet job promoters have not so far built up a position in the great debate in which they have an equal voice with the better established anarchic libertarians, welfarers and worksharers. Being dispersed and thin in numbers and without any recognizable professional or institutional base they have scarcely been in a position to establish an identifiable school of thought. There is a critical size problem which has to be overcome before the momentum can begin.

Looking forward

Job promoters, being like actors in some unseen play, await their curtain call. Their parts are already inscribed upon the historical programme. Their turn has yet to come. But the moment of arrival is near, for two forces are now combining to suggest that job promoters are at last working in tune with public opinion rather than against it.

The first major factor that strengthens demand for their cause is the way in which the dislocation of the labour market has gained public attention. It is not uncommon to find job vacancies more numerous than the unemployed available to fill them, yet the unemployed are ineligible or unwilling to move into the jobs on offer. This costly paradox strikes the economically active tax-paying public as increasingly unacceptable. In both economic and moral terms the case for removing unemployment benefit and replacing it with guaranteed work and/or training and other ways of gaining income in return for activity is likely to gain general support. There can scarcely be any illusions about the difficulties of bringing about such a radical transformation of the social system. But the prospect becomes appealing and challenging in neighbourhoods where the size of the problem looks manageable.

The second factor which is advancing the case for the job promoter is the growing call, detectable on a global scale, for local autonomy. Major issues that arise in any particular vicinity have been customarily treated as being part of a wider national or even world problem – a view that spells passivity. The rival approach is to downplay the importance of global conditions and to press for local solutions to local problems. That outlook is co-terminous with a belief in decentralization, local government and local decision-making.

A growing demand for local autonomy has become a real force in the world today as people have reacted against bureaucracy, the failure of big government and inefficiency. A new political consciousness has set the scene for a reaffirmation of the intimate relationship between people, the community and a healthy society.

With the timing of their appearance now opportune, job promoters are likely to increase their numbers as soon as a programme of guaranteed work and training becomes a declared alternative to welfare payments for the fit and able. At that moment a new political philosophy is required. No goal is achievable unless people are persuaded that it is worthwhile. Such a programme must have its advocates ready to stand their ground against the competitive claims of anarchic libertarians, welfarers and worksharers.

But the principal demand for job promoters will arise for professional reasons. Every new venture is beset with technical snags. Unless they are overcome the programme will falter.

Special skills are needed to work up local projects that have business viability and can provide new jobs. New skills in assessment will have to be developed to diagnose the problems of the under-employable and to handle their training and eventual placement. And, lastly, new forms of accountancy arrangement will need to be entered into whereby a better estimate can be made of the net cost of a programme that successfully transfers into real jobs those who would otherwise need continuing public support.

Such was the vista of the future that these rediscovered papers prompted as we set out to follow our packing cases to their awaited lodging.

The apprenticeship that had been served was over. The skills and learning that an apprentice acquires are of uncertain value until their applicability has been tested in different settings. The future moves on and, as it does, destinations change. The world is full of discontinued ventures. What will be continued and discontinued? Aye, that is the question.

Postscript

This book has been written in the belief that the world is on the brink of a major change in the way in which it treats the problems of the unemployed. The themes on which this book is based are that unemployment can be treated directly by special measures rather than depend on the indirect effects of fiscal and monetary strategies; that the focus of attention should begin to move from financial capital as the prime mover in job creation to people issues with special reference to the key groups — those who cannot secure jobs for themselves and those with the flair to create jobs for others; that a new profession to generate jobs is an urgent requirement; that the zero unemployment is an option in some places, if locally managed; that social and employment security systems need to be reconstructed; and that the starting point for any major revision in approach will occur, in the first place, at a moral and philosophical level.

The sceptics will argue that as we are largely in the grip of natural forces, the world will carry on much as before. But while my testimony may be discounted on how I see the future shaping, there are now signs of a strange ship just visible on the horizon, even if as yet we can see only the tips of a funnel and the masts. The forces likely to bring about change in our current society may be nearer than is supposed.

Perhaps it is a sign of the times that, as this book was nearing completion, there came into being a professional pressure group operating from St George's House, Windsor Castle under the title UK Full Employment. Its convenor and inspirer was Peter Ashby, Employment Research Fellow at St George's. The Group arranged a series of consultations, involving 25–30 experts, ranging from university professors to experienced practitioners and officials from government ministries. Each consultation lasted two or three days and I had the pleasure of attending two in the series. The Group has drawn up both long term objectives and an interim programme which it believes to be immediately applicable. One of these programmes called Trainfair is designed to provide a guarantee

185

that training will lead to paid employment whether in the public or private sectors for all of its unemployed intake. The course would run for a maximum period of two years and would involve training, work experience and job applications.

That full employment in a capitalistic society is both morally desirable and economically and technically possible has not hitherto, to my knowledge, gained the support of such a nucleus of well-informed opinion.

These are mere beginnings. But they could become harbingers of more widely held views. Should that happen, a very different world is in prospect before us.

Further reading

Further reading

Addison, John, *et al.* (1979). *Job 'Creation' or Destruction.* Six essays on the effects of government intervention in the labour market. London: Institute of Economic Affairs.

Ashby, Peter (1989). *Citizenship, Income and Work: A report on three consultations.* Windsor: St George's House.

Beenstock and Associates, Michael (1987). *Work, Welfare and Taxation.* London: Allen & Unwin.

Bell, D. A. (1984). *Employment in the Age of Drastic Change.* Tunbridge Wells: Abacus Press.

Cassels, John (1990). *Britain's Real Skill Shortage and What to do About it.* London: Policy Studies Institute.

Clarke, Roger (1982). *Work in Crisis.* Edinburgh: Saint Andrew Press.

Fothergill, Stephen, Gudgin, Graham (1982). *Unequal Growth: Urban and regional employment change in the UK.* Oxford: Heinemann Educational Books.

Ginsburg, Helen (1983). *Full Employment and Public Policy: The United States and Sweden.* Lexington, Mass. and Toronto: Lexington Books.

Handy, Charles (1984). *The Future of Work.* Oxford: Blackwell.

ILO (1985). *World Employment Programme Research in the 1980s.* Geneva: ILO Publications.

Jacques, Elliott (1982). *Free Enterprise, Fair Employment.* Oxford: Heinemann Educational Books. New York: Crane, Russak and Company Inc.

Pederson, Peder J., Lund, Reinhard (eds.) (1987). *Unemployment: Theory, policy and structure.* Berlin and New York: Walter de Gruyter.

Perry, P. J. C. (1976). *The Evolution of British Manpower Policy.* London: BACIE.

Minford, Patrick, *et al.* (1983), *Unemployment: Cause and Cure.* Oxford: Martin Robertson.

Sinfield, Adrian (1981). *What Unemployment Means.* Oxford: Martin Robertson.

Whiting, Edwin (1987). *A Guide to Unemployment Reduction Measures.* London: Macmillan.

Subject index